JAMES BURGH, SPOKESMAN FOR REFORM IN HANOVERIAN ENGLAND

Carla H. Hay
Marquette University

D1590983

University Press of America™

Library of Congress Catalog Card Number: 79-89204

For Carl B. Cone,

mentor and friend,

with deep appreciation

ACKNOWLEDGMENTS

I am indebted to several people for their assistance at various
stages in the preparation of this study.

The topic was originally suggested to me by Professor Carl Cone of
the University of Kentucky who generously shared his own research with
me and critiqued the initial draft of the manuscript. From my first
days as his student in English Constitutional history, he has been a
stimulating force in my intellectual and professional development. For
all of his many kindnesses, I am deeply grateful.

At a critical stage in its evolution, the manuscript also profited
from the thoughtful comments of Professor Eugene Black of Brandeis University. Professor Black has since been extremely generous in supporting my application for various grants and fellowships. His help is all
the more appreciated because it was offered in a true spirit of academic collegiality at a time when his administrative responsibilities
made it most difficult to render such assistance.

Ultimately, however, this book has largely been made possible by
the sustained support of my colleague and spouse, Professor Robert P.
Hay of Marquette University. His own work in American popular ideology
during the revolutionary and early national period has had a significant impact upon my methodology. And on a personal level he has been
willing to sacrifice a humane existence so that this study could be
completed and others could be undertaken.

I would also like to thank G.R. Barbour and Barbara L.H. Horn of
the Scottish Record Office; R.P. Bateman of the Central Library, Stoke
Newington, England; R.G. Cant of St. Andrews University; R.E. Clifford
of Oxford University; Elizabeth Cuthbert of the Royal Archives, Windsor
Castle; A.J. Tait of the Sandeman Public Library, Perth, Scotland; and
Christine Vane of the British Museum for kindly responding to my
queries on James Burgh.

Finally, my special thanks to Mrs. Janet Black and Mr. Perry
Raines for their efforts in preparing the manuscript for publication,
and to the _Journal of British Studies_ for permission to reprint material which appeared in that publication.

Carla H. Hay

TABLE OF CONTENTS

Introduction:

THE MUCH NEGLECTED MR. BURGH

The period of Whig supremacy in the history of Great Britain has been characterized as "an oasis of tranquility between two agitated epochs."[1] All British citizens were not as satisfied with their so--ciety as this description implies. The self-styled Real Whigs or Com-monwealthmen constituted one particularly vocal, if none too numerous, group of critics who deplored popular complacency. The first genera-tion of Commonwealthmen emerged shortly after the Glorious Revolution. The third and final generation came to the fore in the age of the American Revolution.

As their name implies, the Commonwealthmen traced their ideo-logical antecedents to the Interregnum. The core of their philosophy can be found in the writings of James Harrington, John Milton, March-mont Nedham, Edmund Ludlow, Algernon Sidney, Henry Neville, and Andrew Marvell. These Real Whigs espoused the right of resistance, separation of powers, freedom of thought, religious toleration, the secularization of education, and the extension of the rights of Englishmen to all mankind, including the less privileged sections of British society. Viewing the Glorious Revolution as one episode, rather than the climax of efforts to redress injustice and thwart tyranny, they advocated re-forms including the extension of the franchise, reapportionment of legislative representation, annual parliaments, rotation in office, and the exclusion of placemen and pensioners from the House of Commons. They were critics of party, but their own lack of organization did much to frustrate their efforts.[2] It was in America rather than in England that their ideas found most fruitful expression.

The place of the Commonwealthman tradition in the intellectual history of Great Britain received scant attention until recent years.[3] With the outbreak of the American Revolution, Englishmen were less in-clined to speak of the reform which some had demanded in the early 1770's. The French Revolution hardened uneasy resistance to change in-to organized repression on the part of the government. The movement for reform died in a fervid flurry of patriotic adversion for every-thing tainted by a similitude to French liberalism. A generation later reform agitation re-emerged, armed with the new rhetoric of an age beset with problems unknown to eighteenth century radicals. In the

3

interim the Commonwealthmen passed into relative obscurity. With the exception of a Locke or a Shaftesbury, most of the Real Whigs were consigned to historical oblivion.

The dissenting schoolmaster, James Burgh, is one such neglected Commonwealthman. Burgh dedicated one of his books "To the Good People of Britain of The Twentieth Century"[4] in the hope that they would place a higher premium on his efforts than did many of his own generation. And ironically, it is only in the present century that this educator and influential propagandist of political radicalism has received a degree of recognition by scholars engaged in specialized study of the eighteenth century English reform movement and its connections with the American Revolution. In these circles, Burgh's magnum opus, the Political Disquisitions, is now distinguished as "perhaps the most important political treatise which appeared in England in the first half of the reign of George III" and "the standard source book for reform propagandists in the 1780's."[5]

Despite such encomiums, Burgh has remained a vague figure in eighteenth century studies. The full scope of his career as a reformer has never been adequately studied.[6] Undoubtedly the nature of the primary sources pertinent to such a study has discouraged researchers. Succinct sketches by contemporaries Andrew Kippis and John Nichols constitute the core of the meager available biographical data. There are no known Burgh diaries, papers, or correspondence. Burgh did not share his age's fascination with letter-writing. He much preferred "one hour's conversation" to "twenty letters" and believed it was "vain to think of doing anything" by such "ticklish weapons" towards "clearing up a point in dispute."[7] Any investigation of Burgh must rely on his published works. But the style and format of these compositions are formidable obstacles to their thorough analysis. Didactic, discursive, and frequently dull, these "grab-bags" of information offend modern literary tastes, although they were widely read in Burgh's day.

Once tackled, however, Burgh's writings disclose a surprisingly fulsome picture of their author. More importantly they prove valuable indices of shifting currents in eighteenth century society, in the broadest sense of that word. Burgh's diatribes on morals, mores, and revealed religion struck a responsive chord in a people for whom God was still very much alive. An increasingly literate age took keen interest in his discussion of education and his manual on rhetoric. His comments on women and children reflect what Lawrence Stone has characterized as the rise of "affective individualism."[8] Likewise, his statements on such topics as legal reform and poor relief highlight a growing humanitarianism as well as an interest in more efficient and effective government. Although Burgh's political views are better known than other facets of his thinking, even here a closer inspection is warranted. In particular, a study of the process whereby Burgh became a political radical points up aspects of the parliamentary reform movement that have not been sufficiently appreciated.

Part I of the following discussion will trace the process whereby a moralistic young immigrant from Scotland became one of the foremost spokesmen for reform in Hanoverian England. Part II will delineate the development of Burgh's ideas on religion, education, society, and politics. The result will hopefully bring James Burgh into sharper historical focus and further illuminate the broadbased assault by eighteenth century reformers on established institutions and attitudes.

PART ONE:

THE MAKING OF A RADICAL

CHAPTER I:

A MORALIST IN BABYLON

Exhultation! Whigs reveled in their triumph. Gone, but assuredly not forgotten was the stultifying pall of intrigue that had so recently hovered over the English metropolis as men, ravenous for power,
harried a dying queen. Tory hopes that her Hanoverian successor would
establish a broad-bottomed ministry proved specious. George I remembered and rewarded those Whigs who had loyally defended the Act of
Succession from Tory attacks. As the year 1714 drew to a close, Whigs
dared to dream of completely crushing their political foes in the ensuing parliamentary elections. Tory folly would make their goal a
reality. The rule of the Whig oligarchy was at hand.

Far removed from this political scene the family of Andrew Burgh[1]
was preoccupied with other concerns. By year's end their number would
increase with the birth of a third child whom they named James. Se-
questered in the small community of Madderty among the mountains of
Perthshire in Scotland, the Burghs could hardly anticipate that this
son would play an important role in the distant world of the Whig oligarchy.

The infant James was too young to remember his first encounter
with that world of politics, intrigue, and ambition. But no doubt as
he grew to manhood he was frequently regaled with tales of the "Fifteen" when Jacobites led by the Earl of Mar advanced as far south as
neighboring Perth. The Burghs were anti-Jacobites, as indeed were most
Scottish Presbyterians. James Burgh early imbibed their loyalty to the
House of Hanover--a loyalty he tenaciously clung to until his death and
vigorously asserted when Jacobitism again reared its anarchic head in
the "Forty Five."

With the exception of the "Fifteen," nothing eventful disturbed
the apparent tranquility of James's youth in rural Madderty. His family
occupied a position of respect in the community. A highly educated man
Andrew Burgh was minister of the parish Church of Scotland and, as was
common to presbyteries, served with his congregation's approbation.[2]
All of his life James Burgh was concerned with moral issues. His preoccupation is eloquent testimony to the force of his father's example.

Likewise, James's unusually advanced opinions on women bespeaks the influence of a forceful mother. Margaret Burgh was the daughter of William Robertson of Gladney, Scotland, and the aunt of the famous Scottish historian.[3] A rare anecdote from James's childhood provides a telling glimpse of Margaret as an authority figure in the household. The episode also underscores the family's social status. On one occasion James treated his nursery maid rather severely. Upon being reprimanded by his mother, he observed that he was a "gentleman" and the maid "only a servant." His mother rejoined that a child of twelve was inferior to every "well-behaved grown-up person."[4]

Nursery maids had work aplenty in the Burgh household. Following their marriage on August 13, 1703 Andrew and Margaret Burgh set about observing the Biblical admonition to "be fruitful and multiply." In addition to two older brothers, John and David, James had eight younger brothers and sisters: William, Margaret, Ann, Mary, Helen, Christian, Susan, and Grizel.[5] The family must have been a happy one for in later years James Burgh always spoke enthusiastically about marriage and large families.

Details of the family's finances are unavailable, but the nursery maid incident together with the family's educational background suggest that they were reasonably affluent. Both Andrew Burgh and his eldest son John obtained degrees from St. Andrews University. James also attended the University.[6]

James Burgh first ventured into the classroom as a youngster attending the local Madderty grammar school. There "he discovered such a quickness and facility in imbibing literary instruction that his master" predicted "his scholar would soon acquire all the knowledge which it was in his power to communicate."[7] Following grammar school, James enrolled at St. Andrews with the intention of becoming a clergyman of the Church of Scotland. No better commentary on Andrew Burgh's character is needed than his two sons' decision to pattern their professional lives after his. Unlike his brother John, however, James never received a university degree.[8] Ill health prematurely terminated his stay at St. Andrews. Although denied a ministerial career, James Burgh reflected throughout his life the moral concern and evangelism of the cleric. The classroom and the literary forum would be his pulpit as surely as the parish church at Madderty was his father's.

Young James was no more successful in his second attempt at a lifetime's profession than in his first. Having recently inherited a "handsome fortune" from his brother John, he entered the linen trade on the advice of friends. All too soon he demonstrated the commercial naivete that consistently characterized his discussion of economic issues. Injudicious grants of credit to his customers cost him his newfound business and his bequest.[9] James Burgh never forgot this unpleasant excursion into the market place. He later remarked:

> Whenever . . . any Person in Distress desires
> you to assist him with your Money or Credit, with-
> out offering you a direct Security, consider with

yourself, whether the Sum is such as you may spare,
without detriment to your Affairs; and if it is
not, by no Means venture it in the Hands of your
nearest Relation: for <u>lent</u> Money is almost always
<u>lost</u> Money, and the Person, to whom it is lent, is
hardly ever the better for it. At the same time,
if you can in such Cases prevail with a number of
other Friends to join with you in assisting a good
Man, so as the Sum lent, or engaged for by each,
may be moderate, and the Burden may fall the lighter
for being divided; or if you can any other way be of
Advantage, without endangering yourself; never think
you can take too much Pains for the Service of distressed Worth.[10]

Viewed from a broad perspective, this experience highlights the basic
flaw of the moralistic Burgh. His idealism fostered fervor, but it
also encouraged a certain naivete and superficiality. His "common
sense" perspective on situations too often bespoke an unduly simple
approach to life's complexities. Thus Burgh's painful encounter with
the commercial world encouraged his future insistence that economics
be included in a young man's educational curriculum, but his discussion
of economic problems never reflected any degree of sophistication. All
too frequently he was the enthusiastic moralist offering panaceas for
intricate problems.

Having lost his capital, Burgh was once more a young man in search
of a livelihood. His quest prompted him to hazard the highways and
highwaymen of the United Kingdom in the long and difficult journey
south to the great metropolis of London.[11] Henceforth England was his
home. Burgh's sojourn suddenly transposed him from a rural community
where most people shared his national origins and religious beliefs to
a pluralistic society with which he was often at odds.

Samuel Johnson once acidly remarked to Boswell that "the noblest
prospect . . . a Scotsman ever sees is the road which leads to England!"[12] Johnson's comment pointedly underscores the prejudice against
Scots that was all too common in England. The slurs cast at George
III's Scottish favorite, Lord Bute, are but one of the most virulent
examples of such feelings.[13] The young Burgh, newly arrived in London,
brogue still pronounced, was no doubt painfully sensitive to this hostility. Quite naturally, he wanted acceptance in his new home. Sub-
suming regional loyalties in a patriotic regard for the British nation
as a whole, he identified himself as a Briton and hailed the British
as the "<u>greatest</u> people in Europe!"[14] Yet his Scottish origins would
always set him apart in England. Although Burgh prospered, he could
never quite belong. He must have felt particularly uncomfortable at
the time of the "Forty Five" and later during George III's reign when
anti-Bute feeling again fanned anti-Scot sentiment. Responding to this
prejudice, Burgh exhorted Scots and Englishmen to abandon their mutual
hostility and cement in spirit the political bond forged between them
by the Act of Union of 1707. Though not unaware of Scottish failings,
Burgh believed that the English, overly prone to xenophobia, were primarily responsible for the continued antipathy between the two races.

11

Such discord was folly in Burgh's eyes. It could only work to the advantage of Britain's natural enemy--France.

> The minds of the railers against our north-
> ern brethren are so narrow, that they can take
> in but half this little island . . . Our times
> have, I suppose, exhibited the first instance of
> persons setting up for patriots upon the avowed
> principles of making one half of their country
> enemies to the other half . . . One would suspect
> that they who set up, and keep up, the division
> between the two kingdoms, must have a warm side
> to <u>France</u>. For the union between the two kingdoms,
> which some among us seem desirous to be dissolved,
> was one of the severest blows <u>France</u> has ever suf-
> fered, as being the effectual shutting of the back
> door, by which she annoyed <u>England</u>, the most
> fatally.[15]

Burgh's admonition was ill attended. Prejudice against Scots prevailed throughout his lifetime.

In England Burgh joined the ranks of a religious as well as a
national minority. Gone was the community respect accorded a Church
of Scotland minister and his family. Burgh's Presbyterianism placed
him outside the fold of England's established Anglican Church. He was
now a Dissenter: by definition a "non-conformist," by law a second
class citizen. Not until 1689 had the right of Dissenters to practice
their faith been legalized in England. As late as 1714 legislation
had attempted to undermine Dissent by destroying the schools which nurtured it. Although the Schism Act was quickly repealed, the Test and
Corporation Acts denied Dissenters the right to hold local and national political offices until 1828. Occasional conformity and annual legislative grants of immunity rendered these laws ineffectual, but they
were nonetheless onerous reminders of the dissenting community's legal-
ly inferior status. The requirement that students at Oxford and Cambridge subscribe to the thirty-nine articles of the Anglican Church
further limited Dissenters' rights. These restrictions encouraged a
critical perspective towards English society among Dissenters. Particularly sensitive to libertarian issues, they were in the forefront of
eighteenth century reform movements.[16] Sharing their sense of alienation, James Burgh would be there too.

Burgh's estrangement from the mainstream of English life was also
furthered by his impressions of the English capital--one of the two
greatest metropolitan centers in all Europe. His fellow Scotsman,
James Boswell, has left a memorable account of his own introduction to
London:

> When we came upon Highgate hill, and had a
> view of London, I was all life and joy . . . my
> soul bounded forth to a certain prospect of happy
> futurity. I sang all manner of songs . . . I

found that to live would require great economy.[17]

Undoubtedly, Burgh shared Boswell's youthful exuberance upon arriving in the English capital. Likewise, both young men would be awed at the sophistication, density, and luxury of London life in comparison to their backward homeland. Much more than his profligate countryman, however, the self-righteous Burgh was also shocked, even outraged by these conditions. Reared amidst the rural tranquility of Madderty in a Calvinist home where assuredly industriousness, self-denial, and rectitude were cherished virtues, he was horrified at the frivolity and licentiousness so visible in the city's congested streets. His natural inclination towards loyalty to his adopted home warred with his finely honed moral sensibilities. He gloried in London's greatness, yet was repulsed by its apparent wickedness. His parochialism was obvious in the distress he expressed over the possible migration of industry from London to sections of the empire where living costs were lower.[18] Yet he emotionally castigated the English Babylon for its turpitude.

> O London, London, how hast thou degenerated!
> Where art now those happy Days when thy Greatness
> and Superiority to the other Cities of England, con-
> sisted more in thy superior Virtue and Piety, than
> in thy enormous Wealth, Trade, and Magnificence.
> Thou art the Chief of the Cities of the Earth; thy
> Merchants are Princes; thy Commerce is extended
> from Sea to Sea, and from the Rising to the Setting
> of the Sun. Thy Riches have exalted thee to Heaven;
> beware lest thy Pride humble thee to the Dust. For
> when thy Sins have once brought thee the Hour of
> thy Destruction, it will not be in the Power of thy
> Riches, thy Commerce, or thy mighty Fleets, to pro-
> tect thee; much less will the infamous Tools and
> Panders to thy Luxury and Pleasures, serve to come
> between thee and the Vengeance which hangs over
> thee.[19]

Convinced by life in London that public and private virtue was imperilled in the land he loved, Burgh's disaffection from English society deepened. Another man might have fled this den of prejudice, intolerance, and iniquity. Not James Burgh. His choice of the ministry as a profession reflected more than parental influence. Burgh was an activist whose concept of Christian commitment made him a natural crusader, born to strive for the hearts of men. His experience in England provided the focus for his energies. His sense of alienation from English society encouraged his evolution as a radical reformer.

Burgh had come to England in search of a livelihood. His career as a reformer was necessarily a secondary occupation. He first found employment in London as a corrector of the press for the eminent printer, William Bowyer. An industrious young man, Burgh supplemented his income by making indexes during his leisure hours. His association with Bowyer was a particularly fortuitous one. The printer was familiar with a wide variety of influential people. Through him, Burgh met several "respectable friends who were highly serviceable to him in his future plans of life." Arthur Onslow, Speaker of the House of Commons, was especially helpful. Burgh was frequently obliged to bring Onslow the proof-sheets of the Commons' vote which Bowyer printed.[20] Possibly his contact with Onslow gave Burgh the opportunity to observe first hand many of those legislative practices which he later criticized so vehemently.

Burgh quit his job with Bowyer after a little more than a year. As Andrew Kippis remarks, his work in the printing establishment could not have been very congenial to a man of Burgh's intelligence and disposition.[21] He went to Great Marlow in Buckinghamshire where he served as an assistant in the town's free grammar school. Teaching would be Burgh's life-long profession. Most probably, practical pressures more than personal penchant prompted Burgh to take his first teaching position. He was, after all, approaching thirty and still in search of a permanent occupation. That his quest ended in the classroom is revealing. Burgh found in an academic situation the opportunity to mold minds and save souls that had been denied him in the Church. His industriousness, capacity for study, affection for children, and administrative ability complimented his ministerial instincts and made for a successful career. During his tenure at Great Marlow, the school's enrollment is supposed to have increased "considerably." But Great Marlow offered Burgh little opportunity to meet people with whom he shared common interests. He had only one close friend there. That anonymous gentleman, "a man of piety, and of extensive reading in divinity, though no classical scholar," was indeed well suited to Burgh's own "turn of mind" and may be responsible for Burgh's first turning author.[22]

Published anonymously in London in January of 1745-46, <u>Britain's Remembrancer: or, The Danger not over</u> was occasioned by the Jacobite rebellion of 1745.[23] Burgh had been brooding over the luxury and license of English society for several years. He saw in the "Forty Five" a vindication of his own moral outrage. The episode immediately raised the spectre of divine retribution in his mind. Convinced that the triumph of Jacobitism would be disasterous to the United Kingdom, Burgh interpreted the "Forty Five" as a solemn warning of future catastrophe to the English people should they fail to purge themselves of the corruption which was enervating the nation. As the bulwark of Protestantism, England had enjoyed providential protection in previous years. But the "Almighty Governor of the World" would not be trifled with. Although the Lord had stayed his righteous wrath by causing the Rebels to tarry in the North until the English army, speeded by unseasonable East winds, could return home and revive the faltering courage of dispirited South Britons, England could not long depend on such divine generosity. Burgh called upon each "particular Rank in the Nation, to exert themselves in their publick and private Stations for bringing about that general Reformation which is necessary for averting a final and extirpating Judgment." Only then would the <u>real</u> danger confronting the island be over.[24]

Although offensive to modern tastes, this emotional exhortation was immediately and _immensely_ popular in Britain and in the colonies. By 1754 six to eight editions had been published in England, Scotland, and Ireland and over 10,000 copies of the tract had been sold.   There were four American editions, the first being published by Benjamin Franklin in 1747.   The pamphlet was "ascribed to sundry Bishops; quoted by both the Clergy and Dissenting Ministers in their pulpits; and universally allowed to be a seasonable and useful tract" that ought to be "attentively read and considered by every family."[25]

Britain's Remembrancer's auspicious reception initiated a literary career that spanned thirty years and resulted in a variety of pamphlets and books that kaleidescope life in eighteenth century England. Burgh was always ambivalent about his writing which he consistently characterized as a "bye-business." Prompted by his early misfortunes to lead a life of retirement, he insisted that he had no ambition to be an author:

> I have never taken the pen in hand, but when I
> have been desired or prompted to it; and if I
> have got ten pounds by all I have published, I
> have got ten thousand . . . my own employment is
> my supreme pursuit, and . . . it is not an itch of
> scribbling that has occasioned my being so often
> in the press; but that I have been partly drawn
> and partly dragged into it.[26]

Yet in a moment of candor Burgh also confessed his aspiration to accomplish something noteworthy and to the public's advantage. Writing provided him with the means to do so. He reasoned that:

> men of abilities, in the most private stations,
> are capable of serving their country, if not by ac-
> tion, yet by suggesting useful hints to those, whose
> stations give them an opportunity of action; and of
> improving, by their conversation and writings, the
> minds and manners of their countrymen.[27]

Convinced that England teetered precariously on the precipice of moral degeneration and thus national destruction, he repeatedly resorted to his pen to alert his countrymen to their peril.

Created in his limited leisure time, Burgh's compositions were little more than unpolished first drafts. Poorly organized, they were chronically repetitive and frequently rambled from one unconnected topic to another. Arguments were developed in a haphazard, almost stream-of-consciousness fashion. Burgh's diction was simple and direct. His occasional attempts at eloquence generally sounded maudlin.   Contemporary critics politely called him to task for these defects.[28] Asserting that his teaching duties left him insufficient time for polishing his literary style, Burgh testily countered their criticism with the rejoinder that the subject matter rather than the mode of expression determined the essential worth of any book. A volume which prompted the public to examine "the foundations of established nonsense;

. . . to correct . . . errors in principle or in practice;" to curb
vices and to pursue "whatever is virtuous and praiseworthy" deserved
the public's careful attention.[29] Unquestionably Burgh believed his
own writings met these criteria and for the most part the public
agreed.

Initially Burgh's educational limitations obliged him to rely
heavily on his own observations for the information he conveyed to his
readers. Only an occasional quotation or reference to Scripture or
ancient history bolstered his arguments. A rigorous and variegated
course of extensive reading, however, soon provided him with a wealth
of information. Diligently he compiled abstracts of all he read.[30] His
mature works reflected a growing familiarity with an impressive array
of eminent authors. Lengthier quotations, more numerous and varied
references to such authorities were increasingly frequent in his studies. He relied most heavily on histories to document his arguments,
including the works of Hume, Robertson, Catharine Macaulay, Bishop
Burnet, Voltaire, and the Universal History. Typical of the neoclassi-
cal age were his repeated references to the history of the ancient re-
publics, their virtuous customs, eventual moral degeneration, and con-
sequent destruction. Scriptural allusions appeared throughout his
works, but were most numerous in his early writings. He also frequently
cited political philosophers such as Aristotle, Plato, Cicero, Locke,
Harrington, Bolingbroke, Thomas Gordon, John Trenchard, and Charles
Davenant. No doubt Burgh felt, and with some justification, that such
allusions added considerable weight to the observations and suggestions
of a mere schoolmaster. There is no evidence that contemporaries
found his device disconcerting. On the contrary, the practice was a
popular one.[31]

The dearth of company in Great Marlow agreeable to Burgh's "liberal taste" prompted him to move in 1746 to Enfield, located about eleven
miles north of London in Middlesex county. There he served as an assistant in the academy of a Mr. Kenross. At the end of Burgh's first year,
Kenross advised him that he was squandering his talents as an assistant and generously offered to help Burgh finance his own academy.[32]

Kenross's willingness to hazard personal funds in Burgh's behalf
both affirms Burgh's academic abilities and bespeaks his appealing personality. At first acquaintance Burgh impressed people as a somewhat
stiff and assertive individual of obvious intelligence and shrewdness.
His reserve reflected a serious man who thought in terms of duty and
responsibility. Viewing men as moral agents whose primary goal was
rectitude, not happiness, Burgh was disinclined towards frivolity or
levity. Always the moralistic, even priggish schoolmaster, he tended
to catechize friend and foe alike as if they were pupils in his classroom. A "positive" man, he was blunt, forthright, even aggressive in
enunciating his opinions. He confessed to speaking "too eagerly" and
acting "too vigorously" on some occasions so that his enthusiasm sometimes alienated people. Burgh's friends forgave these foibles in light
of his many attributes. An intelligent, spirited conversationalist
with a wry sense of humor, he played an "entertaining" part in social
gatherings. Although a moral absolutist, he was open to the opinions

16

of others. His preoccupation with duty rendered him industrious, reliable, and trustworthy. Most endearingly, he was a loyal, generous,
warm-hearted man whose righteousness was tempered by a deep concern for
the welfare of others.[33] This was the James Burgh that Mr. Kenross
knew and offered to subsidize.

    With Kenross's backing, Burgh became master of his own academy at
Stoke Newington, Middlesex, in 1747. The school prospered rapidly, a-
betted no doubt by the publication of Burgh's first educational tract:
Thoughts on Education, tending chiefly to recommend to the Attention of
the Publick, some Particulars relating to that Subject; which are not
generally considered with the Regard their Importance deserves.[34] By
1750 Burgh was obliged to seek larger quarters to accommodate the increasing number of pupils who sought to study under his tutelage. He
moved to nearby Newington Green where he resided for the next twenty-
one years.[35]

    Newington Green was a particularly amiable neighborhood for a man
of James Burgh's tastes and disposition. Located about three miles
north of London, the area was a noted stronghold of Dissent. It was
also a pleasant suburban retreat for Londoners who came there for cakes
and ale on May Day. Spring Gardens, located between the Green and
Ball's Pond, was a popular recreational attraction. A square of respectable houses surrounded the Green, three sides of which together
with the enclosed center ground were in the parish of St. Mary's,
Islington. The north side of the square was bounded by the parish of
St. Mary's Stoke Newington. Located on the southeast corner of the
Green, Burgh's new home was embellished with a playground, kitchen gardens, and orchard.[36]

    The focal point of life at Newington Green was the chapel, "a sub-
stantial brick building, of nearly square form, with the high, tiled,
projecting roof, common at its era . . .." It was built in 1708 "for
the use of Protestant Dissenters and the worship of Almighty God." Originally, the congregation was Presbyterian, but drifted towards Unitarianism, a common occurence in the eighteenth century.[37] In 1756 the
eminent Arian, Richard Price, began conducting morning and afternoon
services at the Green chapel.[38] Dr. Price and Burgh rapidly developed
a fast and firm friendship that lasted until Burgh's death. Under
Price's sway, Burgh began to rethink the Presbyterian faith in which
he had been reared. Eventually, Burgh too became an Arian.

    Price, however, was not Burgh's sole source of companionship at
Newington Green. Many of the area's inhabitants were tradesmen and
merchants who desired a rural retreat easily accessible to London.
Financially comfortable, such individuals shared with Burgh a sympathy
for the Whig party and a latitudinarian outlook on theological questions.[39] Newington Green offered Burgh a haven from the "culture
shock" he had heretofore experienced in England. From the security of
the Green he could sally forth to wage the battles of the Lord, comfortable in the assurance that respite and understanding always await-
ed him there.

The year after his arrival at the Green, Burgh married. In choosing a helpmate he was affected by several considerations which typified a new kind of marital relationship that emerged in the seventeenth and eighteenth centuries: the "companionate marriage."[40] Burgh shared the assumption common to most ages that domestic cares were a woman's primary concern. Nature had designed the female to be wife and mother. But his conception of how a woman could best fulfill these roles reflected the views of an increasingly vocal minority of English men and women who rejected the stereotype of women as pretty, frivolous creatures and argued instead that women, like men, were rational, moral creatures whose sexual roles demanded intelligence and spiritual maturity, more than physical allure. Burgh believed that a woman interested in attracting the admiration of the "Judicious" should adorn her mind, rather than beautify her person. She should employ herself "in the Works of domestic OEconomy, Charity Vertue [sic], and Piety," rather than be preoccupied with "Plummage . . . Pleasures and Diversions." He was especially scandalized by the presence of women at the theatre, finding it inconceivable:

> That a Lady . . . [could] frequent the luscious
> Theatre, be a Witness of all the Scenes of Impurity,
> and give Ear to all the shameless Lewdness of that
> Haunt of Vice and Obscenity, without having her Mind
> debauched and polluted, which is the surest Prelude
> to the debauching of her Person.[41]

Undoubtedly, Burgh's thinking was strongly influenced by his homelife in Madderty. In part his attitude reveals a priggishness about pleasure that was rooted in his Calvinistic upbringing. It also bespeaks his mother's influence. A minister's wife, Margaret Burgh must have been decorous in dress and diligent in the performance of her domestic duties. As is common with young men, Burgh assuredly patterned his ideal woman after his mother's example. Moreover, Burgh's stance suggests a phenomenon common in the history of modern feminism. A marked percentage of feminists, especially in America, were nurtured in the house of Calvinist ministers. Prizing education as an essential tool in the attainment of salvation, these men encouraged the intellectual development of sons and daughters alike. Feminism flourished in such an environment.[42] Given Andrew Burgh's educational and religious background, it is most probable that this father of six girls presided over a home whose women enjoyed a status unusual in the eighteenth century. In turn, his son grew to manhood accustomed to view women in an unusually commendatory light.

Burgh found his ideal helpmate in Hannah Harding, a widow four years his senior. The circumstances of their courtship are unknown. The widow Harding was a woman of some means and social position. Burgh was apparently sensitive about her affluence. He several times observed that:

> If between the two married persons, there be
> upon the whole enough for a compatible subsistance
> according to their station, and temper of mind, it

signifies very little, whether it comes by one
side, or the other, or both.[43]

That Hannah Burgh had never been the local Belinda seems evident,
for Burgh strongly advised against marrying a noted beauty "unless you
intend to give up the whole Peace and Happiness of your Life for a
Honey-Moon. There is not one of a Thousand of them that is sufferable,
through Vanity." Her husband prized Hannah for other qualities. According to the couple's friend, Andrew Kippis, she was "a woman of excellent sense and character, who zealously concurred with [Burgh] in
promoting all his laudable and useful undertakings." In addition to
the "excellence of her understanding," she was remembered for the
"goodness of her heart . . . [her] serene and chearful [sic] temper,"
her piety and benevolence.[44] In choosing his bride, Burgh had recognized that:

> Those marriages . . . are likely to be crowned
> with all the happiness this state admits of,
> where a due regard is had to the qualities of
> the mind, to personal endowments, as an agreeable
> appearance, and a suitable age, and prudential con-
> siderations; and where either the one or the other
> is neglected, misery is the consequence to be
> looked for.

Even so, marriage demanded constant effort on the part of both partners:

> Married people ought to think nothing trifling
> or of small consequence, that may please or
> disgust one another . . . Cleanliness, dress,
> compliance; every little piece of obsequiousness
> and tenderness; consulting one another upon every
> trifle, however obvious; commendations of one
> another's judgment or taste, if expressed with
> address, and without the appearance of flattery;
> yielding every point, if possible, before there
> be time to dispute it; these are the arts by
> which love is kept alive for life.

That his was a happy and successful union is affirmed in Burgh's warm
rhetorical query:

> What can be conceived more perfect in an
> imperfect state, than an inseparable union of in-
> terests between two persons, who love one another
> with sincerity and tenderness; who mutually desire
> to oblige one another; and who can with the utmost
> freedom unbosom to one another all their joys and
> all their griefs, whereby the one may be doubled
> and the other divided?[45]

Following his marriage, Burgh soon settled into an established
though far from stultifying routine. He spent the major portion of his

time fulfilling his responsibilities as teacher and headmaster.[46] His academy[47] was not the first such institution to flourish at Newington Green. Charles Morton had operated a highly successful school there in the latter part of the seventeenth century.[48] Dissenting academies enjoyed a reputation for academic excellence and curricular innovation. That Burgh's school was representative of this tradition is indicated by his various educational tracts. Assuming these treatises reflected personal experience, his academy served thirty to forty pupils, many of whom boarded at the school. Its curriculum was broad in scope, ranging from the classical languages to anatomy and astronomy. The focal point of the curriculum was instruction in Scripture and Christian doctrine. The spiritual welfare of his charges took precedence in Burgh's mind over any other consideration. The breadth of his academy's course of study required from its master a general and comprehensive familiarity with many disciplines, rather than an intensive knowledge of any one particular subject. Thus much of Burgh's time was devoted to widening his own intellectual horizons. He read extensively on a variety of subjects with particular emphasis on historical and political treatises. These he collected into folio volumes which would aid him in his capacity as teacher and author.

Burgh believed that the success of an educational institution could only be measured in terms of the "real and substantial care and visible improvement of [its pupils]." Unbiased by parental weakness, a schoolmaster such as himself could serve as an "impartial and prudent governor" in the best interests of the students.[49] Burgh was far removed from the stereotyped instructor who sternly and unfeelingly wielded a pandybat on his charges. His solicitude for his pupils' spiritual and intellectual welfare was intense and sincere. He once lamented:

> My heart sinks within me at the Thought, that
> a Soul, I have had the care of, should ever be in the
> least Danger of final Ruin; that one, whom I have la-
> bored to fit and prepare for Usefulness in this Life,
> and for Glory in a better, should have the least
> Chance of degenerating so far, as to become a Nusance
> [sic] on Earth, and a Vessel fit for Destruction here-
> after. Should I ever see any of those, whose amiable
> Form, in the Years of Youth and Innocence, has so often
> delighted my Eye, and softened my Heart with Tender-
> ness next to that of a Parent; should I ever see any
> of them spoiled, and debauched with Vice and Folly;
> should I ever see those Eyes, which I have so often
> viewed with Pleasure, and fancied I have seen in them
> the Dawning of every manly Virtue, inflamed with Lust
> or Drunkenness; should I hear that Tongue, whose
> innocent Prattle has so often charmed me, uttering
> Impieties, or Obscenities; or find that Mind, whose
> Faculties I endeavoured to cultivate with useful and
> ornamental Knowledge, and to enrich with every vir-
> tuous Principle, debased and sunk with Falshood [sic],
> Sensuality, or Covetousness, and my noblest Work

defaced and ruined; or should I hereafter . . . see
a Soul, in whose everlasting Happiness I hoped to
triumph, and which I thought to have among others for
a Crown of rejoicing to me in the great Day of Retribution, driven out from God and Bliss, and condemned
to the Punishment, prepared for the irrecoverably
Wicked--O fearful Prospect! O startling Thought!
The Horror of it overpowers me.[50]

The depth of Burgh's feelings is easily understood. Having married
late in life, the Burghs were childless. Burgh undoubtedly regretted
this. He had grown up in a house filled with the sounds of children.
Moreover, in accord with the eighteenth century notion that the
strength of a country was directly proportioned to its population, he
passionately believed citizens had the moral obligation to serve the
state by augmenting its numbers.[51] In the classroom Burgh found the
family he could not father himself. His skill as a schoolmaster was
reflected in his academy's prosperity.[52]

     Burgh's success as a teacher was only achieved by diligent appli-
cation and occupied most of his time. Rising early, he studied before
breakfast. Morning prayers were followed by long hours in the classroom. Since Burgh's was a boarding school, supervision of his scholars
continued until their bedtime. In the evenings, such time as Burgh
could husband from these responsibilities was devoted to reading, writing, and "looking into his affairs." After a light supper, "generally
without any animal food," he prayed, then retired early.[53] In addition
to his academic obligations, Burgh played an important role in the
Newington Green community. Together with Thomas Rogers, Samuel Richards,
John Dunn, and William Palmer, he served as trustee of the Green
chapel.[54]

     What little leisure this schedule afforded was spent in a variety
of simple pursuits. On some days Burgh and his wife enjoyed Sunday
dinner or afternoon tea with their good friend Dr. Price.[55] Burgh
passed many of his spare moments with his numerous friends and acquaintances. Sharing a spirited conversation, a pleasant walk, a horseback
ride, a song, a harmless joke, or a game of bowls with congenial company constituted the "whole luxury of life" for him.[56] His circle of
friends and acquaintances is impressive in its scope and prestigious-
ness. His writings introduced him to a variety of individuals that a
schoolmaster, even a prosperous one, would ordinarily never know. He
was understandably proud, even somewhat boastful about these relationships. References to them are liberally sprinkled throughout the
Political Disquisitions, as if by way of testamentary on his lifetime
achievements, and include such famous figures as James Boswell, Benjamin
Franklin, David Hume, and Adam Ferguson.[57]

     Burgh early counted among his friends two influential men who
played important roles in his career: the "inestimable"[58] Stephen Hales,
a noted scientist who was Clerk of the Closet to the Princess Dowager
Augusta and Chaplain to Prince George, and Thomas Hayter, Bishop of
Norwich and Preceptor to the young princes for a short time after

the death of Frederick Prince of Wales . Most probably Burgh's writings
occasioned his introduction to these gentlemen. In 1749 Burgh transcribed a lengthy essay entitled <u>Directions, prudential and moral, for</u>
<u>the use of the youth at a boarding school in Stoke Newington</u> and gave
it to three or four of his students for their edification. Impressed
with its reception he had a private edition of 1,000 copies printed for
distribution to his future pupils and to various bishops and "eminent"
persons for presentation to "young people of rank." Hayter subsequently used this manual of homilies and recommended readings in the instruction of his princely charges.[59] About this same time friends persuaded
Burgh to assist in raising money for an orphan by publishing a poem he
had written earlier. Dedicated to George Lyttelton, politician, humanitarian and literati, <u>An Hymn to the Creator of the World. The Thoughts</u>
<u>taken chiefly from Psal. civ. To which is added in Prose, an Idea of</u>
<u>the Creator from His Works</u> poetically recapitulated the familiar tale
of man's creation, fall from grace, and redemption. Reminiscent of
Fontenelle, it concluded with a sophisticated prose commentary on features of Newtonian physics. Stephen Hales would certainly have found
this piece interesting, as did Benjamin Franklin who reprinted major
portions of it in <u>Poor Richard's Almanac</u> for 1753 and 1754.[60]

      Whatever the circumstances that led to Burgh's acquaintance with
Hales and Hayter, the relationship was a significant one for the
schoolmaster. In 1751 at their behest he published <u>A Warning to Dram-</u>
<u>Drinkers, being an Account of the dreadful Effects of that Vice upon</u>
<u>one who was formerly addicted to it</u> as part of the campaign to curb the
legal sale of inexpensive distilled liquors, such as gin.[61] Of greater
consequence, during the ensuing year Hayter introduced Burgh to the
Princess Dowager.[62] A private citizen whose social insignificance far
removed him from the elite grandeur of the Court, Burgh was overwhelmed
when "that most amiable and illustrious Princess" took notice of him
"in a manner far . . . above what . . . [he] could have thought of or
expected."[63] Naturally predisposed out of deference to view the Princess favorably, Burgh was encouraged in this attitude by the Princess's
personality. She shared his censorious perspective on contemporary
morals. Convinced of the efficacy of the royal example in forming the
manners of the people, Burgh heartily applauded the Princess's interest
in the "general advancement of Truth, Virtue, and Religion" and her
"pious Cares in forming [her] lovely Offspring to virtue and to glory."
Unabashedly, he asserted that "Malice itself, struck silent, stands
awed by [her] native goodness and unaffected greatness of Mind." He
lauded her as the "Best of Comforts, and of Parents" whose honor would
one day "shine conspicuous on the role of fame" and who merited a
"place among the celebrated names of <u>Arria</u>, <u>Cornelia</u>, <u>Porcia</u>, <u>Marcia</u>,
<u>Attia</u>, <u>Aurelia</u>, and others, the glory of the amiable sex, whose charms,
other than of paint or dress, or ostentation, will ever bloom with un--
fading splendor."[64] Burgh apparently visited the Princess several
times and on one occasion was even introduced to the future George III.
Most probably the meeting failed to impress the young prince, but James
Burgh remembered. He long retained an image of George as an "artless
honest-hearted" young man [65] and was markedly disinclined to criticize
him publicly. In part his reluctance reflected a dilemma Burgh shared
with most eighteenth century Englishmen. His was an age in which

opposition and criticism of the Crown still smacked of treason. If corruption in public places prevailed, it was not through the personal connivance of the king. He was more ill-advised than ill-intentioned. But more than convention accounts for Burgh's attitude toward the King. There is something of the schoolmaster loathe to recognize the failings of a beloved pupil in his stance.

Burgh's kind reception by such important personages as Hales, Hayter, and the Princess emboldened him to dream of making a substantial contribution to the moral betterment of English society. At some point around 1752 or 1753 he wrote to Hales to suggest the possibility of conducting a public inquiry by able writers into the chief points of Lord Bolingbroke's pamphlet on the authority of the Scriptures. Hales supported the idea. Circular letters were written, printed pleas for such a project were distributed, and meetings with bishops, eminent laymen, printers, and booksellers were held. The scheme was encouraged by "an illustrious female character," undoubtedly the Princess, and "a noble lord, who . . . presided over the education of a young family of supreme dignity[,] . . . two eminent persons [who] have since been treated by some in a manner particularly genteel."[66]

Burgh's primary goal was the establishment of a Grand Association:

> consisting of persons conspicuous for their
> characters, and stations, who could easily have
> procured the assistance of all the able peers in
> the three kingdoms for carrying on a periodical
> publication in support of virtue and truth; and
> held it in their power to give a general turn to
> the sentiments and manners of twenty millions of
> people.

Conjoined with this plan was a proposal to formulate under the auspices of the Association:

> a complete System of political knowledge,
> drawn from history and biography, antient and
> modern, from the best political writings of all
> ages and countries, with whatever could be obtained
> by searching records, memoirs, state-papers, nego-
> tiations, law-books, codes, antient and modern, ob-
> servations of travellers, treatises on government,
> commerce, and all manners of subjects connected with
> them, etc. the whole to be digested in the briefest
> manner under heads, and printed, or if not, at least
> written out fair into volumes, for the use of the
> then H___ appar__t . . . that, in all cases of dif-
> ficulty, He might have somewhat more certain to de-
> pend on, than the precarious and contradictory coun-
> sels of men, who might be themselves mistaken, or
> might be interested to deceive Him.[67]

The first fruit of these plans was "The Free Enquirer," a

multi-authored series of essays coordinated by Burgh under the pseudo-nym of "T. Trueman." Appearing weekly in the General Evening Post over a two year period, the articles were concerned primarily with the de-fense of revealed religion and the preservation of public virtue.[68] The movement's initial momentum, however, was not sustained. Other than "The Free Enquirer," its only specific result was the publication of Dr. John Leland's A View of the Deistical Writers that have appeared in England during the last and present century (1754-56).[69] This was a far cry from Burgh's vision of the Association's potential achievements. In October of 1754, wearied by bearing major responsibility for the organ-ization and frustrated by the apathy of others, Burgh indicated his in-tention to withdraw from "The Free Enquirer." Although convinced that "so extended a publication, in favor of truth, carried on periodically, has been of service, and may be made of greater," he challenged "those persons, to whom the plan of these Essays was communicated at the time when the design was first projected" to guarantee their continuation.[70] His appeal went unanswered. "The Free Enquirer" and the Association passed into oblivion. In subsequently commenting on the Association's failure, a disillusioned James Burgh wrote:

> I did not then know the world, nor those, who
> make the most noise in it, so well as I do now. If
> I had, I should have saved myself some trouble, expence,
> and disappointment for I should have concluded that
> the majority of that rank [the eminent leaders of
> England] were so happily disposed that nothing was
> likely to engage them to associate, but some object
> suitable to their sort of magnanimity, as a cock-match,
> a horse-race, the preservation of the game, or the
> preservation of the court-places.[71]

Burgh was further dispirited about this time by his encounter with the unsavory side of the publishing trade. All too frequently printers pirated literary works, especially anonymous ones like Burgh's, and sold them without the author's permission. Such was the fate of Burgh's Directions, prudential, moral . . . which was illicitly printed by a Mr. Read in 1752 under the title of Youth's Friendly Monitor; or, the affectionate schoolmaster: containing his last pathethic farewel [sic] lecture to his young pupils, on their entrance into a busy world; and their diligent pursuit after new employments: together with a post-script, pointing out, for their serious perusal, such particular books, as must necessarily enlarge their ideas, and form their minds to an early regard to virtue and religion. The work was warmly endorsed by The Monthly Review as "one of the best performances of the kind . . . [the Review] had ever seen," and enthusiastically recommended for "the perusal of all young persons."[72] Nonetheless, Burgh was indignant when he discovered Read's injustice many months later. By then, however, Read was a "piteous" man oppressed with many debts and Burgh charitably decided to overlook his offense until he discovered that two reputable booksellers had reprinted Read's edition. Burgh first sought to pur-chase all 1,500 of their copies and, failing that, to persuade them to restore his own more modest title to their edition and publicly to dis-associate Burgh from any complicity in the piece's publication. His terms were refused. Outraged, Burgh financed an authorized edition to which he appended Theophilus, a sketch of a fictitious model for youngster's emulation. He explained the circumstances which occasioned the new edition and in advertisements warned that henceforth those who pirated or disfigured any of his works would do so at their own peril.[73]

The only encouraging event in an otherwise depressing year was the publication of Burgh's first major study, The Dignity of Human Nature. Written in response to the plaudits bestowed on Youth's Friendly Monitor when first privately circulated and like that essay initially intended solely for the edification of his pupils, the work was offered for public sale because Burgh could not afford the printing costs involved. His unpleasant experiences with Read undoubtedly explains why he abandoned his customary anonymity and published the work under his own name. Dedicated to the Princess Dowager whom Burgh felt best exemplified, excepting Prince George, the true dignity of man, The Dignity of Human Nature proposed:

> to shew what is truly great, ornamental or
> useful, in life; to call the attention of mankind
> to objects worthy of their regard, as rational and
> immortal beings, to give a brief, but comprehensive
> account of the certain and established means for
> attaining the true end of our existence, happiness
> in the present and future states.[74]

A loosely organized collection of pithy observations on human nature that was enhanced with salient bits of advice on how an individual could best conduct his secular and spiritual affairs, this lengthy tome was extremely well received. Published in late March of 1754 after a publicity campaign no doubt reserved for books thought to have significance and/or popular appeal, the work was simultaneously carried by five booksellers.[75] Although expensive at 10s.6d., it was in wide demand both in England and in America.[76] The Monthly Review described the book as a "sensible and useful performance" abounding in "many just and interesting observations." Andrew Kippis thought the study a "capital" one that "would ever deserve to be put into the hands of young people." He made no distinction between the relative merits of The Dignity of Human Nature and the Political Disquisitions when he implied that Burgh's reputation as an author rested on these two publications.[77] To a more sophisticated age, Kippis's evaluation is incomprehensible. To his generation, however, The Dignity of Human Nature was justly reputed "a very celebrated work."[78]

Yet the popularity of the study could not compensate for the considerable strain its production had imposed on Burgh. Although a man of tremendous energy, he was exhausted by the professional, personal, and literary obligations of the past four years, and despondent over his encounters with grandees and unscrupulous printers. Never having intended to make writing his career, he resolved not "to undertake any work of such a size" again. Himself forty years old, he recommended that an individual not embark on "any great design" after that age.[79] And for the remainder of the decade Burgh followed his own advice. He concentrated his energies on his academy, writing only two pamphlets during that period.[80]

CHAPTER II:

THE MORALIST POLITICIZED

A disillusioned James Burgh reacted to the failure of his association scheme by withdrawing within the comfortable confines of Newington
Green. But permanent retirement was impossible for a man of his moralistic disposition. His religious conviction in the feasibility of moral regeneration precluded his becoming a confirmed cynic. George III's
accession to the throne quickly rekindled Burgh's crusading ardor and
riveted his attention on the political scene. Encouraged by an invet-
erate optimism that was bolstered by his earlier contact with the youthful monarch, Burgh assumed that the throne was now occupied by a "patriot king" who would usher in the millennium. His expectations, albeit
exaggerated, were shared by many of his fellow citizens and actively
encouraged by the new sovereign.[1] The advent of the young king initiated
a "rising expectations" syndrome in English politics. Studies of the
period have largely ignored this important ingredient in the emotionally charged atmosphere of the 1760s.[2] But as Burgh's case demonstrates,
the frustration of those expectations helped fuel the extraordinary hue
and cry that greeted political actions during the early years of the
reign.

The first British ruler in Burgh's lifetime born and bred an Englishman, the young king cultivated a reputation for piety and patriotism that naturally prompted men of Burgh's disposition to anticipate a
new probity in politics, a rebirth of rectitude throughout the land.
Coinciding with the conclusion of a war that considerably augmented the
territory and commercial potential of the royal domain, George's accession seemed to harbinger a period of unparalleled greatness in British
history. What wonders might be accomplished in a reign of possibly
fifty years. Faction would cease; manufactures would prosper; "public
and private Virtue and true Religion, . . . [would] again raise their
drooping Heads; . . . Luxury, Infidelity, Corruption, and Perjury, . .
[would] sink to the regions of darkness, whence they first arose; and
. . . Heaven . . . [would] again smile propitious on these once highly
favoured nations."[3]

How keen the disappointment of men like Burgh as their dreams became nightmares. Instead of another Moses, George became the focal

point of party strife in a power struggle that seemed to stimulate
rather than stymie corruption. The king's attempts to purge the government of party and corruption and to exercise his constitutional prerogative to select his own ministers obliged him to utilize the very political tactics which he opposed in principle, thereby aggravating, rather than eliminating party rivalries. Faction flourished; civil liberties were assaulted; manufactures were imperilled by an imperial policy
that threatened the survival of the empire.

This unhappy turn of events politicized James Burgh. Prior to
George III's accession, Burgh had scarcely mentioned politics. Thereafter political themes increasingly preoccupied his writing which he
resumed shortly after the new reign began. Frustrated in his unrealistic hopes that George III would be the instrument of national regeneration, horrified by the ministry's very real foibles and blunders, Burgh
gradually became convinced that his country was teetering on the brink
of tyranny and deemed action to be imperative lest the nation's liberties, already dangerously undermined, be completely subverted. Such a
disaster would be doubly damnable. Not only would the victory of tyranny mean the demise of political freedom, it would occasion the waning
of English commerce for "where liberty is restrained, commerce languish-
es." The country would decline from its pinnacle of greatness. Under
such circumstances Burgh projected an unhappy future:

> I see, _____ how shall I write it? _____
> I see my wretched country in the same condition as
> France is now. Instead of the rich and thriving
> farmers, who now fill, or who lately filled, the
> country with agriculture, yielding plenty for man
> and beast, I see the lands neglected, the villages
> and farms in ruins, with here and there a starve-
> ling in wooden shoes, driving his plough, consist-
> ing of an old goat, a hidebound bullock, and an
> ass, value in all forty shillings. I see the once
> rich and populous cities of England in the same
> condition with those of Spain; whole streets ly-
> ing in rubbish and the grass peeping up between
> the stones in those which continue still inhabited.
> I see the harbours empty, the warehouses shut up,
> and the shopkeepers playing at draughts for want
> of customers. I see our noble and spacious turn-
> pike roads covered with thistles and other weeds,
> and scarce to be traced out.[4]

Burgh's last years were dominated by a crusade to alert the nation to
its peril.

Burgh was sustained and encouraged during these troubled years by
those "friends of liberty," the Honest Whigs. A club that met on al-
ternate Thursday evenings at St. Paul's Coffeehouse in London, this coterie had apparently been organized by John Canton, Fellow of the Royal
Society, electrician, and former schoolmaster. Comprised mostly of
nonconformists (although Jonathan Shipley, Bishop of St. Asaph, is said
to have belonged), its apparently fluid membership consisted largely

of clergymen, teachers, and doctors. Participants in addition to Burgh included Richard Price, Joseph Priestley, Benjamin Franklin, James Boswell, Andrew Kippis, William Rose (schoolmaster, critic, and co-founder of The Monthly Review), John Hawkesworth (dramatist, essayist, and editor), John Stanley (composer and organist), Peter Collinson (merchant and naturalist), Dr. Joseph Jeffries ("a supporter of the Bill of Rights"), William Watson (physician to the Foundling Hospital), Matthew Maty (principal secretary of the Royal Society and principal librarian of the British Museum), Peter Templeman (keeper of the Reading Room at the British Museum), James Parsons (doctor and philolgian), Sir John Pringle (President of the Royal Society and a prominent physician), John Fothergill (the Quaker philanthropist), Dr. Samuel Morton Savage, Dr. Thomas Amory (who succeeded Price as morning preacher at Newington Green in 1770), Dr. Philip Furneaux, Mr. Ebenezer Radcliff, Mr. J. Collings, and Mr. James Densham.[5]

The most intimate sketch of the club's activities has been provided, appropriately, by James Boswell. Describing a meeting of September 21, 1769, Boswell noted that the assembled group had access to some wine and punch on a table. Some members enjoyed a pipe. Conversation was carried on "pretty formally, sometimes sensibly, and sometimes furiously." Supper was served at nine and consisted of such items as apple puffs, rarebits, porter and beer. In all, the gathering cost each member about 18d. On this particular evening, "much was said . . . against Parliament." Frequently Boswell facetiously suggested that "as it seemed to be agreed that all members of Parliament become corrupted, it was better to chuse [sic] men already bad and so save good men."[6]

Burgh joined the Honest Whigs in the early 1760s. They were a particularly congenial group for a man of his intelligence, interests, and conversational skills. They shared his distrust of the turbulence and corruption of the English metropolis. For the most part they were alienated from the established Church and thus were barred, at least theoretically, from active participation in politics. Accordingly, they were able to subject their society to the critical appraisal of the outsider. "Their faith was science, education, and the application of the principles of correct reason to the problems of the day. Earnestly dedicated to doing right, they believed in the power of moderate sense and knowledge to improve the lot of their fellow men."[7] Their political creed was best summed up by the pamphleteer Thomas Gordon who identified a true and independent whig as one who:

> scorns all implicit faith in the state, as well
> as the Church. The authority of names is nothing
> to him; he judges all men by their actions and be-
> haviour, and hates a knave of his own party as much
> as he despises a fool of another. He consents not
> that any man or body of men shall do what they
> please. He claims a right of examining all publick
> measures, and if they deserve it, of censuring them.
> As he never saw much power possessed without some
> abuse, he takes upon him to watch those that have
> it; and to acquit, or expose them, according as

they apply it to the good of their country,
or their own crooked purposes.[8]

The influence of the Honest Whigs upon James Burgh is difficult to
measure. Burgh once remarked that "the only Value of the Opinion of
others is, That it may serve to confirm the Judgment of a Man's own
Conscience." But he also asserted:

> nothing more forcibly warms the mind to a
> love of goodness, or raises it more powerfully to
> all that is truly great and worthy, than the con-
> versation of wise and virtuous men. There is a
> force in what is said _viva face_, which nothing in
> writing can come up to.[9]

Although in the vanguard of a select group of reformers of whom the
Honest Whigs were representative, Burgh was less an original thinker
than an eclectic intelligence. In the heat of debate or in the cool
reasonableness of friendly dialogue, his thoughts on a multitude of topics were nurtured, molded, or crystallized. He formalized in print
ideas that had been bantered about, mulled over, analyzed, and discussed
by himself and his friends over many a Thursday evening glass of wine
or Sunday afternoon cup of tea. He was propagandist and popularizer of
a group viewpoint.

When Burgh renewed his literary career in late December, 1761 there
was no hint of his impending emergence as one of Britain's foremost
spokesmen for political reform prior to the American Revolution. The
Art of Speaking[10] is typical of his earlier focus on educational and
moral themes. It was the last of his works to have this exclusive emphasis.

Criticisms of English oratory, especially clerical delivery, were
widespread in the early eighteenth century. Addison had complained:

> Nothing could be more ridiculous than the
> gestures of most of our English speakers. You
> see some of them running their hands into their
> pockets as far as ever they can thrust them, and
> others looking with great attention on a piece of
> paper that has nothing written on it; you may see
> many a smart rhetorician turning his hat in his
> hands, moulding it into several different cocks,
> examining sometimes the lining of it, and some-
> times the button, during the whole of his harangue.
> A deaf man would think he was cheapening a beaver;
> when perhaps he was talking of the fate of the
> British nation.[11]

To improve oratorical training in England, two schools of elocutionary
theory were developed in the latter half of the century. One group emphasized a flexible approach to oratory. Generally styled the "natural" school, this group relied on broad precepts and stressed

comprehension of whatever was to be read or spoken. Thomas Sheridan was the foremost exponent of this philosophy. The second school, reflecting neo-classicism's concern with methodizing nature through the formulation of rigid rules, offered elaborate instructions for satisfying virtually every demand which might be made on the orator. The Art of Speaking is usually described as an example of such a mechanical approach to rhetoric.[12]

Initially the volume was intended to be simply an inexpensive collection of rhetorical exercises drawn from the best writers in prose and verse for use as a school-text. Upon reflection, Burgh broadened the scope of the work so that it might be profitably used by students, adults, and clerics interested in developing or enhancing oratorical skills.[13] He prefaced the practice exercises with a sixty-two page essay containing general observations on the importance of rhetoric and the means of acquiring facility in speaking.

The Art of Speaking was the most widely circulated of Burgh's volumes. It went through eight editions in England. The Monthly Review described it as "a laudable attempt to excite greater attention to an important part of education than is generally paid to it."[14] The colonial response was equally enthusiastic. The first treatise on speech ever published in America, it had at least ten editions there.[15] Advertisements noted:

> The general reception and approbation which
> this work has met with in Great Britain and Ire-
> land, not only as a school book, but as a private
> preceptor in the study of elocution, sufficiently
> evince its merit . . . The author of this work,
> a Gentleman of distinguished reputation in England,
> has ennobled his memory by the great pains he
> has taken, and the judgment he has shewn both in
> the easy yet sublime rules he has laid, and the
> lessons he has selected for the purpose of acquir-
> ing a graceful elocution: and whoever will care-
> fully attend thereto cannot fail of attaining two
> of the first accomplishments of a Gentleman, that
> of reading and speaking gracefully.[16]

James Burgh's importance in the development of speech education was long underestimated. Recent studies have rectified this injustice. The introductory essay to The Art of Speaking "was read by [Thomas] Sheridan, paraphrased by [John] Walker, anthologized by [William]Scott, pirated by an American publisher, quoted by [Gilbert] Austin, and recalled in one way or another by elocutionists [including Noah Webster] for over a century."[17] Burgh is now recognized as one of the "four early writers who gave the elocutionary movement its first distinctive framework."[18]

Within months of The Art of Speaking's publication, Burgh completed the first of his compositions to give close attention either to foreign or domestic politics. Never published, its existence apparently unknown to contemporaries and posterity, "Remarks Historical and Political . . . Humbly presented to the King's most excellent Majesty," is an intriguing composition that provides the most thorough available exposition of Burgh's theory of monarchy. Implicit in the work is his first uneasy apprehension--sparked by the growing contention over Lord Bute and the pending peace negotiations concluding the Seven Years War --that George might prove less a king than Burgh had anticipated. The obvious haste with which Burgh and his wife transcribed the manuscript suggests that the schoolmaster hoped to influence the king's thinking on these controversial issues.[19] Burgh justified his audacity on the grounds that he had earlier promised the recently deceased Stephen Hales to "write out, and from time to time" present to the King "whatever observations . . . made from books, or other wise" which seemed "in any degree worthy" of George's attention. He secretly submitted the manuscript to the king in August of 1762, with assurances that "being in temper and circumstances independent," he expected no compensation for his efforts.[20]

In the "Remarks" Burgh boldly lectured the new monarch on his moral and political responsibilities as if he were an adolescent schoolboy in the classroom at Newington Green. Strongly influenced by Bolingbroke's _Patriot King_, Burgh claimed that the people would "deify" George if he championed the cause of virtue. Hopeful that the demise of the Pitt-Newcastle coalition augured the decline of ministerial influence, he exhorted George to "be a King" and personally resume the powers guaranteed England's monarch by the country's "mixed" constitution. Although acknowledging George's prerogative to choose Lord Bute as his chief advisor, Burgh urged him "to see with his own _eyes_, rather than those of _others_." Perhaps his previous contact with the King gave Burgh an appreciation of the young man's diffidence for he assured George that he had "no occasion to be at a loss for the _real state_ of affairs, or for the best advice, his kingdom can afford. History and political books . . . [were] open before him. By them he . . . [might] master the wisdom of the mighty dead." In any case, politics was "only _common sense_ applied to matters of public concern."[21] On the subject of the pending peace treaty, Burgh reported that "the friends of the gov.ᵗ" earnestly hoped "the next to come may be _less_ obnox. to just _blame_, than the two _last_." He warned that if a "less advantageous peace" than the people expected was concluded, the blame would be attributed to those "who promoted contin.¹ meas.ˢ." Convinced that "forbear.ᶜᵉ on the part of Brit. will alw.ˢ produce insol.ᶜᵉ on that of France," Burgh boldly proposed his own peace terms. These included indemnification for British losses in this and the previous war, a limitation on the number of French warships, and commercial concessions that would give Britain preeminence over France.[22]

When Burgh dispatched this amazing manuscript he apparently consigned it to oblivion. There is nothing to indicate that the King read it.[23] Certainly during the next few years little in his conduct fulfilled Burgh's expectations. But despite royal unresponsiveness to his advice, Burgh doggedly persisted in his efforts to influence governmental policy. Quitting the avenue of private suasion, he returned to the familiar path of appealing to the reading public. Much more involved in radical agitation than has been generally appreciated, he produced a variety of publications that expanded with increasing urgency upon themes enunciated in the "Remarks."

Published in 1764, An Account of the First Settlement, Laws, Form of Government, and Police of the Cessares detailed a blueprint for colonial development which Burgh hoped would be applied in the territories acquired during the recent war.[24] This epistolary exercise provides the most specific exposition of Burgh's remedies for the evils he believed affected English society. Approximating a modern planned community in its mathematical organization, the Cessares' settlement epitomized a Commonwealthman's ideal of "mixed" government, a Dissenter's ideal of religious freedom, and a Calvinist's ideal of moral rectitude, absteemiousness, and industry. Burgh rather smugly concluded that "a better form of government, where the liberty and happiness of every individual is more carefully consulted; where every tendency to vice and licentiousness is more effectually discouraged; and where more care is taken of the right education of the children" could not be found than in the land of the Cessares.[25] One of the very few reformist utopian studies printed in eighteenth century Britain,[26] the Account of the. . . Cessares was ignored by reviewers, newspapers, and the public. Burgh was ill prepared by his previous literary successes or his sense of Christian activism to cope with such indifference. As was the case a decade earlier, his enthusiasm for reform soon gave way to intense frustration, exaggerated by exhaustion and his own unrealistic expectations. His mood was at its ugliest after the almost simultaneous publication of two disparate works, neither of which engendered the interest he anticipated.

In early spring of 1766 Burgh brought out volume one of Crito, a collection of essays on religious toleration, contemporary politics, Rousseau's educational theories, and the metaphysics of evil. Whereas the Account of the . . . Cessares had obliquely criticized English society by extolling the virtues of a utopian community, Crito made no such pretense. Burgh hoped his pointed comments would stimulate controversy as a prelude to reform. The volume attracted some attention in the press,[27] but Burgh deemed the response woefully inconsequential. His summer involvement in another abortive association further heightened his distress at public apathy.

In August Burgh became the spokesman for an anonymous group of public-spirited gentlemen who hoped to assist the poor by reducing the exorbitant price of foodstuffs in London. From 1750 until 1790 English agricultural prices rose between 50 and 75%, largely in response to the growing pressure on food supplies made by a bourgeoning population. Increasing profit margins encouraged farmers, the chief beneficiaries of these rising prices, to enclose at least 2,000,000 acres and reclaim an additional 3,000,000 acres of waste lands during this period. Periodically, this upward price trend was exaggerated by the whims of nature. So it was in 1766 and 1767, a time of "general, if not acute, dearth." Severe winter frost and heavy spring and summer rains led to a partial failure of the crops. Sheep-rot forced up the price of mutton and animal foodstuffs in general were in short supply due to the scarcity of

fodder. Food riots were widespread.[28] London newspapers were barraged
with letters of complaint which evidenced particular concern for the
plight of the poor. Monopolists were popularly singled out as the culprits responsible for the distressing rise in the cost of living.[29]
Burgh and his associates shared this conviction.[30]

Arguing that the law was too inflexible to deal with the current
emergency, Burgh's coterie organized the Provision Society whose purposes were three-fold: (1) "To bring Butcher's Meat to the London mar-
kets, free from the unjust profits laid upon it by interlopers, between
the breeder and the consumer;" (2) to indemnify persons who would be
willing to testify against Forestallers, Regrators, etc; (3) to check
the premature destruction of young cattle and sheep by premiums and
"other means." To accomplish these goals the Society solicited sub-
scriptions of at least ₤20. Once ₤5,000 had been pledged a general court
would be called to elect a governing committee of twenty-four which
would be responsible for purchasing "in the cheapest manner" full-grown
cattle and sheep. The animals would be driven to London where they would
be penned, slaughtered and dressed for sale, in part to retail butchers
at prices set by the Society and in part directly to consumers "for
ready money only."[31]

Burgh delineated the Society's proposals in an anonymous pamphlet
published in August. Although The Monthly Review approved the "useful
design" and recommended it to the "attention and encouragement of the
public,"[32] the organization apparently expired from insufficient support. Burgh's bitterness was acute. With the ire of a prophet scorned,
he railed against the public's apathy in volume two of Crito which appeared the following May. Indignantly charging that "whoever attempts
any thing toward reformation, is sure to become the butt of universal
ridicule . . . [as] a Quixote, a castle-builder, a dreamer," he caus-
tically complained:

> time was when people were ashamed of being publicly
> branded; and it was thought necessary to answer
> a writer who presumed to insinuate, that governors,
> either in church or state, were culpable. What was
> the consequence? Why a controversy was set on foot:
> Matters were thoroughly examined: Truth came out:
> The eyes of the people were opened: . . . the wings
> of tyranny and priestcraft were clipped. How much
> wiser we; who walk off, as quietly as so many
> cowards after a kicking . . . Thus the honest
> writer's good advice is neglected, and the evil re-
> mains uncured.[33]

Such indifference prompted Burgh to dedicate Crito's second volume to
the "Good People of Britain of the Twentieth Century" in the hope that
they would hold him in higher estimation than did his own generation.
After rambling discursively over a variety of political issues, he resumed his discussion of evil and concluded with a defense of Christianity's rationality.

Ironically, volume two of Crito provoked greater interest than its less vitriolic predecessor. The prestigious _Gentleman's Magazine_ commented that it included "many sensible and important remarks upon subjects that are worthy of universal attention." Lengthy excerpts were reprinted in _The Monthly Review_ and in _The London Chronicle_. One correspondent with the latter approvingly noted that _Crito_ was "calculated to put almost all sorts of people out of humor with themselves, with one another, with established opinions, and established practices."[34]

The volume's tone might account for this level of interest. More probably the hypertensive Burgh, overextended by his literary, civic, and professional obligations, had been precipitate in concluding that his ideas had not found a receptive audience. Disaffection with English society, and with the government in particular, was deepening. The John Wilkes affair[35] and the Stamp Act crisis served as the seedbeds for a parliamentary and imperial reform movement that gained impressive momentum in the next ten years. As the author of _Crito_ Burgh early established himself as a spokesman for that movement and earned an important place in its vanguard.

Stirred by the events of the next few years Burgh quickly recovered from his lapse into cynicism. Although he continued to berate his countrymen for their degeneracy he never again engaged in the scathing sarcasm of _Crito_. He had been disappointed in his hopes that _Crito_ would have an ameliorating impact on the parliamentary elections held in 1768 and took advantage of the publication of James Boswell's _Account of Corsica_ to upbraid his fellow citizens for "courting the yoke and bowing their necks to a set of encroaching grandees." Deliberately, however, he concluded with the optimistic observation that he did not yet despair of the Commonwealth.[36]

Burgh's comments earned him an introduction to Boswell through the offices of the printer Charles Dilly.[37] Thereafter, Boswell frequented the Honest Whigs, but proved less a friend to liberty than Burgh initially supposed. Dilly, however, was typical of the growing number of reform-minded Britons with whom Burgh associated, a circumstance reflecting the close ties within the radical community. The printer subsequently published Burgh's radical manifesto, the _Political Disquisitions_. An intimate of the radical historian, Catharine Macaulay, Dilly may also have initiated Burgh's friendship with that lady. In the winter of 1768-1769 Burgh frequented her salon, a popular rendezvous for radical reformers, and spiritedly exchanged political views with men like the colonial physician, Benjamin Rush, and Mrs. Macaulay's brother, John Sawbridge.[38] A newly elected member of parliament, Sawbridge was fast emerging as a major figure in the latest controversy engendered by the perpetually provocative John Wilkes. Burgh too became embroiled in that cause celebre.

The ambitious and dissolute Wilkes first provoked popular interest in 1763 while editing a vitriolic opposition newspaper, the _North Briton_. He used the publication to launch a scurrilous attack on Lord Bute, the ministry, and the treaties concluding the Seven Years War. In retaliation the government unwisely resorted to a general warrant to obtain evidence against Wilkes for seditious libel and subsequently sought his imprisonment, even though he was a member of parliament and immune from arrest. This obstacle was overcome by securing Wilkes's expulsion from the Commons which prompted the rabble rouser to flee to France. Wilkes returned to England in 1768, impecunious, and bent on escaping his creditors in the halls of Westminster. Failing in his bid for election to parliament from London, he succeeded in Middlesex county. The ministry refused to acquiesce in this affront and Wilkes was denied his seat, only to be reelected by his Middlesex constituents. This happened at three successive elections until Commons declared the minority candidate, Colonel Henry Lawes Luttrell, duly elected.

Climaxing a series of controversies that began with Lord Bute's ministerial career and included the Stamp Act crisis, this latest example of ministerial effrontery galvinized radicals into overt political action and generated an organized extra-parliamentary reform movement. Wilkes became a popular hero. Sawbridge and others organized a fund for his relief and initiated a petition movement in the summer of 1769 to vindicate the constitutional rights of Wilkes and the Middlesex freeholders.

Moralistic radicals like James Burgh did not find Wilkes an attractive standard bearer for the reform movement.[39] Burgh had earlier criticized the folly of those who so intemperately supported such a dissolute demagogue.[40] Nonetheless, in the current controversy Burgh agreed with Richard Price's observation that while Wilkes was a seamy individual, "the question which he had been the occasion of moving was of such a constitutional magnitude, that his private character ought to have no influence on the decision of it."[41] There was absolutely no doubt in Burgh's mind that the people had the irrefutable right to elect whom they saw fit as their representatives. In denying Wilkes his seat, parliament was arrogating privileges and powers never granted it by the ultimate source of sovereign power: the people.[42]

In Burgh's opinion, however, the controverted Middlesex election was only the most notorious instance of parliament's unconstitutional conduct. Petitions for the dissolution of parliament and the removal of the ministry might redress the grievances of one man and one county. They would not rectify the fundamental constitutional imbalance that gave rise to such assaults on the liberties of Englishmen. To persuade the petitioners to lobby for substantive constitutional reform Burgh published twenty letters in The Gazetteer and New Daily Advertiser, one of London's most widely circulated daily newspapers.[43] This forum allowed Burgh's radical ideas to reach their largest audience ever. Given his friendship with Mrs. Macaulay and her brother, the intriguing possibility exists that Burgh began this series at their prompting. If so, his action would underscore the political sophistication of the reformers and in particular their skill in manipulating public opinion through the press.

Using the pseudonym "Constitutionalist," Burgh argued that the constitution had been subverted and that the House of Commons was:

> too much under the influence of the Court, that

elections have been too much at the command of
the Peerage; and that, accordingly, our p_____ts,
instead of proving as they ought the <u>defense</u> of
the <u>people</u>, against the bad effects of . . . administration, and the dread of ministerial tyranny,
have been little else than the outworks of corrupt
<u>Courts</u>, and the sanctuary of bad Ministers.

If the constitution was to be restored, three reforms were essential:
annual parliaments in which no individual could sit more than once in
seven years; adequate representation with parliamentary seats appor-
tioned to each county on the basis of the taxes paid by its inhabitants
and with the franchise accorded to every contributor to the window-tax;
and the exclusion of all placemen and pensioners from the House of Commons.[44]

Alternating on the front page of the <u>Gazetteer</u> with correspondence
from such notables as "Junius" and Junius Americanus," the "Constitutionalist" letters provoked considerable attention.[45] Burgh was immense-
ly gratified. In order to make his ideas accessible in greater detail
to "gentlemen of property, influence and integrity," he at first resolved to publish the "Constitutionalist" letters in a pamphlet or pock-
et volume,[46] but on reflection apparently decided to expand the series
into a comprehensive survey of conditions in Britain and in the colonies.
The <u>Political Disquisitions</u> would be the result.

Burgh's intention to include the colonies in his projected study
reflected the conviction of radicals that the issue of colonial taxation
provided another major instance of government's flagrant violation of
the rights of Englishmen. Unfortunately, preoccupation with the Wilkes
affair left little time during the winter of 1769 for government's critics to respond to the latest crisis in the ongoing dispute over colonial
taxation. When parliament reconvened after its Christmas recess the
ministry intended to recommend the repeal of most of the Townshend customs duties, instituted in 1767. Opponents of the duties objected that
anything less than their total repeal would undermine the American boy-
cott of British goods initiated to protest the duties and thereby tacit-
ly sustain the reprehensible principle of taxation without representation. Burgh shared this concern. He was undoubtedly encouraged in doing so by his "incomparable" friend and fellow Honest Whig Benjamin
Franklin. Burgh had great respect and affection for the American and
valued his friendship as "one of the most fortunate circumstances" of
Burgh's life.[47] Franklin was deeply involved in the lobbying effort on
behalf of total repeal of the Townshend duties. Possibly at Franklin's
behest, Burgh too became active in this cause. He temporarily suspend-
ed the "Constitutionalist" letters in late December, 1769 and joined the
debate over repeal. Beginning January 4, 1770 he published eleven letters under the pseudonym "The Colonist's Advocate" in the <u>Public Adver-</u>
<u>tiser</u>, another renowned London daily.[48] The series catalogued colonial
grievances against the mother country and succinctly recapitulated the
familiar arguments against taxing the colonies. "The Colonist's Advocate" letters were "the most considerable effort" waged in the press on
behalf of total repeal.[49] The cause, however, proved hopeless. With

the triumph of partial repeal imminent, Burgh terminated the series March 2nd and resumed the guise of "Constitutionalist."

Burgh's last letters as "Constitutionalist" vigorously disputed Edmund Burke's recently published party tract, Thoughts on the Cause of the Present Discontents, thereby highlighting a growing rift in the ranks of government's critics. Burke was the spokesman for aristocratic reformers like the Marquis of Rockingham who were bent solely on curbing the king's political power while their own remained intact. Radicals like Burgh and his friend, Catharine Macaulay (who wrote the most effective rejoinder to Burke's pamphlet) were adamantly opposed to Burke's argument that parliamentary reform would be unnecessary if public confidence was reposed in a "firm combination" of party men like the Rockinghamites.[50] Such ideological differences and the exigencies of practical politics disrupted the reform movement and prevented sustained cooperation among its adherents during the next few years. By contrast the ministry, now under the conciliatory direction of Lord North, demonstrated considerable deftness in defusing the petition and reform movements and resolving potentially explosive issues such as the reorganization of the East India Company. The Boston Tea Party ended North's idyll. War with the colonies reinvigorated the cause of reform in England, ultimately climaxing in the 1780s with the organization of an abortive extra-parliamentary association movement.

Despite the bleakness of reform's prospects in the first years of North's administration, Burgh persisted in his determination to publish a multi-volume survey of:

> the most interesting Political Points agitated in
> these Times, in order to open the eyes of the People,
> and enable them to guard against their most danger-
> ous Enemies, viz. Tyrannical Princes, Designing
> Ministers, Corrupt Parliaments, and False Patriots;
> by determining from authentic History, and the
> Opinions of many of the best Politicians of var-
> ious Ages and Nations, the true Principles accord-
> ing to which the British Empire ought to be gov-
> erned, and the Deviations from those Principles, com-
> mitted by Kings, Ministers, or Parliaments; and by
> exhibiting Instances of Impositions on the People by
> their pretended Friends, and pointing out the dis-
> tinguishing Marks of true Patriotism.[51]

In order that "no important historical fact nor valuable political remark" pertinent to his discussion might escape him, Burgh undertook a rigorous course of reading in English history, political tracts, parliamentary debates and statutes, and contemporary newspapers and magazines. He aspired to make his magnum opus a work of objective scholarship, but in fact was consistently uncritical in his use of sources that confirmed his opinions.[52] The tome proved to be the least polished of Burgh's works--a circumstance which reflected the obvious haste in which it was written. In part that haste was apparently attributable to Burgh's hope that the publication would influence the outcome of the general election

due in late 1774 or early 1775.[53] But Burgh's race to complete the
Political Disquisitions anticipated a deadlier event than an impending
election.

A general feeling of ill health had prompted Burgh to quit his
academy sometime after August 26, 1771 and move to a house in Colebrook
Row in neighboring Islington. Shortly thereafter he was diagnosed as
having a stone in his bladder. The pain from this infirmity became ex-
cruciating. Nonetheless, to his friends' astonishment, he continued for
a time to attend services at the Green Chapel, to tutor privately, and
to work furiously on the Political Disquisitions. In the last months of
his life he was obliged to restrict his social contacts to members of
his immediate family and to an occasional visit from admirers such as
Josiah Quincy, Jr. who were drawn to Colebrook Row by Burgh's reputation
as a political radical.[54] Only at the very end did he relinquish his
writing, having completed three of the projected six volumes of the
Political Disquisitions.[55] This study was Burgh's most important and
comprehensive endeavor and a fitting climax to his literary career.

In contrast to a racy and inexpensive pamphlet such as Common Sense,
the Political Disquisitions was costly, staid, and very long.[56] Nonetheless, the work achieved considerable notoriety on both sides of the Atlantic. Those who could not purchase it might borrow it from a friend
as did the Rev. Peter Cunningham, Curate of Eyam.[57] Libraries made the
work accessible to others. The Bristol Library's copy was borrowed 38
times by 1784.[58] And excerpts in numerous periodicals, newspapers, and
other popular writings[59] made the work familiar to an extensive audience
that stretched from the backwoods of Kentucky to the provinces of England.[60] Even the Dutch were acquainted with the Disquisitions.[61]

In Britain the Disquisitions enjoyed the plaudits of the review
journals. Typical was the reaction of The Scots Magazine:

> This work cannot fail of being highly useful to
> members of parliament, and all those who are de-
> sirous of acquiring a knowledge of the principles
> and defects of the British constitution; as the
> most valuable materials on these subjects are here
> collected from the best authorities, and arranged
> in methodical order.[62]

Understandably, however, the work received its most enthusiastic
reception in reform circles. Boswell rather superciliously noted that
it was "much valued by . . . republican reformers," although he found
it "quite adverse" to his own "gentlemanly system."[63] In such quarters
the Disquisitions immediately became a classic text with well nigh the
authority of Scripture. Few would have agreed with Jeremy Bentham's
characterization of Burgh's tome as "a well meant but superficial performance." Far more typical was the opinion of the Reverend Samuel
Parr, L.L.D., Curate of Hatton and Prebendary of St. Paul's who when
asked whether he had read the Disquisitions replied indignantly: "Have
I read my Bible, Sir?"[64]

At some point almost every major figure in the reform movement had
occasion to acknowledge their indebtedness to Burgh's magnum opus.   It
served two purposes for them. First and foremost it was a fund of information, a tremendous reference work. Burgh had drawn together all
of the ideological threads of reform thought, all of the facts, figures,
and examples necessary to document the reformers' case. Again and again
reformers cited the Disquisitions to prove their points or referred
their audiences to the work for a more extended discussion of a particular issue. Describing Burgh as an "excellent author" and one of the
public's "best friends," the celebrated republican historian, Catharine
Macaulay, quoted at length from the Disquisitions to demonstrate the
folly of taxing America. Likewise, in his famous speech of March 21,
1776 advocating parliamentary reform, John Wilkes relied heavily on
Burgh's discussion of the inadequacy of representation in the Commons.
Burgh's friend Richard Price invoked the Disquisitions for the same purpose. Tom Paine referred the readers of Common Sense to the work should
they seek a detailed explanation of the value of "a large and equal representation" in a state. Both William Pitt the younger and the Duke of
Richmond apparently studied Burgh on this same subject. One of the
leaders of the Association movement of the 1780s, John Jebb, advised a
meeting of Middlesex freeholders in 1779: "Let any unprejudiced person
consult the 'Political Disquisitions' of the late excellent Mr. Burgh;
let him attend to facts, which must have fallen within his proper knowledge; and he may possibly be inclined to doubt, whether an english [sic]
house of commons is in being at this instant." Capel Lofft, Jebb's colleague in the radical Society for Constitutional Information, relied on
the "excellent Burgh" for an exposition of the "abuses which have destroyed the Representation of the Commonalty." Lofft praised Burgh as
a "man who devoted his time, his health and life to the service of the
community and who submitted talents, of unusual vigour and acuteness, to
the painful office of compiling authentic evidence for their information
on points of universal concern." In fact the Society for Constitutional
Information was so convinced of the Disquisitions's importance that it
published and distributed excerpts from the work gratis.[65]

     But the Disquisitions was more than a reference work to document
preconceived opinions. It was also a source of inspiration for the radicals. Major John Cartwright, one of the primary progenitors of the
Association movement of the 1780s, was considerably indebted to the plan
Burgh enunciated in the Disquisitions for the creation of a national
association. In his highly influential essay, Take Your Choice, Cartwright made numerous references to the Disquisitions and advised his
readers to:

               either recollect or read what is proposed in the
               conclusion of the Political Disquisitions, con-
               cerning a GRAND NATIONAL ASSOCIATION FOR RESTORING
               THE CONSTITUTION. It would be impertinent to re-
               peat what is there written. I will only endeavor to
               throw in my small contribution towards removing the
               difficulties of carrying such a scheme into practice.[66]

Cartwright's colleague, John Jebb, likewise devised an association plan based on Burgh's model. And still another participant in the reform movement, Granville Sharp, took his "cue" from Burgh's Disquisitions when advocating that counties "elect, instruct, and supervise members of Parliament."[67]

Although after the onset of the French Revolution, the Disquisitions's influence gradually waned along with the reform movement itself, it continued to be esteemed by reformers well into the nineteenth century. Samuel Taylor Coleridge relied heavily on it in 1795 for his Bristol lectures against the Two Bills, subsequently published as The Plot Discovered. Likewise, William Hazlitt cited Burgh extensively in his 1807 "Reply to Malthus's Essay on Population," as did John Rutt in his annotations to the 1832 edition of Joseph Priestley's works. Speaking in 1815, William Morgan, Richard Price's nephew, observed that the Disquisitions "abounds with the most important information on the extreme defectiveness of the national representation, and cannot fail to be admired by all who wish to restore the constitution to its original purity." Such sentiments prompted a Scottish bookseller to remark as late as 1842 that the work was held "in high estimation."[68]

In 1794 the radical journalist Daniel Isaac Eaton announced his intention to publish James Burgh's collected works in a series of Political Classics that would also include the writings of Algernon Sidney, William Lord Russel, Milton, Locke, Harrington, Thomas More, George Buchanan, Montesquieu, Paine, Price, and William Godwin. Eaton noted that in their works these "judicious Philosophers" had "laid down such principles of government, which must flash conviction on the most despotic mind, and which have lived, and will ever live, to immortalize their names till time is no more."[69] Undoubtedly, it was on the strength of the Political Disquisitions that Eaton included Burgh in his litany of Commonwealthmen heroes. Eaton's tribute aptly indicates the place of prominence and respect that James Burgh enjoyed within the late eighteenth century English reform movement.

The Disquisitions earned Burgh the esteem of American patriots as well as English radicals. Whereas English enthusiasts of the work proved a relatively ineffectual political minority, their American counterparts effected the Atlantic community's most successful revolution. This circumstance permitted the Disquisitions to exert a very real, albeit incalculable influence on the formation of the new American republic.

In the turbulent years immediately prior to the American Revolution colonial patriots and English radicals very deliberately courted each other's support and solicitude. Catharine Macaulay's home, for example, became a notorious rendezvous for Anglo-American dissidents. There James Burgh spiritedly discussed current politics with Americans like Benjamin Rush. The colonial agent, Arthur Lee, joined the Bill of Rights, Society to proselytize for America and arranged for complimentary copies of American pamphlets to be sent to reformers like Mrs. Macaulay and the Earl of Shelburne. In turn English radicals initiated correspondences with colonials and sent complimentary copies of radical literature to the Patriots. The English publishers Charles and Edward Dilly served as a clearing house for many of these exchanges. It was Edward Dilly who sent John Dickinson the first two volumes of Burgh's _Disquisitions_ "as a small token" of the author's respect for Dickinson's "Patriotic Virtue."[70] John Adams also received a complimentary set, perhaps through Dilly's offices, and was so impressed that he successfully worked to make the _Disquisitions_ "more known and attended to in several parts of America." He informed Burgh that his volumes were "held in as high estimation by all my friends as they are by me. The more they are read, the more eagerly and generally they are sought for."[71]

Possibly at Adams's or Dickinson's[72] instigation an American edition of the _Disquisitions_ was published on a subscription basis within sixteen months of the English. In itself this unusual feat indicates how very quickly the work achieved a reputation in the colonies as a radical manifesto. The list of subscribers underscores this fact. Aptly characterized as a "Who's Who in the American Revolution," it included George Washington, Thomas Jefferson, John Hancock, John Dickinson, Samuel Chase, Silas Deane, Robert Morris, Roger Sherman, and James Wilson.[73] Undoubtedly acquisition of the _Disquisitions_ was essentially a patriotic gesture for most of these Founding Fathers who would find in the work ample reinforcement of their prejudices and preconceptions. Both John Dickinson and Thomas Jefferson, for example, already owned the work prior to subscribing to the American edition.[74]

Those sets of the American or English editions made available to the American public by booksellers were highly recommended in advertisements such as that appearing in the _Pennsylvania Packet_ of June 12, 1775 which characterized Burgh's tome as "a very useful and interesting work, particularly necessary at this time for all the friends of Constitutional Liberty, whether Britons or Americans." The Philadelphia newspaper printed lengthy extracts from the _Disquisitions_ "for the benefit of those who have not yet those useful books."[75] Writing as "Novanglus" in the _Boston Gazette_, January 30, 1775, John Adams described the second volume of the work as "a book which ought to be in the hands of every American who has learned to read." With such endorsements, the _Disquisitions_ quickly became "fashionable reading."[76] In light of the general scarcity of currency in the colonies, a situation compounded by the uncertainty of events in 1775, the popularity of a costly work like the _Disquisitions_ is particularly remarkable. The evidence suggests that even "common" folk were familiar with it.[77]

In the main the _Disquisitions_ initially proved so popular in the colonies because it bolstered the position of patriotic Americans on the eve of rebellion. Burgh's sympathetic response to colonial complaints was understandably reassuring. But his discussion of strictly American affairs, albeit trenchant, constituted only sixty-seven pages in a treatise totalling one thousand four hundred twenty pages. Obviously, Burgh's appeal to colonials went beyond his comments on their particular grievances. His fulminations against a corrupt ministry and an inequitable system of representation which threatened the independency of the House of Commons and the preservation of a balanced constitution confirmed colonial fears of a "comprehensive conspiracy against liberty throughout the English-speaking world."[78] Writing in March 1776 under the pseudonym of "Cassandra," James Cannon, for example, cited Burgh and

Obadiah Hulme when he contended that "'the British constitution is so effectually undermined by the influence of the crown, that the people of Britain have no security for the enjoyment of their own liberties.'"[79] Bernard Bailyn has illuminated the significance of the Commonwealthman tradition in the formation of American revolutionary ideology. The Political Disquisitions climaxed over fifty years of agitation by Commonwealthmen whose criticisms and proposed reforms were seriously attended to by the Americans.

With the advent of peace, the appeal of the Disquisitions persisted. As was true of its English admirers, its American enthusiasts viewed the Disquisitions as an important political treatise of enduring significance and recognized authority. Thomas Jefferson, for one, included the work, together with the writings of Locke, Sidney, Priestley, Montesquieu, and De Lolme in a course of recommended reading for James Madison and James Monroe. He made the same recommendation to Thomas Mann Randolph in 1790 and to Bernard Moore in 1814. He also included the Disquisitions in his 1824 catalogue for the University of Virginia's Library. And in 1803, while President, he "urged" the work on Congress.[80]

During the constitutional debates waged on a state and national level in postwar America the Disquisitions was invoked with impressive frequency to substantiate widely divergent views. The scope of the work permitted federalists, anti-federalists, and local factionalists to select those of Burgh's arguments that suited their own purposes, ignoring any points to the contrary. James Madison cited the work in his "Additional Memorandum for the Convention of Virginia" and in Federalist 56. In fact the Disquisitions was one of the few books directly cited in The Federalist. Although he did not share Burgh's aversion to standing armies, James Wilson, a federalist, used the Disquisitions in his defense of the people's right to choose their governors. In contrast antifederalists emphasized Burgh's strictures against power, standing armies, and infrequent elections. The work was a "major" source of antifederalist thought. One antifederalist correspondent with The Independent Chronicle and Universal Advertiser sounded the key-note of antifederalist opinion when he observed: "It was wisely said by Burgh in his political disquisitions, all power is arbitrary; meaning all power naturally inclines to an arbitrary conduct." In his refutation of James Wilson's defense of standing armies, "A Democratic Federalist" suggested that the future supreme court justice read "the excellent Burgh in his political disquisitions, on this hackneyed subject, and then say whether you think that a standing army is necessary in a free country?" Another correspondent, discussing the magnitude of the task confronting the constitutional convention of 1787, hinted at his own political principles when he praised critics of the English constitution, such as Burgh and Tom Paine, and roundly criticized John Adams for his excessive enthusiasm for English institutions. Such was Burgh's reputation that even in a frontier state like Kentucky his name was invoked to resolve a dispute over popular ratification of the new state constitution. Defending such a manifestation of popular politics, "H.S.B.M." cited the Disquisitions and styled Burgh "the best of English authors." Although another correspondent with The Kentucky Gazette rebutted Burgh's argument, he shared "H.S.B.M."'s regard for Burgh, characterizing him as an individual "of the most exalted character." As late as 1807 the "young federalist" Abijah Bigelow utilized lengthy quotations from the _Disquisitions_ to bolster Bigelow's critique of political parties.[81]

The only sour note in this chorus of compliments was sounded by Burgh's former admirer John Adams. In 1774 Adams had described the _Disquisitions_ as the "best service that a citizen could render to his country at this great and dangerous crisis, when the British Empire seems ripe for destruction, and tottering on the brink of a precipice." By 1789 the growth of antifederal sentiment led Adams to qualify his judgment. Writing to Richard Price, Adams explained the circumstances which prompted him to write his _Defense of the Constitution_, published in 1787:

> It appeared to me, that my countrymen were running wild, and into danger, from a too ardent and inconsiderate pursuit of erroneous opinions of government, which had been propagated among them by some of their ill informed favourites, and by some writings which were very popular among them, such as the pamphlet called Common Sense, for one example, among many others; particularly Mrs. Macaulay's History, Mr. Burgh's Political Disquisitions, Mr. Turgot's Letters. These writings are all excellent in some respects, and very useful, but extremely mistaken in the true conception of a free government.[82]

Adams's judgment is telling evidence of the _Disquisitions_'s influence during the formative years of the American republic.

Although at his death James Burgh had various materials at hand suitable for posthumous publication, the _Political Disquisitions_ was the last of his writings to be shared with the public. Burgh was released from "the tortures . . . which he bore with uncommon patience and resignation" on August 26, 1775. He was buried in Bunhill Fields, the traditional resting place for Dissenters.[83] In his will, after directing that all of his "just debts and funeral expences be fully paid and satisfied," he bequeathed the residue of his estate to his "dearly beloved wife Hannah Burgh" whom he named as his Executrix.[84] Hannah Burgh survived her husband by thirteen years. On November 22, 1788, she too was interred at Bunhill Fields.[85]

Several sources tersely took note of Burgh's death,[86] but, not without some forethought perhaps, the man provided his own most appropriate epitath:

> I thank Heaven, I have endeavoured to honour virtue and truth, and to detect and disgrace corruption and villany. I have unburdened my own conscience. I have delivered my own soul. I have sounded a loud and distant alarm. I have endeavoured to raise the standard of liberty higher, and to unfurl it wider than has been

attempted by any private person before.
Whether my well-meant attempt will prove effectual for rousing you [my countrymen] from
your long and dangerous lethargy, remains to
be seen.[87]

Thus ended a lifetime devoted to the service of others. The young
Scot who had ventured to England in search of a livelihood had found
not only opportunity to make his fortune but occasion to exercise those
evangelistic instincts he had acquired during his Presbyterian upbringing. Shocked by the prejudice, intolerance, and corruption he encoun-
tered, he endeavored to foster the moral regeneration of English society. Often a frustrating experience, that moral crusade gradually involved Burgh in political reform as well. His pen was the instrument
whereby he sought to champion reform. His writings were his legacy to
the public.

PART II:

THE MANY FACES OF JAMES BURGH

CHAPTER III:

THE MAN OF FAITH

Fame, fortune, art, politics, or sensual gratification govern the
lives of many men. The mainspring of James Burgh's character and conduct was a moral code grounded in his religious convictions. It dominated his personal and professional relationships and occasioned his
literary career. Neither Burgh nor his writings can be understood a-
part from this reality.

Burgh's preoccupation with religious and moral issues in no wise
seemed strange to his contemporaries nor was it unusual among his fellow Commonwealthmen. Quite the contrary. The popularity of Burgh's
publications on these subjects and the critical acclaim accorded them
indicate the appeal of such themes to many of Burgh's generation. And
as Colin Bonwick has observed, Commonwealthmen in particular were "dominated and controlled" by religion. "It suffused their entire understanding of political morality and behavior and nourished their con-
ceptualization of social and governmental processes."[1]

Reared in the Calvinistic Church of Scotland, Burgh imbibed moral
and religious attitudes in many ways reminiscent of a sixteenth or seventeenth century Puritan. But he lived in a century characterized by
growing secularization. His was an "age of reason" and affluence--a
time when the intelligentsia repudiated traditional religion and Mammon
seemed to threaten moral values. Burgh was keenly sensitive to these
changes--although no more so than a Wesley exhorting the masses to return to the religious fundamentals of the past or a Jefferson extolling
the simple virtues of a pastoral society. In his own life and in his
writings Burgh attempted to reconcile the faith of his fathers with the
new verities of their posterity. The result is a telling commentary on
the tensions inherent in a culture posed between two value systems.

The crux of Burgh's problem as an intelligent eighteenth century
Christian derived from the fact that he was himself a man of reason as
well as a man of faith. As such he rejected the traditional notion
that certain Christian doctrines were mysteries beyond man's comprehension and affirmed that "no man ever _believed_ or _disbelieved_ what he
did not understand."[2] To be tenable, faith must be rational. Yet in

his attempt to demonstrate Christianity's resonableness, Burgh labored under serious handicaps. He lacked the intellectual depth and rigor necessary for such discussion. His commentary was superficial and imprecise. He failed to define his terms and argued on the basis of unwarranted presuppositions. Viewing reality starkly in terms of good and evil, he was prone to simplify situations. Moreover, he was seemingly oblivious to contradictions in his thinking or to shifts in his opinions. Nonetheless his religious commitments impelled him to grapple with profound philosophical questions, sometimes with sorry results. In the process some of his own beliefs underwent dramatic metamorphosis. While for the most part he remained committed throughout his life to the moral precepts of his Calvinist heritage, he ultimately deviated from certain of its theological rudiments. His experience was not unique, especially in dissenting circles. Protestantism in general and English Dissent in particular encouraged a spirit of individualism that easily led to doctrinal diversity. Moreover, the fluidity of dissenting thought reflected in Burgh's example fostered a critical perspective conducive not only to religious diveristy, but to deviation from other orthodoxies.

Burgh's earliest writings indicate that during his first years in London he was still largely influenced by the religious upbringing he had received under his father's tutelage. His perception of God and of man's relationship to his Creator was in no wise unusual. He defined the Deity as "the All, the Whole, the Perfection of Perfection," the necessary uncaused first cause whose existence could be rationally demonstrated from the wonders of nature. Man as a creature of this beneficent Supreme Being was indebted to Him for all happiness and destined for Immortality. In return for God's munificence it was man's "indispensable duty" to worship the Deity publicly, to seek His favor through prayer and "to learn and obey his laws." Although Burgh heartily endorsed private religious devotions, he maintained that the public expression of such sentiments was especially useful in inculcating a sense of one's obligations to God.[3]

There was never any question in Burgh's mind that organized Christianity was the most valid expression of man's religious needs and duties. He maintained that Christianity contained truths "unexceled in importance." It provided a "rule of life superior to all others, in its being absolutely perfect and complete, wanting nothing proper for the complex performance of _every_ social and relative duty, and fixing the only acceptable way of worshipping the One Supreme." Moreover, Burgh always believed that Protestantism was the only legitimate manifestation of the Christian faith. He asserted that there was as much difference between Catholicism and Protestantism as "between Darkness and Light; between incredible Absurdities and certain Truths; between diabolical Cruelty and heavenly benevolence; between Satan and Jesus Christ." Popery was "the worst thing in the universe, hell only excepted." It was the Antichrist.[4]

Despite such strong statements Burgh was a consistent and staunch advocate of religious toleration. Believing that an individual's religion was the private concern of his conscience and God, he argued that:

> there is no <u>Heresy</u> so <u>bad</u>, nor so <u>contrary</u>
> to the spirit of Christianity, as to believe it
> to be proper or lawful to <u>hate</u> or <u>persecute</u> a fel-
> low creature and a brother for an <u>Opinion</u>, which
> he declares, in the simplicity and sincerity of
> his heart, he has impartially <u>examined</u>, and thinks
> he finds to be <u>agreeable</u> to the sense of Scripture.[5]

Unlike most proponents of religious toleration, Burgh did not except Catholics from this liberty. Although he described papists as the "most persecutable people he knew," he nonetheless defended their right to worship freely. He argued that the removal of restraints on their religious exercises would significantly dampen the ardor which persecution encouraged in their ranks.[6] He did not specifically recommend the extension of such freedom to Jews and other non-Christians, but the tenor of his arguments suggests that he would have supported such a policy.

A logical corollary of Burgh's belief in religious toleration was his antipathy to established Churches. While resident in Scotland, it is unlikely that Burgh was particularly distressed by the incompatibility of established churches with the principle of religious toleration. His father, after all, was a minister of the established Church of Scotland. But in England Burgh's affiliation with a religious minority undoubtedly sensitized him to the drawbacks of established churches. Most probably, his increasingly bitter denunciation of such institutions was directly related to his association with a growing number of dissenting clergymen and schoolmasters whose preferment and status were restricted by their alienation from the Anglican Church. Burgh came to characterize established churches as the "ever faithful coadjutor" of tyrannical rulers and politicians, and their clergy as generally "the greatest enemies to all kinds of reformations," "the most narrow-minded and most worthless set of men in every country." Describing the Anglican Church as a "monopoly of fat livings," he charged that many of its clergy were imbued with secularism, even "Immorality." Surely there was more to the ministry than the pursuit of income, pluralities, and preferment or reading learned and elegant sermons on theological technicalities over velvet cusions.[7] Maintaining that the only legitimate function of the civil magistrate in the sphere of religion was the maintenance of peace among diverse sects, Burgh exhorted public-spirited politicians to support religious toleration by repealing such discriminatory legislation as the Test and Corporation Acts. He even took his case to the King, urging George III to support the movement against enforced subscription to the thirty-nine articles of the Anglican Church.[8] Neither King nor Parliament responded to his appeals. Their failure to do so contributed to Burgh's disenchantment with contemporary politics. He was particularly distressed by the legislature's rejection of the Feathers Tavern petition. He viewed parliament's action as one more unhappy manifestation of that body's disregard for popular rights.[9] His reaction pointedly underscores the confluence of religious and political liberties in the minds of many Dissenters.

Well aware that many men did not share his enthusiasm for Protestant Christianity on the grounds that it defied reason, Burgh repeatedly asserted that no doctrine <u>fundamental</u> to the Christian faith violated the dictates of reason. He likewise defended the validity of Scripture wherein was found the sole rule of Christianity. Revelation was an aid to reason as a telescope was an advantage to the eye. He dismissed contradictions between Scripture and scientific or historical knowledge with the observation that since the purpose of revelation was not to make men "philosophers," most probably the Holy Spirit saw no necessity in inspiring the sacred authors "with any knowledge not directly necessary for improving men's hearts and lives." Certainly if intellectuals such as Newton, Locke, and Samuel Clarke were satisfied with the validity of Christianity, its compatibility with reason must be obvious.[10] Such arguments begged the question.

Burgh first expressed reservations about fundamental tenets of his Calvinist heritage in 1754. In the <u>Dignity of Human Nature</u> he mused about the propriety or efficaciousness of Christ's suffering for sinful man, lamely concluding that the redemptive character of Calvary was a mystery which man could probably never fathom. Whether consciously or not, he also implied misgivings about Christ's nature. Although referring to the Messiah as the Son of God, he casually commented that Christ was highly exalted as a result of his submission to death, thereby seeming to suggest that Christ did not enjoy the Father's fulness of perfection.[11]

Perhaps Burgh's doubts were sparked by conversations with his neighbors at Newington Green. Certainly Richard Price, a noted Arian, must have had a momentous impact on Burgh's thinking. After 1756 Burgh spent unnumerable Sundays listening to Price's sermons at the Green chapel. Given such influences, whether imperceptibly, or after much anguished soul searching, Burgh came to reject trinitarianism and the expiatory character of Christ's death because of their illogicality. He publicized his position on both issues in <u>Crito</u>.

Extremely brief, Burgh's case against trinitarianism had a certain persuasiveness. He questioned "whether He, whose God and Father the <u>Almighty</u> is can be properly said to be the <u>Almighty</u>; whether the <u>Almighty</u> has a <u>God</u> and <u>Father</u>; or whether the <u>Son</u> of God is the <u>Father</u> of the Son of God." He noted that "the Scripture-writers, having never subscribed the Athanasian creed, though a good sort of clergymen, in their little way, do every where represent our illustrious Deliverer as <u>subordinate</u> to the <u>Almighty</u>, whom they style his God and Father." It would not be:

> a whit more absurd to put the virgin MARY into the
> Tr___ty, or Godhead, than <u>any</u> <u>other</u> being whatever.
> All beings are <u>equally</u> distinct from, and <u>inferior</u>,
> to the Supreme; the S_n as much as the virgin; the
> virgin as much as a worm. For <u>all</u> beings, but the
> One supreme only, are <u>finite</u>; and there must ever be
> an <u>infinite</u> distance between <u>finite</u> and <u>infinite</u>.

Burgh concluded that many men who "do constantly pay solemn worship to H__y, bl__d and gl__s Tr___ty," were (with Newton, Clarke, Locke,

52

Whitby, Emmlyn, etc.) . . . satisfied, that it neither is, or can be true."[12]

Like Richard Price, Burgh had become an Arian Christian who viewed the Messiah as the divine Son of God, elevated above all men, but subordinate to the Father. Although Arianism was a waystation to deism for some men, Burgh never became a deist.[13] Despite his frequent descriptions of the Deity as the Creator, or even the "infinite Author of the universal oeconomy," he never deviated from his early and quite explicit repudiation of deists as an "unhappy set of men, who reason as a person might be expected to do, who was born with the wrong side of his brain upwards." His abiding belief in the "continued Divine superintendency over the natural and moral world," the efficacy of prayer, the reality of revelation, the defectiveness of the human condition, and the validity of miracles was incompatible with the deistic concept of an impersonal divine watchmaker.[14] Most certainly Burgh would have agreed with the London Evening-Post's correspondent who defended the Reverend Theophilus Lindsey against a similar charge of deism:

> If names must needs be given to distinguish, the
> only one that can properly be given to Mr. Lindsey,
> is that of an Unitarian; but if that should not
> suffice, because it lacketh a sting in its tail, call
> him a Socinian. But deny not to a disciple of Socinus,
> what you allow to the deluded followers of an assumed
> infallible guide; for a belief of Christianity, under
> however different or contradictory interpretations, ex-
> cludeth all propriety of the character of Deist.[15]

A conversion such as Burgh's to some form of unitarianism frequently occurred in eighteenth century dissenting circles. Considerably more controversial and far-fetched was Burgh's attempt to rationalize the Redemption. Tradition argued that man's sinfulness necessitated the Redemption. Burgh came to reject this rationale as unjust and illogical in that it implied a fundamental flaw in the Divine scheme of creation. In the stead of such so-called Calvinistic reasoning, he offered a lengthy and involuted discourse on the nature of evil in the world.[16] The results ranged from the prosaic to the absurd.

Burgh began with the orthodox assumption that rectitude is the Creator's greatest attribute. From there he reasoned that the moral character of God could only be reflected in moral agents, distinguished from the animals by their capacity for abstract reflection and free to choose between good and evil in their quest for virtue, the ultimate goal of mankind. Yet Almighty Goodness could not be presumed to have introduced vice into the world in order to test man's virtue. Nor is the heinousness of vice diminished because good may accidentally result from it. Evil is just that and thus contrary to the Divine Will. In no wise unusual thus far, Burgh's argument rapidly deteriorated as he attempted to explain God's response to evil in the world. Burgh reasoned that since God knew that man was capable of sin, He would surely have provided means for man to atone for his offenses short of an extraordinary intervention in human history. That being so, what then was the Messiah's mission? Burgh concluded that Christ was not sent as God's emissary to redeem man from the consequences of his own free will choice of evil, but to rescue man from the influence of an invisible malevolent agency--Satan. Anticipating the incredulity his thesis provoked, Burgh insisted that if Scripture is interpreted literally when it speaks of a Messiah, then it must be interpreted literally when it refers to evil forces in the world hostile to man. He even went so far as to suggest that possibly Satan had poisoned the world's atmosphere thereby making mankind more prone to certain moral faults than would otherwise occur. At the least, natural evil resulted from demonic influence.[17]

Nowhere are Burgh's shortcomings as an amateur theologian and philosopher more painfully obvious than in this sorry attempt to rationalize a theological problem that had plagued and baffled far wiser men. That Burgh ventured into this intellectual quagmire is a rather poignant and pointed reflection of the ideological pressures a man of faith experienced in an age of reason. In his attempt to justify faith, he became mired in incredible absurdities. His struggles were sarcastically derided by one anonymous reviewer of _Crito_ who regretted that Burgh had expanded a valuable commentary on contemporary affairs into an unsuccessful exercise in metaphysics. Even the usually laudatory Andrew Kippis dismissed Burgh's discourse on evil as "peculiarly fanciful and groundless."[18]

James Burgh's changing concept of God is most interesting for what it says about the impact of rationalism on traditional Christianity. His relatively static view of man as a moral creature, imbued with free will and rationality for the purpose of reflecting Divine rectitude, is most significant for what it says about Burgh's own philosophy of life. His belief in free will underlay his defense of both religious and political liberty. Only in an atmosphere of responsible freedom could man truly function as an independent moral agent. His conviction that rectitude was the goal of man's existence occasioned his criticisms of contemporary corruption. His sense of man's responsibilities within the Divine scheme of creation motivated his sallies against the social and political ills of his day. His belief in the intelligent design of creation and the rational character of man prompted him to grapple with the most intricate philosophical, social or political problems in the assurance that they were intelligible and thus soluble. In no wise a relativist, Burgh maintained that there were certain moral absolutes grounded in the unchangeable nature of God and that truth, moral or otherwise, resides in the thing perceived and not in the mind perceiving. Qualifying John Locke, he further asserted that certain truths are self-evident. That is, they are "not collected or deduced, but intuitively perceived, or seen by the mind." For Burgh, such truths were just as validly the objects of the mind's perception as those presented to the mind by way of the senses. Despite Burgh's failure to define his terminology with precision and the brevity and unsystematic character of his remarks, the tenor of his argument implies that moral truths fall into this category. Believing that moral truth was "in no respect naturally more vague or precarious than mathematical; but equally fixed and clear to superior minds," Burgh was confident that man could ascertain the moral absolutes by which his life should be governed. Moral conduct would be the necessary consequence of this intellective process. An individual would never pursue a course of action clearly perceived as evil or erroneous. Only if an individual's perception of truth proved inaccurate would he mistakenly choose evil or error in the belief that it was a good or a truth. Burgh recognized that all too often man's perception of the truth was indeed distorted. Passion beclouded reason. A subscriber to the Popean concept of a ruling passion, Burgh observed that "a man's ruling passion is the key by which you may let yourself into his character, and may pretty nearly guess at his future conduct." Although valid in themselves, passions had to be ever regulated by the perceptive faculty lest they lead man into error or sin. The development of the perceptive faculty, the inculcation of an adequate concept of morality in less than "superior minds" was the task of education.[19] Burgh's conviction that such instruction was essential to the formation of a moral, incorruptible society and body politic is the rationale underlying his academic and literary careers as well as his repeated advocacy of moral associations "in support of virtue and truth."[20]

CHAPTER IV:

THE EDUCATOR

After several false starts in other occupations, the practical
problem of making a living led James Burgh to the classroom. There he at
last found a profession congenial to his talents and interests. Teaching
provided an outlet for his intellectual curiosity, frustrated evangelism
and familial instincts. As an educator Burgh demonstrated an innova-
tiveness that merits recognition. Not peculiar to himself, his theories
and programs for the education of youth were advocated by a limited circle of British reformers, many of whom were Dissenters like Burgh.

"Throughout the eighteenth century, dissenting academies were the
most important feature of English education."[1] The dissenting educational tradition was stimulated by the Act of Uniformity of 1662.[2] In addition to excluding Dissenters from the educational seats of orthodoxy--
Oxford and Cambridge--the Act prompted widespread defections from the
Church of England. Rather than violate their consciences by subscribing
to the oath of religious conformity prescribed by the Act, over two thousand clerics resigned their places in the Anglican establishment. Many
of these turned to teaching, both as a livelihood and as a means of dis-
seminating their heterodox religious beliefs, even though such instruction was illegal. Academies designed as alternatives to the Anglican
universities sprang up throughout the country. Perhaps a score existed
by 1689. They enjoyed the widespread support of the dissenting community. Dissenting thought affirmed the inherent right of a child to receive an education so that he might better perform his moral and civic
duties.[3] If the normal educational channels were either inaccessible or
unattractive to the Dissenter, then he would create a second educational
system in harmony with his own needs and philosophy.

At first such academies were conducted on a domestic plan. Dependent on the lives and fortunes of their founders, at their deaths the
schools frequently dissolved or migrated elsewhere. The Toleration Act
of 1689, however, premitted Dissenters to teach in their own schools
with relative impunity, provided they adhere to certain formal require-
ments.[4] Thus better equipped academies established or supported by various organized societies, such as The Presbyterian Fund, The Congregational Fund Board, or the Coward Trust, began to emerge. Frequently

such academies came to be largely controlled--especially in matters of doctrine--by the funding agency. Eventually, in order to mitigate the inconvenience caused by migration and to achieve a large measure of independence from external financial agencies, the institutional type of academy with its own trustees and subscribers came into being. Commonly, such institutional academies, together with private ones like Burgh's, were open to all students, whereas academies supported or controlled by a Fund were mainly or exclusively theological.

Initially academies reflected the traditional classical university training of their first masters. By the beginning of the eighteenth century, however, they were distinguished from most other English schools by an increasingly practical emphasis on preparing students for life in the world, both in a spiritual and secular capacity. This utilitarian orientation reflected the close association between English Dissent and the burgeoning world of English commerce and resulted in extensive curricular reform, much of it patterned after the example of neighboring Scottish universities. In addition to such traditional mainstays of classical education as logic, ethics, Greek, Latin, Scripture, theology and mathematics, course offerings were expanded to include modern languages, history, geography, certain sciences, elocution, and bookkeeping. In consequence, academies enjoyed a reputation during the eighteenth century for educational innovation. This, together with the generally superior quality of their scholarship and lower fees in comparison to the universities, made them attractive to Dissenter and non-Dissenter alike.

His writings would indicate that James Burgh's academy exemplified the dissenting educational tradition at its finest. Burgh brought to the classroom attitudes common to the dissenting community that his personal experience reinforced. The son of a highly educated minister, Burgh undoubtedly prized education even more than the average Dissenter. His brief tenure at St. Andrews had exposed him first-hand to the advanced pedagogy of Scottish universities. Likewise, even though Burgh never developed any economic sophistication, he could appreciate because of his own business misfortunes the importance of a practical education that equipped one to deal with life's realities. His friendship with the merchants and tradesmen who resided at Newington Green further encouraged his awareness. As a self-employed schoolmaster he was unrestrained in his choice of texts or instructional methods and could bring these diverse influences to bear on his teaching. His classroom could serve as a laboratory for testing new educational theories and procedures which Burgh could reject, modify, or adopt as experience dictated. Because Burgh chose to share these experiences with the general public, his significance for the history of eighteenth century education goes beyond the example of his Newington Green academy. He was an important exponent of an educational philosophy that challenged the medieval and Renaissance ideals that dominated eighteenth century education.

Typically, it was his concern for public morality that prompted Burgh to publish his 'thoughts on education.' Provoked by the Jacobite rebellion of 1745 to speak out against the corruption of his day, Burgh noted the crucial role that education played in promoting or inhibiting immorality. Yet, echoing an increasingly popular contemporary theme, he asserted that England could take little comfort in her educational system. He charged that English youth were being perverted, and that nowhere did the "Irreligion of the Age," the root cause of English ills, "appear more shocking . . . than in the Modern Education of Youth." It was notorious, Burgh contended, that "the Immorality of the Youth of one of our Universities is grown to such a Height, that it deserves at this Day more properly to be stiled [sic], the Seat of the Vices, than of the Muses."[5] Nor were the prospects bright that the situation would soon be remedied.

Accordingly, Burgh determined to acquaint the public with the educational needs of the age in hopes of rectifying a dire situation. Subsequently, this weighty topic was given consideration in most of Burgh's other writings and was the primary concern of Thoughts on Education (1747) and Youth's Friendly Monitor (1754).

Burgh's view of the state of learning in England was not altogether pessimistic. With many of his contemporaries he believed in the progression of human knowledge. He thought men of his own generation were better educated in certain respects than those of an earlier age. He was particularly enthusiastic about the increase in scientific knowledge and lauded Newtonian physics as "the summit and pinnacle of knowledge, the utmost reach of human capacity."[6] Burgh was also impressed with the greater diffusion of knowledge in England: "The present is by no means an age for indulging ignorance . . . We find more true knowledge at present in shops and counting houses, than could have been found an age or two ago in universities." But Burgh attributed this achievement to the influence of such periodical essays as the Spectator, the Tatler, and the Guardian, rather than to English schools. By treating learned subjects in a familiar style, "cleared from the scholastic rubbish of Latin and Logic," so that "people of plain common sense might comprehend [them]," the "elegant and ingenious" authors of these essays had significantly broadened the intellectual horizons of the reading public. Likewise, the public exhibition of experiments in London and in other major cities had "greatly contributed to the spreading a taste for knowledge among the trading people, who now talk familiarly of things, their grandfathers would have thought it as much as their credit was worth to have been thought to know."[7]

It was the practical thrust of these informal educational mediums that attracted Burgh. Reflecting the dissenting community's belief that the objectives of education were essentially utilitarian, Burgh defined those goals as:

> The accomplishing a person in such parts of knowledge
> as may be useful for qualifying him to pass decently
> and comfortably through the present life; . . . The
> right directing him how to prepare himself for the
> everlasting duration after this life is at an end,
> teaching him how to improve and ennoble his nature,
> and putting him in the way of attaining the favour

of his <u>Master</u>, which is only another phrase for <u>perfect happiness</u>.[8]

Together with such educators as Thomas Sheridan and Joseph Priestley, Burgh viewed the second objective as primary. He believed that the individual concerned with eternal perfection was obligated to develop his capacity for perfection while in the mortal state. Since "no rational mind will, or can rise to any high degree of perfection in any state whatever, and continue in ignorance," education was a vital element in attaining spiritual excellence.[9] Moreover, Burgh maintained that the very nature of the intellect prevented the individual, concerned with salvation, from neglecting this "active and restless principle." As conceived by Burgh, the intellect engaged in a continual search for happiness. It would pursue either "the objects of Sense, to wit, pleasure, Power, or Riches, or those of the Mind, to wit, knowledge, Virtue or Religion."[10] That a person should actively seek happiness in the second alternative and cultivate the rational rather than the sensual faculties seemed obvious to Burgh.

These principles underlay the syllabus of education outlined by Burgh in his writings. As he acknowledged, his proposals somewhat resembled those delineated by John Milton in <u>Of Education</u>. The two were in general agreement about the physical environment of study, although Burgh envisioned a school of about forty pupils in contrast to Milton's academy of one hundred fifty. Both men criticized the excessive emphasis on the study of Greek and Latin that was common in English schools. Both thought education should begin with easier subjects and gradually progress to more difficult disciplines. Burgh's plan, however, is distinctive in its concern with the education of children from pre-school age to about eighteen, whereas Milton's is designed for boys from twelve to twenty-one. Moreover, not sharing the poet's interest in preparing a man to function skillfully in war as well as in peace, Burgh, unlike Milton, largely neglected a program of physical recreation and exercises in the use of weaponry. Finally, Burgh's proposed curriculum is developed in more detail than Milton's and is broader in scope. It included instruction in religion, reading, spelling, grammar, composition, Latin, Greek, French, rhetoric, geography, chronology, government, logic, natural science, economics, dancing, fencing, riding, music, and drawing.

Burgh prefaced his syllabus with some acute observations on child psychology that are remarkably modern-sounding and most probably reflect John Locke's influence.[11] He noted that a child's education began even before enrollment in school. From the time a youngster learned to speak until he was four or five, it was essential that parents endeavor to form his temper "to meekness and obedience, regulating the passions and appetites[,] habituating the mind to the love and practice of virtue," and encouraging his desire for self-improvement and his curiosity or thirst for knowledge. Should "this work be neglected by Parents till the age of Six be past, it need hardly be attempted at all: for the mind soon acquires a sturdiness and obstinacy that is not to be conquered."[12] Although Burgh shared the eighteenth century's belief in man's fundamental rationality, he was keenly aware of the irrational side of man's nature.[13] Children should not be allowed to follow their own instincts, for many of those instincts were frivolous, if not immoral. Youngsters required direction from an early age in order to develop their rational and moral faculties. Yet, despite his conviction that children needed guidance and discipline from adults, Burgh did not approve of corporal punishments for childish transgressions. He believed that confinement, dieting, prohibition from the amusements enjoyed by other youngsters, and disgrace were more effective disciplines.[14]

In the contemporary controversy over where a child should be educated, Burgh agreed with those theorists who believed a youngster should be educated outside the home.[15] He vigorously rejected Rousseau's proposal that fathers educate their sons. Burgh thought many fathers were either too illiterate or too indulgent to assume such a weighty responsibility.[16] Instead, he recommended that children be entrusted as soon as feasible to the care of a teacher who possessed a "general and comprehensive knowledge of the various branches of learning and the proper methods of acquiring them." Such a schoolmaster should be even-tempered and noted for "exemplary virtue, good breeding, knowledge of the world, and of languages, writing, accounts, book keeping, geography, the principles of philosophy, mathematics, history, and divinity." Disengaged from other pursuits and unbiased by paternal weakness, he would serve as an impartial and prudent governor of the real interests of his charges and would instruct them in "all the branches of useful and ornamental knowledge, suitable to their ages, capacities, and prospects" with special emphasis on "what will make them useful in this life and secure the happiness of the next."[17] Ideally these purposes could best be served if pupils lodged with their teacher and were educated in the company of other children. The expense of such a private boarding school assumed a certain affluence among the student body. Whether consciously or not, Burgh tailored his theories for a middle or upper class student.

Although developed in more detail than Milton's plan, Burgh's syllabus was little more than a catalogue of subjects to be studied by children at various ages, together with suggestions of appropriate texts and supplemental readings. Otherwise tedious reading is only occasionally redeemed by Burgh's explanation of the propriety of certain curricular proposals.

Religious education was crucial to Burgh's curriculum. Aware that intellectual maturity varied in youngsters, he recommended flexibility in determining when to initiate a child's education in specific disciplines. In the case of religious instruction, he believed that the mind could comprehend "very noble and extensive moral views" at an early age. Normally, a toddler of three or four could grasp the concept of God as Supreme Creator and should be introduced to this perspective on the Deity in the home. He would thus be able by the age of seven or eight to receive daily classroom instruction for an hour in the principles of prudence, morality and religion. Burgh recommended informality on these occasions as a stimulus to learning and particularly urged that questions from the pupil be encouraged. The student of ten to fourteen years would study various a posteriori proofs of God's existence.[18] Next he would investigate the nature of God and of man's relationship to the Creator. Burgh believed that the pupil's familiarity with God's

handiwork easily enabled him to understand the Divine attributes if
they were discussed in language appropriate to his years. To facilitate
such study Burgh recommended using secular disciplines such as geography
and astronomy. The analysis of man's relationship to God should include
a demonstration of Christianity's validity. In this endeavor, Scriptural passages which Burgh delineated, supplemented by readings from Gro-
tius (On the Truth of the Christian Religion), Locke (The Reasonableness
of Christianity), and Samuel Clarke (Evidences of Revealed Religion)
would prove useful. Burgh was certain that at the conclusion of this
course of study, most young people would be confirmed in a belief in
God and in Christianity for:

> whenever Christianity is fairly proposed, undis-
> guised and uninjured by the inventions of men,
> with all its evidences and all its excellences
> set in a strong and proper light, it will not fail
> to produce conviction in any teachable and un-
> prejudiced mind.[19]

Simultaneous with this religious instruction, Burgh's student was
to undertake a course of general studies that would prepare him "to
pass decently and comfortably through the present life." Burgh recommended judiciousness in formulating such a program. As no one could
learn everything, an individual should choose that which was most appropriate to his station in life.[20] A tradesman's son had more need of
bookkeeping than of dancing. A foundation in certain disciplines, however, was essential to all for "without general education, a person
finds himself on every occasion at a loss in carrying on those improve-
ments of mind without which man is a mere animal."[21] Burgh was particularly critical of the customary termination of the education of a
merchant's son at fifteen or sixteen before this course of general education had been completed.[22]

Reading, of course, is the basic educational tool. Burgh believed
that a child aged four to six and "of good capacity" could learn to read
distinctly.[23] At the same time the youngster should be introduced to
spelling, punctuation and the rudiments of Latin.

The emphasis placed on the classical languages by traditional
schools was frequently attacked by educational innovators, including
Burgh[24] who believed the study of Latin could only be justified on the
grounds that a knowledge of Latin, one of the foundations of the English
language, facilitated the pupil's understanding of English. For this
reason he included the classical language in his curriculum. On the same
grounds he justified instruction in Greek, but deferred its study until
the student was about twelve. In learning Greek the Westminster Grammar, the New Testament, and the writings of Socrates, Plato, Homer or
Demosthenes could be used to advantage.[25]

In even the most progressive institutions modern languages received
slight attention and where offered were generally optional. Thus Burgh's
inclusion of French as a regular part of his curriculum was unusual.[26]
Describing the language as one "which no gnetleman, or man of business,

can be without," Burgh recommended that students begin its study at ages six to eight.[27]

By the age of ten Burgh's pupil began to concentrate on public speaking. The importance Burgh attached to this subject is amply documented in his volume on The Art of Speaking. He believed that "there is no earthly object capable of making such various and such forcible impressions upon the human mind, as a consummate speaker." While "very indifferent matter well delivered will make a considerable impression . . . bad utterance will defeat the whole effect of the noblest composition." Simultaneous with his study of rhetoric a student should focus on composition and spelling. As an aid in developing the art of writing, Burgh suggested Pope's Essay on Criticism "from which . . . may be drawn a general view of the requisites for a well-written piece."[28]

Arithmetic and geometry were proposed as appropriate subjects for the youth from his twelfth to his eighteenth year. Burgh recommended Fisher's, Wingate's, Hill's, or Well's books on arithmetic and Cunn's or Simpson's books on Euclidean geometry as suitable texts.[29]

At fourteen or fifteen Burgh's pupil began the study of geography and history. Both subjects were among the most neglected disciplines in eighteenth century schools.[30] In challenging this contemporary neglect Burgh argued that a knowledge of geography was valuable for men of all ranks and professions:

> The statesman can have no distinct ideas of the
> interests and connexions of foreign nations; the
> divine no clear conception of Scripture or ecclesi-
> astical history, nor the merchant of the voyages
> his ships are to make, the seats of commerce and
> means of collecting its various articles; nor indeed
> the private gentleman bear a part in common con-
> versation, without understanding the situations,
> distances, extent, and general state of kingdoms
> and empires. In a word, he who does not know geog-
> raphy, does not know the world.[31]

Similarly, he defended history as the "key to the knowledge of human nature," and the "great instructor for all ranks in life." Although restricting classroom instruction in history to chronology and the outlines of universal history, he recommended that an intensive study of this discipline be undertaken privately upon graduation from school.[32]

In the majority of dissenting educational institutions, instruction in the principles of constitutional government and the liberties of press and people, including the right of resistance, found a place in the curriculum.[33] Burgh's own academy was undoubtedly no exception to this generalization. Certainly his educational tracts called for such instruction. Reflecting his Commonwealthman proclivities, he suggested that a youngster from his earliest years be exposed to a "rational set of political principles, and taught the love of liberty and . . . [of his] country, and consequently the hatred of Popery, Tyranny, Persecution,

Venality, and whatever else is against the interest of a free people."
Political factionalism should be singled out for particular opprobri-
um.[34]

Interestingly, Burgh's commitment to Commonwealthman cant was also
reflected in his defense of economics as an important academic discipline. With unabashed exaggeration Burgh charged that financial folly
brought on by economic ignorance frequently induced men to make corrupt
bargains with the Court as an alternative to fiscal embarrassment. He
reasoned that a familiarity with economics could prevent such disaster.[35] In addition to this novel apologia, more obvious arguments could
be adduced to justify economics. Certainly Burgh's own unhappy business
venture gave him a keen appreciation of the practical need for instruction in economics and related subjects, such as bookkeeping.

However involuted and farfetched Burgh's own intellectualizing
might occasionally be, he nonetheless prized logic and included it in
the curriculum of the sixteen to eighteen year old. Stressing the utility of this subject, Burgh noted its value in promoting a discerning
judgment. Dewatt's book on logic and some of the less challenging sections of Locke's Essay on Human Understanding, which, not surprisingly,
Burgh particularly admired, were recommended as texts. He also suggested
that the works of Thomas Hobbes and Hebrew Hutchisson be studied as examples of the subtle abuses of rational argument.[36]

Burgh placed especial emphasis on the natural sciences in his educational scheme. He was very much a man of his age in his high regard
for science as his poetic Hymn to the Creator of the World indicates. In
his syllabus Burgh reflected the contemporary emphasis on experimenta-
tion as an avenue to knowledge. He recommended a series of experiments
in mechanics, hydrostatics, pneumatics, optics, astronomy, and chemistry.
Hopefully, such a program whetted the curiosity of students and incul-
cated in them a "taste for knowledge" that would motivate them when a-
dults to continue their intellectual development. Ever the moralist,
Burgh even speculated that such experiments might rival taverns, theatricals, and less innocent amusements as sources of adult entertainment.[37]

Committed to the Calvinistic work ethic, Burgh was, in fact, ever
wary of the various ways in which men recreated. He reluctantly admitted such frivolous pursuits as dancing, fencing, riding, music, drawing
and the other elegant arts into his curriculum, but on a conditional
basis. He believed that such interests should only be indulged in accord with the particular circumstances of parent and of pupil and then
always in moderation. None should be of primary interest, given what
Burgh felt to be their less serious nature.[38] He described music, for
example, as a "bewitching art, and one way or another . . . hurtful to
most people, who delight in and practice it." Moreover, it demanded
natural aptitude. Where there was "genius" for it, it should be "very
sparingly indulged."[39] For reasons he kept to himself, Burgh asserted
that dancing was a subject best pursued in youth. He admitted that
drawing was an "ingenious accomplishment," but one that had the supposed
disadvantage of straining the constitution, especially the eyes.

Although personally disapproving of fencing, Burgh thought that a man who wore a sword ought to know how to use it.[40]

Burgh concluded his syllabus by recommending that a student who completed this wide-ranging course of general studies be sent forth into the world armed with a personal letter from his schoolmaster. Among other things this missive should warn the graduate against the perniciousness of Deism. More importantly, it should contain an extensive list of reading designed to promote the graduate's continued intellectual growth, for education was a life-long process.[41]

Most of Burgh's remarks on education dealt with the intellectual development of young gentlemen. He did not, however, entirely neglect the subject of female education. Although Burgh unhesitatingly affirmed that women were naturally intended by the Creator to be submissive to men and that their only rational ambition could be to function as "loving wives, prudent mothers and mistresses of families, faithful friends, and good Christians," he did not believe that women were either the intellectual or moral inferiors of men. They could and should be educated in those academic disciplines which prepared them for their naturally ordained roles. He found contemptible his society's emphasis on the female's physical allurements and boldly urged that ladies be informed that "(contrary to the vulgar error) it is a woman's conduct and behaviour, not her shape and complexion, that determine her character and value." Instruction in needlework, the toilette, playing the spinet, and speaking French were trivial substitutes for the development of the "more valuable beauties of the mind, to wit, Good nature, Prudence, Virtue, and Religion." Plays, cards, romantic novels, and poetry were "utter ruin" to the fairer sex. Instead, young ladies should be educated at home in such subjects as recitation, writing, grammar, history, arithmetic, and geography. Consistent with his belief that utility should be the measure whereby a student determined his curriculum, Burgh reasoned that such subjects as science, while within the grasp of the female intellect, were irrelevant to her ordained vocations of wife and mother and thus need not be studied by young ladies.[42]

Burgh's remarks were reflective of a substantial body of opinion that affirmed the relative equality of the sexes and lobbied for an upgrading of female education. The subject was discussed with impressive frequency in books, newspapers, and periodical reviews.[43] The prominence of the bluestockings and of political radicals like Catharine Macaulay and Mary Wollstonecraft[44] further supports the thesis that during the century an important shift in attitudes towards women occurred at least within the middling ranks of English society. The subject is far too complicated to pursue within the context of this study. But as in so many other instances, James Burgh's appeal for an amelioration of female education placed him solidly within the ranks of enlightened reformers.

Burgh's educational theories have heretofore received little attention, yet they reflect some of the most progressive thinking current in his day. His ideas on education have held little fascination for political historians preoccupied with his opinion on political reform and they have apparently been largely unknown to historians of education, perhaps because they were published anonymously or as part of a broader study. In his own day, however, and for several decades after his death, Burgh's "thoughts on education," especially as elucidated in <u>The Dignity of Human Nature</u> and <u>Youth's Friendly Monitor</u>, were well known and well received.[45] They typify an educational philosophy that gradually infiltrated the bastions of educational orthodoxy and revolutionized English education. Many men like Burgh spoke out before such change was accomplished. The repetition of their ideas over the years familiarized the public with the subject of educational reform and eventually secured its widespread implementation. The popularity of Burgh's educational tracts on both sides of the Atlantic suggest that his contribution to this achievement was far from negligible.

CHAPTER V:

THE SOCIAL CRITIC

        Underlying James Burgh's professional and philosophical interest in
education was his firm belief that education was fundamental to the development of judicious and moral socio-political institutions.[1] Sharing
the jaundiced view of his own day that is typical of the moralist, he
was convinced that English society had particular need of the ameliora-
tive effect of education. Together with many of his contemporaries he
believed that his environment was tainted by widespread moral degeneracy.[2] References to the irreligion, luxury, licentiousness and corruption of British society were liberally laced throughout his writings and
those of many another commentator on British mores and politics.[3] According to these critics the corruption of public morality, although a
gradual process, would, if unchecked, undermine social and political
stability. Ultimately the nation would be destroyed:

              The welfare of all countries in the world depends
              upon the morals of their people. For though a
              nation may get riches by trade, thrift, industry,
              and from the benefit of its soil and situation; and
              though a people may attain to great wealth and
              power either by force of arms, or by the sagacity
              of their councils; yet when their manners are de-
              praved, they will decline insensibly, and at last
              come to utter destruction.[4]

Burgh maintained that history afforded numerous examples of this process.[5] His religious sensibilities and patriotism were alike offended
at the possibility that Britain would follow the same path to destruction earlier trod by Greece and Rome.

        Much of Burgh's writing was designed to awaken the public to the
malignancy that he believed threatened its well-being. This fundamental
theme imposes a unity on his discussion of such seemingly disparate topics as masquerades and poor relief. In the course of his thirty year
literary career he had occasion to comment on many aspects of British
life, but always with the purpose of diagnosing moral maladies and

proffering panaceas for their alleviation. Varying in quality and in value, his observations frequently suffered from his tendency toward superficiality and over-simplification. Moreover, his criticisms were largely based on his observations of London life, a circumstance that has obvious pitfalls.[6] But if some of Burgh's remarks reflect a decidedly personal perspective, others, whether accurate or not, were shared by many men on both sides of the Atlantic. And although prompted by an inherently conservative moralistic perspective, many of Burgh's suggested reforms were quite enlightened by contemporary standards.

One of the phenomena of eighteenth century life which Burgh and contemporaries such as Richard Price viewed with particular alarm was the improvement in the national standard of living.[7] The theme is a consistent one in Burgh's writings. Unlike a modern student of economics who thrills at such statistics, Burgh was extremely pessimistic about the long-range effect of ever increasing affluence. He filled his publications with diatribes against luxury. Although willing to concede that "riches do not <u>necessarily</u> enervate a people,"[8] needless to say, he felt that in England such <u>was</u> the case. Instead of being used exclusively for the "purchase of the necessaries and conveniences of life," and for "the relief of the indigent," English wealth was supporting the perfidious growth of LUXURY! And luxury spawned extravagance, sloth, effeminacy, corruption, bribery, a disregard for law, and all manner of vice.[9] It was the first step down the road to moral and political depravity.

That England had taken this first step seemed obvious to James Burgh. Succumbing to the myth of a golden yesteryear, he argued that whereas in the past London streets were supposedly filled "with decent Citizens, dressed in a Garb, plain, uniform, and fit for Business," now they teemed with a "motley Race of English Traders, burlesqued into French Dancing-Masters," whose clothes were "bepatched with Lace, their Hands unsuited for Business by being muffled up in cambrick to the Finger Ends, and their feet crippled by wooden-heeled Shoes of some inches high." With the kind of exaggeration to which the fervor of his crusade sometimes prompted him, Burgh asserted that the homes of the wealthy, though hardly the richest citizens, resembled "palaces" in the lavishness of their entertainments, the numbers of servants, and their general luxuriousness. A tradesman "of the meanest Rank" ate on "gilt China Ware," had "Silver Plate," and enjoyed a choice of "foreign Wines" with his meals. Burgh bemoaned that "vast sums of money are now dedicated to pleasure among us, squandered away upon finery and trifles, lost in gaming, lavished away upon delicacies and profuse entertainments, and dissipated in levity and folly, in sensual gratifications and indulgences," when they should be "employed for the good and happiness of others, in generous and benevolent actions."[10]

The Calvinistic overtones of Burgh's harangue are unmistakable. Although he quarreled with certain doctrines of the Calvinist faith, Burgh never divorced himself from a Calvinistic concept of morality. Few diversions escaped his censure. Intemperance and gambling were obvious targets of his disapproval. "Drunkenness, especially in spiritous [sic] liquors, enfeebles the people, defeats population, shortens life, cuts off multitudes in infancy, lessens the quantity of labor, and hurts the

revenue much more than it benefits it." Gambling aroused avarice, led
to cheating and debased the mind. Worst still, it was a waste of time
and money. Though dancing at private gatherings was acceptable in moderation, public balls were another matter. They served as occasions
where "artful and designing" members of either sex might "lay snares"
for one another which could perhaps "prove fatal." Theatricals likewise
prompted a critical rebuke from Burgh. As late as 1754 he described
dramas as, for the most part, "a heap of wild flights and bombastic
rants;" comedies were "scandalous impurities." Even decorous plays were
indecorously presented. Lewd songs or dances between acts and a "ludi-
crous and beastly farce" at the play's conclusion marred what might otherwise have been an acceptable piece of entertainment. Instead of promoting virtue and religion, most plays were exhibitions of wickedness
and opulence, not fit to be read, let alone viewed. He recommended a
tax on theaters sufficient to discourage the working people from fre-
quenting them. By 1775 the tone of theatrical productions had improved
sufficiently in Burgh's opinion for him to comment that although "modern productions have, generally speaking, as little tincture of religion
as can well be imagined, . . . scarce any age ever deserved more praise
on account of the decency and charity of its theatrical compositions,
and the behavior of the actors and actresses upon the stage, than the
present, if you except the female dancers." Burgh attributed this improvement more to the force of public opinion than to such government
measures as the Licensing Act.[11]

Burgh was of one mind with Henry Fielding in his opposition to another popular amusement--masquerades. He described them as a "piece of
wretched foolery, as ought to be beneath any but children, or mad people." By masking his identity an individual was freed from the fear of
public censure and thus better able to act inappropriately, should he
choose to do so. Indeed, Burgh went so far as to suggest a causal connection between the celebration of masquerades and marital infidelity
which he charged, without verification, was on the increase.[12]

Of those diversions of which he did approve, reading, the conversation of friends, horseback riding, and hunting were most acceptable,
if pursued with moderation. Concerts were unobjectionable, but an undue
interest in music could result in an "expence of time and money, above
what the accomplishment, carried to the greatest length is worth."[13]

Allusions to the judicious use of time and money are sprinkled
throughout Burgh's writings. He remarked that "every eating mouth without a pair of working hands to it, is an atrocious evil in a commercial
nation" and recommended fining people who did nothing useful. His attitude on idleness is perhaps best summed up in his contention that "if
all the idle people in a nation were to die in one year, the loss would
be inconsiderable, in comparison of what the community must suffer by
being deprived of a very few of the active and industrious."[14]

Burgh's admiration for the "active and industrious" partially accounts for an apparent contradiction in his thinking. While on the one
hand he was unalterably opposed to luxury because of its degenerative
effect, he was also an exponent of the Protestant ethic. This

consideration, together with his enthusiastic nationalism, enabled him
simultaneously to fulminate against affluence and to encourage the expansion of English commerce. He justified his stand on the grounds that
"the business is not to give over dealing in the materials of luxury;
but to work them up and export them, making other nations pay for
them."[15]

    Burgh's commitment to the Protestant ethic prompted him to endow
the attributes of the businessman with the sanctity of moral virtue.
His obvious sympathy with England's trading classes is a pointed exception to John Osborne's observation that a distrust of such economic interests was characteristic of the radical reform movement.[16] Describing
merchants as "the most judicious and prudent sett [sic] of men in the
nation" and manufactures as the source of England's greatness and "a
more valuable fund of riches to a nation, than mines of gold and silver,"
Burgh recommended a plethora of government legislation to encourage the
continued growth and prosperity of English commerce: the elimination of
monopolies, such as that enjoyed by the East India Company, once the
trade for which the monopoly had been granted was established; the creation of uniform weights and measures throughout the empire; the promotion of Jewish emigration to England since Jews were good traders; and
the use of machines in manufacturing, whenever they would produce a better, cheaper, and more competitive product.[17] In a more moralistic
vein Burgh also commented extensively on a variety of business practices.
Obviously drawing upon his own unhappy experiences as a trader, he advised caution in lending money to others; suggested that businessmen
have all transactions in writing with clear provision for the arbitration of differences; and warned merchants against over-extending themselves, concluding that if failure did occur, bankrupts should always
pay their debts as soon as feasible.[18]

    Burgh's commitment to the Protestant ethic and his preoccupation
with public morality and its ramifications on social stability not only
prompted his interest in England's commercial classes, but occasioned
his sporadic comments about the English poor. Few contemporary Commonwealthmen and political reformers were much concerned with the plight of
the English poor. Certainly, genuine egalitarianism was alien to their
thinking.[19] Burgh was more typical than not of their attitudes and pre-
occupations. But as a moralist, he occasionally demonstrated an interest in the poor that went beyond the ordinary.

    That Burgh had much personal experience with the poor is doubtful.
His comments on their circumstances have an altogether academic tone.
Burgh accepted the reality of social stratification and never challenged
the traditional argument that socio-economic distinctions were part of
the inscrutable design of Providence. He did, however, reason that
riches created a mere superficial distinction among men. To be grateful
for the bounty of the Creator was Christian; to be insolent was unwarranted, indeed, ridiculous.[20] In his ealier writings, Burgh had little
of a specific nature to say about the poor. Not until the 1760s when
his concern for public mores was rapidly politicized did he seriously
consider their problems. In addition to heightened political consciousness, his interest was undoubtedly stimulated by the fact that this

period was one of increased social unrest attributable to the beginnings
of an inflationary spiral sparked by population pressure on food supplies and aggravated by wartime expenditures.

What particularly distressed Burgh as he surveyed the contemporary
scene in the 1760s was the increase in the numbers of idle poor people.
Idleness and debauchery went hand in hand in Burgh's mind and should always be discouraged. Moreover, since Burgh believed that the population
of England was either stable or declining, he reasoned that an increase
in the numbers of unemployed poor necessarily meant a decrease in the
work force--a phenomenon that would constrict commercial expansion and
erode English greatness. Burgh appreciated that the "industrious" poor
were the "most valuable" class in the nation. They were its "sinews and
strength." It was their labor that provided the rich with comforts and
conveniences.[21] Government should pursue policies that would stimulate
employment among the poor and offset social unrest in their ranks.

Burgh singled out those age-old villains, the monopolist and en-
grosser, as the culprits largely responsible for the current plight of
the poor. His vision of socio-economic relationships was innately conservative. Glorifying individualism, industry, abstemiousness, charity
and rectitude, he was outraged by what he perceived as the greedy attempt of a wealthy minority to exploit the many in pursuit of riches far
beyond the needs of any one man. Such affluence could only corrupt the
few and needlessly deprive the masses. Accordingly, he attacked the en-
grossment both of land and food supplies.

Together with many of his contemporaries Burgh erroneously believed
that enclosure, rather than a population explosion, was primarily responsible for the increase in the numbers of poor people. His naive proposals for the alleviation of this problem reflect an interest in agrarian
reform that was unusual in Commonwealthman circles.[22] Burgh recommended
that legislation be passed limiting the size of an individual farm to a
maximum value of £200 annual rental. Large land owners affected by such
a measure could invest their surplus capital in the Sinking Fund or in
additional farms, each to be leased to a different family.[23] A still
more radical proposal was his suggestion that the Commons be divided a-
mong the "sober and industrious" thereby relieving the poor rates and
encouraging marriage "on which the strength of a nation depends." Five
to seven acres per householder would suffice. As this homestead would
be too small to occupy all of its owner's time, he could still work at
some other trade. His wife and children might engage in domestic industry. Though some would waste this opportunity, the majority, Burgh con-
fidently predicted, would prove "sober and diligent: for as a man op-
press'd with poverty, notwithstanding all his continual labour and care,
naturally gives himself up to sloth and despair; so the having an estate
which he can call his own, is no small inducement to sobriety, industry,
vigour and alacrity."[24]

Burgh's concern with the engrossing of food supplies not only reflected his innate hostility to monopolists, but his distress about the
social impact of high food prices caused by manipulative practices. He
strongly advocated the establishment in every town of public granaries

which could be opened in times of dearth in order to lower grain prices. He also recommended the construction of public enclosures where cattle could be bred and slaughtered and the meat sold directly to the consumer. If necessary, private associations should implement these proposals. Although Burgh was a laissez fairist on the general question of government regulation of imports and exports, he favored government price and profit fixing for certain essential staples and criticized government bounties on agricultural exports, arguing that they contributed to an artificial scarcity that worked undue hardship on the indigent. He also opposed sumptuary taxes on commodities consumed largely by the poor.[25]

Moral and humanitarian considerations were not the only factors motivating Burgh's interest in the poor. He was after all a taxpayer directly affected by the financial burden of supporting an increasing indigent population. Burgh believed that the existing system of poor relief based on the parish was archaic and actively supported its overhaul. He largely favored the recommendations made by a parliamentary committee in 1760. Anticipating the reforms made in 1834, the committee suggested the establishment of a national system of poor relief which would eliminate the local inequities of the present system and would strongly encourage the able-bodied to work. To the committee's suggestions, Burgh added the stipulation that applicants for relief be carefully scrutinized by magistrates who should keep a register of complaints made against the "idle and debauched." Individuals who lived industrious and frugal lives should be assisted. Idlers should be sent to the plantations.[26] Burgh failed, however, to define the criteria whereby the industrious and idle poor might be differentiated, nor did he consider the possibility that magistrates might differ over these terms. Typically, he simply sketched the broad outline of a proposal which he felt constituted a marked improvement over current practice and was either oblivious to or unimpressed with the important practical problems that might be associated with the implementation of his recommendation.

Poor relief was but one feature of the government's effort to maintain social stability that Burgh censured. He argued that the government's entire system for preserving law and order needed reform. Noting that citizens were not safe on city streets and country highways, he urged that the urban watch be increased, that every street and alley in cities and suburbs be lighted, and that a mounted patrol travel the major roads of the kingdom to protect wayfarers (the cost of this endeavor to be paid from a tax levied on travelers at every turnpike). He suggested using paid government informers to expose the moral and criminal offenses of the citizenry; proposed making local communities financially liable for the conduct of their residents; and even recommended the formation of a "grand association for . . . seeing the laws duly executed." Asserting that such laws should be few in number and simple in composition, he further urged the codification of English law to eliminate its confusion and repetition. He was likewise critical of the lethargic pace of judicial proceedings which could be rendered more efficient and equitable if held publicly without charge. Burgh believed that lawyers were particularly culpable for the prevalent abuses of the English legal system. He described pleading at the bar as "a mischievous invention, calculated wholly for the purpose of disguising truth,

and altogether incapable of being applied to any honest purpose." In order to eliminate the economic incentive for advocates to distort the
truth, Burgh thought that ideally they should perform their services
without compensation, apparently from a sense of noblesse oblige. The
judicial process might be further accelerated by referring civil dis-
putes to arbitration upon the request of one of the litigants. When a
case did go to trial, the whim of one juror should not be allowed to
thwart justice in the interest of a unanimous verdict. Moreover, juries
should determine penalties as well as assess culpability. Burgh agreed
with Beccaria that punishments should be "calculated to deter offenders,
and prevent further transgressions." The certainty rather than the se-
verity of punishment provided the real deterrent to crime. As with the
wayward student, so also with the lawbreaker, the shame of punishment
ought to constitute the principal part of retribution. If the offender
felt no shame, the responsibility lay with the government. Either the
punishment was unjust or the culprit hardened and abandoned. In the latter case the government's responsibility, though subtle was more insidious, for Burgh maintained that government was responsible ultimately to
prevent such perversion of its citizenry.[27]

One means whereby such depravity might be avoided was early marriages. Burgh believed that marraige promoted sobriety and responsibility and satisfied the sexual impulse. In addition to its salutary effect on manners, marriage was also vigorously to be encouraged since,
according to eighteenth century reasoning, the strength of the state was
directly correlated to the number of its citizens. The legitimate growth
in the birth rate was thus a goal of considerable importance. Indeed
James Burgh solemnly declared that it was the "indispensable duty" of
all citizens to marry unless physically or prudently unable to assume
this weighty obligation. In his utopian essay Burgh made marriage a condition for citizenship in the land of the Cessares. And in Crito he suggested that voluntary celibacy be heavily taxed.[28] Believing that obstacles preventing early marriages should be eliminated, he denounced the
Marriage Act of 1753 on the grounds that it especially deterred marriages among the poor who got "cold feet" during the time required for publishing the bans of matrimony. Despite his frequent laudatory comments
about the intellectual and emotional gratification of marriage, Burgh
obviously believed, perhaps out of a sense of moral superiority, that the
majority of men were motivated by the irrational passion of the moment
when they determined to wed. For this reason he concluded that prostitution was a particularly grave threat to national well-being as it either satisfied physical desire, thus obviating an important incentive to
marry, or it rendered the company of all females odious to the debauched.
To erradicate this gross moral peril Burgh recommended a modest tax be
levied on all urban householders, the revenues to be used for the apprehension, cure, and training of prostitutes for other employment. In addition, the root cause of prostitution should be attacked. Ignoring or
ignorant of the connection between poverty and prostitution, Burgh simplistically reasoned that today's seduced young virgin was tomorrow's
prostitute. Once deflowered, a young woman often drifted into or was
obliged to turn to prostitution since she was no longer an attractive
marriage prospect. If the law dealt severely with culprits who misled
such innocents, the wellspring of prostitution would dry up. A man

convicted of robbing a virgin of her priceless prize should be obliged
to marry her or find her a husband under penalty of fine, imprisonment,
or banishment.[29]

As might be expected, Burgh no more countenanced illicit sex after
marriage than before. Infidelity destroyed family harmony, possibly resulted in "the introduction of a bastard instead of the lawful heir to
an ample estate," and endangered the eternal salvation of the parties
involved. Yet such gallant behavior was fashionable in certain circles.
Burgh sarcastically offered his own "modest proposal" to deal with vio-
lators of the marriage contract. Adulterers should be flayed. Their
skins could be sold at public auction for conversion into various items.
Burgh was certain many a connossieur would pay handsomely for a pair of
gloves made from the hide of a lady of quality or from that of royalty.
"They must indeed be much more beautiful than the finest <u>French</u> kid."
Burgh speculated that a pincushion made of "such rich stuff" might bring
100 guineas. Admittedly the frequency of adultery would result in a
prodigious glut of such skins, but, given the example of grain engrossers, it should not prove too difficult to create artificial scarcity in
order to maintain a high price. The government could naturally profit
handsomely from this scheme by establishing a hide-office employing com-
missioners at ₤2000 per year and clerks at ₤500, thereby increasing the
number of places at its disposal. Assuredly the hide business would
soon bring the government as much net profit as it was likely to acquire
by taxing the colonies.[30] Unlike its famous model, Burgh's Swiftian
scheme engendered neither controversy nor reform.

Although more seriously offered, still another of Burgh's proposals
for improving the moral tone of English life also failed to attract attention. Ever enamored of the idea of association to remedy public ills,
Burgh suggested in the <u>Political Disquisitions</u> that an organization similar to the Royal Society be established for the general purpose of up-
lifting the manners of the people. Members would be elected from the
ranks of talented, exemplary gentlemen. The group would publish moral
discourses and satires which Burgh with undue confidence felt could not
but have a beneficial effect on public morality.[31] In essence the proposal is a revival of the Grand Association project of the early 1750s.
The later suggestion was no more successful than the earlier one.

Although James Burgh recognized that private citizens such as himself could do much to foster the improvement of public morality, in the
main he saw the task as one requiring legislative action and dependent
upon the example of the upper strata of English society, the natural
leaders of the nation. Again and again since his first impassioned plea
in 1746 that the nation reject the worship of mammon and resume the virtuous ways of some mythic ancestors, Burgh urged the great of the nation
to spearhead a cursade on behalf of public morality. His words seemed
to fall on deaf ears. He observed with heartfelt anguish that:

> Our governors . . . are <u>Christians</u>, and live in
> an <u>improved</u> age. Therefore, they lead their peo-
> ple to laugh at religion and conscience; they play
> at cards on <u>Sundays</u>, instead of countenancing the

public worship of their Maker; they have made
adultery a matter of merriment; they cheat at
play whenever they can; they lead their inferiors
into extravagance and dissipation by encouraging
public diversions more luxurious and more debauched than all that even the orientals exhibited;
and lest shame should in some degree restrain them,
they put on masks, and set it at defiance; . . .
they appear in public with their drabs at their
sides; they are the first and most extensive vio-
lators of the laws themselves have made; they are
the destroyers of the people, without which no
constitution ever stood long.

Yet surely, "no nation ever was very corrupt under a long continued virtuous government, nor virtuous under a long continued vicious administration."[32]   This conviction eventually led James Burgh to devote the
full force of his moralistic fervor to the cause of political reform.

CHAPTER VI:

THE POLITICAL DISQUISITOR

For many of James Burgh's generation, moral turpitude, though certainly reprehensible in itself, was especially dangerous because of its
impact on political freedom. Public morality was a means to a political end. Only so long as the people remained virtuous could liberty
survive. For ultimately who would defend the freedom of the populace
against the encroachments of tyrants if not the people themselves? Yet
the people could hardly ward off political corruption if their energies
were sapped by moral corruption. Liberty necessarily pre-supposed public virtue.[1]

James Burgh never shared that perspective which viewed politics
as the ultimate reality and considered popular mores more important for
their ultimate influence on political institutions rather than for their
religious implications. Public morality remained Burgh's primary concern. But if his moralistic emphasis contrasted with the more secular
perspective of some segments of his reading audience, such philosophical differences mattered little in terms of his specific discussion of
British politics. Whether motivated primarily by an interest in political liberty or moral rectitude, his readers would find his commentary
stimulating and disconcerting.

Preoccupied with the "manners of the people," Burgh had little to
say about political issues in his early writings. Nonetheless, he did
have certain definite political opinions. He viewed government as a
paternalistic institution whose chief responsibility was the maintenance of order and the promotion of public morality and prosperity. His
deference to political authority was pronounced, as was his hostility
to popular violence and to the verbal excesses of government's critics.
He believed that "true liberty is always corrected and restrained by a
proper submission to government." True patriotism manifested itslef
"in a proper reverence to our governors, especially the supreme; even
in cases where we do not see enough (as how should persons in private
stations?) to be able to explain to ourselves, or others, the wisdom
of all their measures." In rare asides he railed against bribery and
perjury at elections and endorsed the secret ballot as a remedy for
these abuses.[2] His political philosophy was an amalgam of Common-

wealthman radicalism and Bolingbrokean conservatism.

When and how Burgh became enamoured of these ideologies can only be guessed at. His introduction to the Commonwealthmen may have preceded his immigration to England. In Scotland, the Glorious Revolution had stimulated keen interest in Commonwealthmen writings.[3] And certainly Burgh's neighbors at Newington Green were acquainted with these works. Burgh's familiarity with Bolingbroke probably developed after his arrival in London and was undoubtedly stimulated by his contacts with Leicester House where Bolingbroke's writings, in particular his essay on a Patriot King, were highly regarded.

Burgh's simultaneous attraction to Commonwealthman and Bolingbrokean ideology was not unusual in the Augustan age. Both philosophies were critical of faction, suspicious of power, and beguiled with the illusion of some mythic yesteryear when right order prevailed. In this regard they neatly suited Burgh's own inclination on the moral plane to censure the present, hark back to the past, and anticipate a regenerated future. There were, however, some fundamental differences between Bolingbroke and the Commonwealthmen that derived from their conflicting attitudes towards John Locke's contract theory of government. Wholeheartedly committed to the concepts of paternalistic government, aristocratic leadership, and the preservation of a social hierarchy based on the great-chain-of-being, Bolingbroke was completely at odds with Locke's "view of men [in the state of nature] 'as equal one amongst another'" and with Locke's emphasis on individual liberties, popular sovereignty, and the right of a people to change their government.[4] Although most Commonwealthmen shared Bolingbroke's social views, they were less logically consistent than he in their attitude toward Locke. Their need to vindicate the Glorious Revolution dictated their allegiance to Locke despite the revolutionary implications of his contract theory for the "mixed" constitution Commonwealthmen so nostalgically exalted. And as Bolingbroke feared, their acceptance of Locke's political principles subtly encouraged a radicalism among the Commonwealthmen that was often at odds with their conservative social attitudes and their sentimental talk of restoring some golden yesteryear.

James Burgh consistently invoked Locke as a mentor. But initially he was far more sympathetic with Bolingbroke's paternalistic vision of an aristocratic government headed by a patriot king who would effect the nation's moral rebirth and encourage its material prosperity than with the emphasis on popular action inherent in Locke's philosophy. Undoubtedly Burgh's upbringing in a paternalistic church that emphasized obedience to authority and social stability encouraged his strong predilection towards aristocratic leadership. Burgh never lost his fascination for Bolingbroke's utopia, but he was gradually disillusioned about the prospects for its realization. His disenchantment was crucial to his emergence as a political radical.

Although not apparent at the time, the first stage in Burgh's metamorphosis into a radical occurred in 1754, the year of his ill-fated effort to organize a Grand Association of "persons conspicuous for their characters, and stations, who could easily have procured the

assistance of all the able peers in the three kingdoms . . . [who] held
it in their power to give a general turn to the sentiments and manners
of twenty millions of people." The station of such men gave them "an
opportunity of action." The failure of his project made Burgh extremely chary of aristocrats, the majority of whom, he determined, were "so
happily disposed that nothing was likely to engage them to associate,
but some object suitable to their sort of magnanimity, as a cock-match,
a horse-race, the preservation of the game, or the preservation of the
court-places."[5] Although Burgh did not write the nobility off completely in his later reform schemes, for the most part he came to identify
them as the villains in his political scenario.

The accession of George III accelerated Burgh's radicalization.
The advent of the long-anticipated patriot king riveted Burgh's attention on the political scene. In the "Remarks Historical and Political"
Burgh repeatedly urged the new monarch to "put himself at the head of
his people to manage, and suppress parties;" to himself assume "the man-
agement of affairs" and "hold the reins of government in . . . [his]
own hands." Noting that "the people have a confidence in the King, as
established for life," whereas "the ministry are in power to day and
out to morrow," Burgh observed that:

> It is a matter of commiseration to see the Sov-
> ereign of the bravest, wisest, most generous
> and greatest people on earth, contented in a
> state of slavish dependence on a junto, whilst
> the whole nation wants nothing so much as to see
> him set free, to put themselves under his imme-
> diate protection and to support him in that inde-
> pendence, which becomes his high station, and
> which stands quite clear of all but the happy con-
> stitution, on which it is founded.[6]

Burgh's "Remarks" clearly reflects his first uneasy apprehension
that the promise of the new reign might not be fulfilled. He was particularly alarmed by the growing factionalism in government. Much of
his political commentary in Crito, for example, was provoked by the
wrangling among Pittites and Butites.

Burgh's abhorrence of party spirit and rabble rousing was a logical corollary of his enthusiasm for a patriot king. He believed that
"no community ever subsisted in peace and happiness, in which the supreme authority was treated with contempt." He wondered "how it is to
be expected, that wholesome laws should take effect in a country, in
which the common notion of liberty is, a privilege of saying and doing
whatever insolence and disaffection may think fit?" He even argued:
"Let the conduct of a government, or of a parent, be what it will, the
subject, who will treat the former, or the son the latter, with open
scurrilous abuse, is to be looked upon as a reprobate, lost to all
sense of common decency."[7] Defining a genuine patriot as one "who
follows virtue for virtue's sake; who serves his country for the sake
of serving his country . . . not himself,"[8] Burgh was extremely skeptical about the patriotism of a party man. Heads of parties seemed to

be much more interested in "the gratification of their own ambition, or avarice," than in the improvement of the nation. Rank and file party men appeared only concerned with getting or keeping places or pensions. As it was "inconceivable" that any party could be always right or always wrong, Burgh concluded that "whoever inclines universally for or against either side, without ever altering his opinion, is either a man of very mean abilities, or has some indirect scheme in view" distinct from the nation's interests. Throughout his career, he reminded his readers of Swift's dictum that "party is the madness of many for the gain of a few." Yet it was commonly maintained that opposition and party were necessary in a free state. Burgh dismissed this maxim with the rejoinder that "nobody ever thought an opposition necessary in a private family, where the heads have nothing but the good of the family in view." Opposition could only be justified when a "junto of artful and pushing grandees" were bleeding the nation. Then one evil required another to expose it. Opposition was an expedient not to be encouraged. Instead, sound politics dictated the elimination of the means whereby a corrupt faction could threaten the general welfare.[9] Burgh never wavered in these convictions.

Frustrated in his exaggerated expectations that the new reign would witness the nation's regeneration, Burgh turned political crusader. He was one of the earliest and most vigorous British spokesmen for radical reform in the decade before the American Revolution. Disillusioned with the drift of aristocratic politics, he increasingly stressed Lockean and Commonwealthman ideology and emphasized popular action as the most viable instrument of reform and regeneration. The Middlesex election controversy gave final confirmation to his fears that the constitution had been subverted, thereby imperilling the liberties of the people and the very survival of the empire. But never fully disabused of his belief in a "Patriot King," Burgh refused to blame his "artless, honest-hearted" young monarch for this horrific turn of events. Although he sometimes spoke of the possible degeneration of the English government into absolute monarchy, Burgh did not subscribe to the thesis that the King was the guiding intelligence behind ministerial machinations. Instead he singled out factious politicians, ambitious and avaricious grandees, placemen and pensioners as the responsible culprits. By implication Burgh believed that George III regrettably remained a rather passive figure in English politics, beguiled and bemused by powerful aristocrats. As late as 1775 Burgh was still exhorting the King to shake off ministerial influence and "think for himself, and . . . speak for himself." The most damning criticism Burgh ever leveled at his young sovereign was to pronounce him culpable for allowing his name to screen the villainies of his ministers.[10]

Burgh's political writings attempted to diagnose the maladies besetting the body politic and the remedies necessary to restore its health. Because most of his political commentary was penned relatively late in his life, there is considerable consistency in his statements. His analysis of the political scene was premised on the conviction that man was divinely fashioned as a free agent and given a free will with which to make moral decisions. Freedom of action in the political sphere was likewise his birthright. The Creator intended "that man should be free." Indeed the Creator was the "glorious patron of liberty."

To serve Him entailed "perfect freedom."[11] Liberty of course could not
be equated with license. The general good always restricted the individual's freedom of action. Whereas licentiousness consisted in:

> doing whatever the will, appetites, and passions
> suggest[,]. . . true liberty desires only the
> freedom of doing what is agreeable to the dictates
> of reason; and the rules of religion: and steadily
> submits to, and cheerfully obeys just laws, en-
> joined by proper authority; and is fully convinced
> that the preserving peace and good order with
> proper reverence to persons in authority, are
> absolutely necessary for the happiness of every
> nation.[12]

If the individual were always mindful of the limits of liberty, governments would be unnecessary. Because men did not consistently follow the
dictates of reason, it became necessary for government to preserve the
general good against the encroachment of selfish interests:

> Did reason govern mankind, there would be little
> occasion for any other government . . . But man,
> whom we dignify with the honourable title of
> Rational, being much more frequently influenced,
> in his proceedings, by supposed interest, by pas-
> sion, by sensual appetite, by caprice, by any
> thing, by nothing, than by reason; it has, in all
> civilized ages and countries, been found proper
> to frame laws and statutes fortified by sanctions,
> and to establish orders of men invested with authority
> to execute those laws, and inflict the deserved
> punishment upon the violators of them. By such
> means only has it been found possible to preserve
> the general peace and tranquility.[13]

The raison d'etre of government was the preservation of the rights,
liberties and happiness of the people.[14] The danger in this relationship stemmed from the very nature of power. Long before Lord Acton ever
penned his famous epigram, Burgh observed that the "love of power is
natural; it is insatiable; it is whetted, not cloyed, by possession."
The temptation of those in authority to extend their influence at the
expense of popular liberties was scarcely resistable. Burgh assured his
readers that "every government will be tyrannical, if they dare." They
"do as naturally tend to despotism, as heavy bodies to their respective
centries [sic]." It was the responsibility of the people to restrain
such natural inclinations. If tyrants succeeded in suppressing the liberties of the people, it was only because popular inertia gave them the
opportunity to do so. "Scarcely any woman loses her virtue, no nation
its liberties, without their own fault."[15]

In analyzing the specific mechanics of Britain's constitution Burgh
subscribed to the widely held notion that power was supposed to be balanced among king, lords, and commons or, put another way, monarchy,

aristocracy, and democracy. In accord with this theory of "mixed government" Burgh identified the king as head of the executive branch of government with the responsibility for enforcing the laws enacted by the legislature, pardoning criminals, and serving as an example of virtue to the people.[16] By implication royal ministers were simply agents in the execution of these tasks. Burgh was less clear on delineating the role of the Lords. According to the commonly accepted interpretation of the "mixed" constitution, the House of Lords exercised a legislative curb on the excesses of popular enthusiasm. But Burgh criticized the Lords' ability to protect their own interests against popular pressures through use of their veto powers. Moreover, he believed that too numerous a peerage threatened the constitutional balance by giving the peers too much influence in the government. In his utopian government peers were not allotted separate representation in the legislature.[17] By contrast, Burgh identified the House of Commons as the most important element in the constitutional triangle because it represented the bulk of the population. Delineating the twofold function of the Commons as "Inquisitorial . . . and legislative," Burgh characterized the Commons as the "principal" part of the legislature in terms of activity and business, while the king and peers were principal in dignity.[18] Frequently when Burgh spoke of parliament, he really meant the Commons.

The authority of all three branches of government was derived from the people. Reflecting the influence of Locke's contract theory of government, Burgh affirmed that "power in the people is like light in the sun, native, original, inherent, and unlimited by any thing human." The authority of all governors was "borrowed, delegated, and limited by the intention of the people, whose it is, and to whom governors are to consider themselves responsible." Only so long as government enjoyed the support of a majority of the people could it function legitimately. Should it pursue a course of action in violation of the popular will it would be a tyranny.[19]

As the ultimate source of sovereignty in the state, only the people enjoyed the right to alter the constitution, either directly by some form of popular action or indirectly through their chosen representatives.[20] The Wilkes affair convinced Burgh that the British constitution had in fact been unconstitutionally altered. The spirit of the constitution had been subverted by a group of men who did not truly represent the interests or opinions of the majority of the people. The government had fallen into the hands of a group of avaricious grandees who controlled the executive as members of the court and who exerted unwarranted influence over the House of Commons because of its unrepresentative character and through the systematic and deliberate use of corruption. As a result of ministerial influence the House of Commons, traditionally the bulwark of popular liberties, had:

> lost its efficiency, and instead of being (as it
> ought) a check upon regal and ministerial tyranny,
> is in the way to be soon a mere outwork of the
> court, a French parliament to register the royal
> edicts, a Roman senate in the imperial times, to
> give the appearance of regular and free government;

but in truth, to accomplish the villainous
schemes of a profligate junto.[21]

Cabinet government was the constitutional innovation that so disturbed James Burgh and many of his contemporaries. Lacking any specific
legislative fiat, the cabinet was nonetheless gradually evolving from
the privy council in response to political needs created by the Restoration and Revolution Settlements. Its development reflected the reduced
prerogative power of the king and the increased importance of parliament. Political expediency, however, mattered little to the moralistic
Burgh. Unaware that the balance of power among king, lords, and commons was always more myth than reality, he viewed the increasing confluence of executive and legislative power in the cabinet (or to use his
broader term, the ministry) for whatever the reason, as a perversion of
a constitutional balance that had, in reality, never existed.[22]

The justification for "mixed" government was that it supposedly prevented the undue amalgamation of power by one branch of government at
the expense of popular liberties. The fusion of executive and legislative power in the court or ministry seemed to pose just such a threat to
Burgh and to the Real Whigs who saw the liberty of the people seriously
imperilled by this innovation.[23] Although such fears appear ridiculous
today in light of the historical development of cabinet government, they
were not altogether unjustified in the eighteenth century, given the
substantial aristocratic resurgence that occurred in England.[24] The assumption that cabinet government could not lead to oligarchical dictatorship at the expense of king and people ignores the fundamental importance of the French Revolution in British constitutional development.
If the French Revolution postponed reform, it also abetted it by inculcating a fear of the people in the aristocracy which made them ultimately amenable to broadening the English political power base. The resolution of the conflict between popular liberties and aristocratic influence lay in the future. The certainty of its occurrence cannot be tak-
en for granted. James Burgh did not do so.

In accounting for what he perceived as the dangerous growth of ministerial influence, Burgh shared the opinion common to radical Whigs
that the Glorious Revolution had failed to plug "all the leaks in the
vessel of state."[25] In particular, inequities inherent in the structure
of the House of Commons facilitated the violation of the popular will
by an unrepresentative minority. Burgh's argument suggests that had
equitable representation in annual parliaments been introduced in 1688
it would have proved practically impossible for ambitious and avaricious aristocrats to extend their influence unduly over the House of
Commons. The failure to implement these reforms was compounded by the
introduction of systematic corruption both in the election of the Commons and in the conduct of its business. Burgh erroneously dated the
beginning of this nefarious practice with William III's reign.[26]

Despite the fact that "every" session of parliament began with a
resolution prohibiting peers from interfering in elections to the Commons, it was "notorious," asserted Burgh, "that very few elections are
carried without their influence," and in some cases without their

complete control.[27] Encouraging the electorate to violate their patriotic responsibilities by selling their votes and to perjure themselves by then falsely swearing under the election oath that their vote was freely cast could not fail to have dire consequences for the nation. Burgh agreed with Humphrey Sydenham's extravagant assertion that:

> what people get by selling their votes at an election, is generally spent in extravagance; and being once led into an extravagant manner of living, few of them ever leave it, as long as they have a penny to support it. By this means they are led into necessities, and having once broke in upon their conscience, by selling their vote at an election, they are less proof against those temptations they are exposed to by their necessities; so that . . . many a poor man in this kingdom has been brought to the gallows by the bribe he received for his vote at an election.[28]

Yet, reprehensible as such electioneering tactics were, the motive behind them was even more insidious. Why should gentlemen "drink with clowns, kiss old women, and expend thousands in obtaining places," if there were not something to be gained from sitting in parliament. Candidates claimed that the "honour" and "opportunity of serving their country" were reward enough for their services. But Burgh was skeptical. "It was as much, and more, an honour to be in parliament in former times, than in ours," yet men were considerably less eager to obtain seats. The position then was not, however, as "lucrative." Could it be seriously doubted that present-day candidates who trampled upon "honour and honesty" by "bribing, gaming, [and] rooking" were more interested in "the filling of their pockets" than in their patriotic duty? Places, pensions and other remunerations for services were the real reason behind the "continual scramble" for parliamentary seats.[29]

These various bribes were the odious means whereby ministers managed parliament at the expense of the people. Whereas in times past the power of the court was exercised through the prerogative, now it manifested itself through influence. "Though the appearance of court-power is taken away, the reality remains, and is perhaps greater than under James I." How much of the people's money was expended in this fashion was difficult to ascertain because funds for these purposes were in large part drawn from the King's secret service account, a "huge cloak thrown over an immense scene of corruption." Burgh estimated that pensions alone amounted in 1760 to Ł1,600,000 per anum. The civil list accounted for another Ł800,000-1,000,000 per year and was calculated to be only one-third of the revenue at the disposal of the ministry. One anonymous source "credibly" informed Burgh that "the whole annual expence [sic] of supporting the Dutch government, is less than the yearly income devoured by some of our single blood-suckers." Were it not for these various sources of ministerial influence, the members of parliament, especially in the House of Commons, would pursue the interest of the country. For in consulting the interests of the country they would be consulting their own interests, did they not have places or pensions to indemnify them and make profitable their disregard of national needs.[30]

Parliamentary corruption then was one tool whereby ambitious and greedy aristocrats had "thrust themselves into power, in order to raise . . . themselves and their families, and to fill their pockets." As a consequence, venality, that bane of moral reformers like Burgh, had "poisoned all ranks, from the bribed voter in a country borough, upwards to the candidate for a place in the great assembly of the nation."[31]

Two other means whereby ministers extended their influence were the national debt and the army. Demonstrating a commercial conservatism shared by such men as Richard Price and David Hume, Burgh frequently bemoaned the supposed precarious state of the British economy occasioned by the national debt.[32] He even went so far as to suggest that the debt, calculated to be approximately equivalent to one-tenth of the nation's capital, be eliminated by voluntary contributions amounting to one-tenth of every propertied person's assets. Realizing that this proposal had little chance of success, he also recommended the sale of honors and titles as payment on the debt.[33] Dangerous in itself to the welfare of the nation, the national debt became even more odious in Burgh's eyes because it augmented the power of the court. "The anxiety of the public creditors, the proprietors of the funds, about public credit is a powerful cause of their shewing a reluctance against all proposals for salutary alterations, or restorations of the constitution."[34]

The army was an even more obvious source of ministerial influence. By increasing the visibility of the army, the Seven Years War undoubtedly helped revive a latent antipathy to the military that was never far below the surface in an island kingdom that reviled the military dictatorship of Oliver Cromwell and exalted the navy as the bulwark of national defense. After 1763 fears of standing armies were further reinforced by continual colonial complaints against British troops stationed in America and by such dramatic episodes as the Boston Massacre and the Massacre of St. George's Field, May 10, 1769, when British troops fired on a crowd of Wilkite supporters. It was within this context that Burgh singled out standing armies as one of the most dangerous instruments of ministerial power.

Protests against standing armies were not unusual in Commonwealthman ranks and Burgh relied heavily on critics like Charles Davenant, John Trenchard and Thomas Gordon to demonstrate the threat that standing armies posed to a free country. "All history," Burgh argued, proved that soldiers were "ever . . . ready to enslave their fellow-subjects; and almost all nations have actually been enslaved by armies." Recklessly asserting that "no nation ever kept up an army in times of peace, which did not lose its liberties," Burgh cautioned that while there was perhaps little reason to fear that George III would use his army for such tyrannical purposes, a less scrupulous prince or minister, supported by a force only one-fourth the size of Britain's army, could wreak havoc with English liberties. Even apart from the threat they posed to popular freedom, standing armies, whether annually or perpetually maintained provided the ministry with several thousand sychophants dependent on the court for their positions. Every officer in the army was thus "an addition to the power and influence of the ministry. And every addition to their power and influence is a step toward aristocracy or absolute monarchy."[35]

Instead of standing peacetime armies, the country should entrust its defense to the navy and to the militia. Reflecting an Englishman's traditional favoritism toward the navy, Burgh noted:

> There is no advantage we have ever gained by war,
> which would not have been greater, and cost us
> incomparably less, if we had kept to the sea.
> For we never can have a nation for our enemy that is
> not commercial, and we can certainly at any time
> force a commercial nation to yield to reasonable
> terms by attacking their commerce, their foreign
> settlements, their coast-towns, their fisheries,
> etc. And by sea we may always command superi-
> ority.[36]

Should armed forces be necessary, a militia drawn from men of property[37] could adequately repel an invasion or quell internal disorders. All that was required was for the militia to be exercised in their own parish periodically during the year by an experienced sergeant and they would be capable of handling any disorder that might arise. Of one thing Burgh was certain: standing armies were neither necessary nor tolerable in a free country.

From Burgh's perspective, the peril posed to popular liberties by the unchecked growth of ministerial influence was demonstrated time and again in the course of George III's reign:

> We have seen in one parliament the power of elec-
> tion of members taken from the people, and usurped
> by the commons; the colonies irritated by taxing
> them without representation; the mother country so
> dissatisfied, that 60,000 petitioned to have par-
> liament dissolved; 600,000 Ł of the people's money
> given, sorely against their will, to pay debts,
> which none, but the ministry, knew to be real, or
> if real, how contracted; the East India company
> deprived of her rights and privileges, without
> pretence [sic] of transgression against government;
> religious liberty refused to two different sets of
> petitioners humbly requesting what all mankind have
> an unalienable right to enjoy, etc.[38]

Of these incidents, the Wilkes affair and the taxation of the colonies were crucial to Burgh's determination that the constitution was overthrown and that a broad-based assault on liberty was underway.

James Burgh's simultaneous involvement in two such seemingly disparate causes as the Wilkite petition movement and the attempt to repeal the Townshend duties pointedly underscores the interdependence of colonial and domestic grievances in the minds of many Anglo-American critics of government. Both episodes were interpreted as part of a larger threat to constitutional liberties that required immediate action. Colin Bonwick contends that radicals were slow to make this connection and as evidence notes that "James Burgh pointed out the parallels but otherwise treated the two questions separately" in the "Constitutionalist" and "The Colonist's Advocate" letters. This argument overlooks the fact that the focus of each series was dictated by a specific political goal. Undertaken to broaden the scope of the 1769 petition movement, the "Constitutionalist" letters were preoccupied with the question of parliamentary reform. Written to secure repeal of the Townshend duties, "The Colonist's Advocate" letters logically concentrated on strictly American issues. Nonetheless, both series make clear Burgh's complete awareness of the interrelationship between colonial grievances and the fate of liberty in England. "The Colonist's Advocate" warned:

> But when it is remembered, that it is an old
> Artifice of the Enslavers of Kingdoms to begin
> with the more distant Parts, surely every free-born
> Subject on this Island ought to be alarmed at the
> late bold Attempt on the Liberties of our brave
> Fellow-Subjects in America . . . For, should an
> encroaching Administration prevail in enslaving the
> Colonies, would they not thence be emboldened to
> subject the Mother-Country to their Iron Rod?

The "Constitutionalist" sounded a similar note:

> Do you not know that our brethren in America have
> been lately treated by our m____ries in the very
> manner in which <u>France</u> would treat England, if
> for our sins, we were conquered by her? . . . Do
> not such tyrannical proceedings in <u>one</u> part of the
> British empire, give cause of alarm, lest they
> should be attempted in <u>others</u>?[39]

One point is true, however. First and foremost colonists were concerned with events in America and English radicals like Burgh with events in England--a fact that Bonwick seems to lose sight of.

From first to last the Wilkes affair demonstrated the ministry's blatant contempt for popular rights, and the dangers inherent in parliamentary tyranny which was "more to be dreaded than monarchical."[40] In condemning parliament's action, Burgh argued:

> The people have certain <u>incommunicable</u> powers,
> which their representatives can upon no occasion
> challenge to themselves. The people alone can
> <u>elect</u> representatives. The whole body of representa-
> tives have not in themselves the power to <u>take into</u>,
> or <u>exclude</u>, or to <u>expel</u> from their house one single
> member, otherwise than according to notorious and

stated _laws_ made by the _whole_ legislative power,
and assented to by the _people_.[41]

If evidence other than Wilkes's case were required to demonstrate
the unbalanced state of the constitution and the threat therein posed
to liberty, the issue of colonial taxation supplied it in abundance. Oscar Handlin has justly noted how the colonies served as a virtuous contrast in Burgh's writing to the corruption of "the Court and of London
society." Handlin's opinion to the contrary, however, Burgh's emphasis
was not on the colonies as an "outpost of liberty . . . resisting the
corruption of British ministers,"[42] but on ministerial corruption and
tyranny exemplified in colonial policy as was also true in the Wilkes
affair. Colonial readers were interested in Burgh's writings because
they sympathized with colonial grievances and bolstered American claims
that they were resisting a tyrannical, corrupt government seemingly bent
on suppressing the liberties of Englishmen everywhere. Burgh was interested in colonial complaints because they confirmed his contention that
the ministry was indeed corrupt and tyrannical. The relationship between Burgh and the colonists was symbiotic.

Burgh offered nothing new in his analysis of the conflict between
the mother country and the colonists. He fulminated against suppressing
colonial charters, giving permanent salaries to governors, and, of
course, taxing the colonies without representation. From a purely practical perspective all of these measures were impolitic and threatened so
to strain relations with the colonies that trade would be disrupted much
to the disadvantage of the mother country. Grenvillian arguments to the
contrary, Burgh asserted on the basis of information supplied by Franklin that a "prodigious commerce" existed between the mother country and
her off-spring and showed every indication of steadily increasing until
the government implemented its new colonial policy.[43]

But practical considerations were not the basic issue. The government's policy violated the colonists' rights as Englishmen and established a precedent that threatened the rights of Englishmen at home. If
colonial charters could be so easily destroyed "the charters of all the
cities and those by which all crown lands are held, may be annihilated."
The taxation of colonists by a parliament in which they had no representation:

> _adequate_ or _inadequate_, is subversive of liber-
> ty, annihilates property, is repugnant to the
> genius of the people, oppressive to their indi-
> gence; it strikes at the root . . . of their
> privileges as _British_ subjects, ever loyal and unof-
> fending; it is . . . ominous to the liberty of the
> _British_ empire, unjust in its principles, . . .
> and pernicious in its operation alike to the
> mother-country and the colonies.[44]

It was no more legitimate for parliament to tax the unrepresented
colonies than it would be for all of the parishes in Middlesex, with the
exception of Islington, to meet in assembly and agree to a tax that

would equally apply to the unrepresented Islingtonians.[45] Taxation required consent, either directly or through representatives. Burgh did not quarrel with the argument that the colonists should assume their fair financial burden. But were they not already taxed by their own assemblies and by the Navigation Acts? Skeptical that anything but the desire to enrich "court-tools" and create new places motivated demands for additional colonial taxes, Burgh maintained that the legitimate needs for colonial subsidies could best be met in the traditional manner of voluntary contributions. If direct taxation was indeed requisite, then the colonists should have a voice in its determination. As delineated in the Political Disquisitions, Burgh's plan for achieving this, although theoretically reasonable, was unrealistic in light of the deteriorated state of Anglo-American relations in 1774-75. He recommended that American agents temporarily sit in a parliament that would fix colonial taxes at a fair percentage of the taxes paid by Englishmen. Colonial consent thereafter to specific tax proposals would not be essential. These same agents could engage in deliberations about the representation of the colonies in future parliaments. Burgh was not sympathetic with the proposition that distance made such representation impractical:

> If the colonies should object, that it will be
> very inconvenient for them to send members from such
> a distance, it may be answered, that so it is for the
> northern parts of Scotland. All these matters of con-
> venience must be as chance orders them. Nor can any
> two parts of a great kingdom enjoy precisely the
> same advantage in all respects.[46]

Although Burgh did not even consider the argument that colonial interests would be overwhelmed in a British parliament, doubtless he would have rejected this objection as well.

Likewise, Burgh did not agree with all of the tactics used by colonials to protest British policy. He characterized the Boston Tea Party as "inexcusable," naively reasoning that all the Americans had to do was "keep firm in their resolution not to buy or drink" any tea. A moral absolutist completely hostile to the Machiavellian theory that ends justify immoral means, Burgh argued that while the government was chiefly to blame for provoking colonial violence, "those who resist in an unjustifiable manner, are not innocent."[47] Had he lived, James Burgh would have appreciated the motives behind the ensuing colonial rebellion. That he would have approved of it is questionable. That he would have regretted it is certain. As with other English radicals, he was a nationalist who prized the British empire and cringed at the possibility of its disintegration.[48]

The naivete of the moralist accounts only in part for Burgh's stand on colonial violence. His attitude also reflects an ambivalence toward the sovereign right of the people to alter their government that was not uncommon in reform circles. Burgh never denied that right, but he felt it should be exercised cautiously and in the interest of promoting better government. At the least such change should not entail "greater inconveniences than the future advantages are likely to balance." The "laws of prudence and morality" should govern such decisions. Within these limits Burgh could envision the people opting for republicanism instead of monarchy or the converse. Yet Burgh also said that even if the will of the majority, admittedly difficult to ascertain upon occasion, was bent on an ill-advised course, governors were obliged to follow its dictates, for whatever the majority chose was "right."[49] Burgh's dilemma was typical of John Locke's disciples. For all of his glowing references to the people and their rights, Burgh shared the fear of the masses that enervated the eighteenth century reform movement. Although he observed that:

> The opposition of a minority to government, backed by a majority, is proper rebellion. The opposition of a majority of the people to an obstinate government is proper patriotism.

he was in fact wary of rebellions:

> It is undoubtedly dangerous for the people to be employed in redressing grievances. It is not safe to teach them to unite, and to give them the means of knowing their own strength. When they go to redressing, they generally do great mischief, before they begin redressing.[50]

Rebellion should be resorted to only in the direst of circumstances. Burgh did not believe the situation in England, or in the colonies yet demanded such radical measures.[51] His position was typical of eighteenth century English reformers and crucial to their ultimate ineffectiveness. In Burgh's own case, his alienation from the mainstream of English society helped spawn a radical reformer. It did not breed a revolutionary. Burgh was sufficiently aggrieved and disillusioned to criticize his society, but because it afforded him enough opportunity for self-fulfillment he was not so disenchanted as to advocate its destruction.

Although Burgh believed that contemporary circumstances did not warrant insurrection, he nonetheless shared the radical opinion that reform must be speedily implemented if liberty was to survive in the empire. Paradoxically, this man whose fundamental precepts were molded by moral conservatism, whose chief goal was the _restoration_ of some mythic Eden, rather than the _creation_ of a brave new world, embraced radical means to achieve his conservative goals. Believing that there was a point in England's past when parliament, despite "_Popish_ darkness" and "extravagant notions of prerogative," labored faithfully for "the public good" and seized "all opportunities for obtaining an enlargement of liberty,"[52] Burgh consistently maintained that the reforms he proposed, while possibly innovative in themselves, were conservative in their intent. Convinced that his reforms violated no moral law, he justified them on the grounds that they would re-establish the balance of power among king, lords, and commons by once more securing the independence of the legislature from the executive. Parliament would again function as Burgh erroneously thought it was originally meant to function: as the representative of the people and the palladium of popular liberties. The paradox of Burgh's position was not unusual among Commonwealthmen.

In enunciating the radical program Burgh attempted to minimize opposition to it by deliberately avoiding the extremism of some. For example, although he had gradually come to share the opinion of a small minority,[53] that republicanism was the most preferable form of government if a state were formulating a completely new constitution, he could not justify the turmoil such a fundamental constitutional alteration would incur in Britain since the present government, if "restored to its true spirit and efficiency," could "yield all the liberty, and all the happiness, of which a great and good people are capable in this world."[54] Thus republicanism formed no part of his proposed reforms.

On the other hand, Burgh admonished the people not to delude themselves that simply replacing one set of ministers with another would adequately redress their grievances and secure their freedom. Unaware or disapproving of the compromise between radical leaders, Grenvillites, and Rockinghamites that prompted the restraint of the 1769 Wilkite petitions, Burgh bemoaned the limited scope of these popular addresses. Particular grievances, such as those delineated in the petitions, were manifestations of more fundamental problems. It was necessary to "restore the spirit of the constitution" by securing "three important alterations, or rather restorations:" annual parliaments with rotating membership, the exclusion of placemen and pensioners from the Commons, and adequate parliamentary representation. Burgh believed these proposals were interdependent. Nothing less than the adoption of all three would suffice.[55] He was not unwilling to compromise, however, on their specific implementation. Common sense tempered his crusading ardor.

The Septennial Act of 1716 had extended the maximum life of a parliament to seven years. According to Burgh, the result was the encouragement of a sense of independence in the representatives incompatible with their roles as delegates of the people. Burgh completely disagreed with the view so eloquently defended by Edmund Burke that members of parliament must follow the dictates of their own consciences, rather than the instructions of their constituents. To such arguments Burgh responded that the members of the Commons were the "servants" of the people. If they were not obliged to implement the will of the people, then they were a "set of despots" and the people were "as perfect slaves as the Turks, excepting the few months of a general election."[56] In _Crito_, Burgh admonished electors not to send "one member into the house, who did not give bonds to be forfeited, if grievances were not immediately redressed."[57] After 1769 reformers frequently demanded such bonds or election pledges from political candidates.

The primary factor, however, governing popular control over representatives was the frequency of parliamentary elections. If parliaments were annual, the opportunity for popular supervision of the legislature would be significantly increased. The eighteenth century's faulty conception of parliament's historical development encouraged Burgh in the delusion that annual parliaments were the "birthright" of the English people. Relying heavily on Malachy Postlethwayt's _Universal Dictionary_ of Trade and Commerce, Burgh observed that initially parliaments were annual and seldom sat for more than a few months. Not until the reign of Henry VIII was their life extended inordinately. Burgh mistakenly indicated that this change occurred because it was "the most effectual means for rendering the members obedient to . . . [the king's] will." The mischief of long parliaments was amply demonstrated during the time of Cromwell and of Charles II. Not until the reign of George I was the life of parliament regularly extended for seven years on the "pretense" of danger from the Jacobites. Certainly such danger no longer existed. Far from being a constitutional innovation, annual parliaments had historical precedent and should thus be restored.[58]

Yet reducing the length of parliament was not sufficient in itself to restore the health of the constitution. If the same men were returned to parliament year after year, what did it matter if parliaments were annual or septennial? Bribery and court influence would continue to flourish. Accordingly, Burgh proposed that members be excluded by rotation from sitting in parliament every year. Initially he recommended that most members be ineligible for reelection for a period of seven years. Commons clerks and a small number of members selected by lot might carry over in the interest of continuity in government. Subsequently Burgh modified these figures to annual exclusion of two-thirds of the membership who would be barred from reelection for three years. By this device parliamentary service would be opened to greater numbers of gentlemen, thus introducing new perspectives into legislative deliberations. More importantly, this tactic would undermine "packing, bribing, canvassing, electioneering, placing, and pensioning of parliament-men; because the parliament, never consisting wholly of the same men for two years together, it would not be worth while for the court to get their iniquitous schemes carried in parliaments, only to remain for one year, and be overthrown the next."[59]

To eliminate completely systematic bribery and corruption of the electorate and of the Commons further required that all placemen and pensioners be barred from the House of Commons.[60] The least controversial of Burgh's proposals, such a measure would abolish one of the most notorious sources of court influence over the legislature. Burgh also favored the Rockingham program of economical reform as a check on bribery,[61] but it was not fundamental to his program.

Burgh was opposed in principle to financial compensation for public service. He attributed much of contemporary political corruption to the practice of "rewarding those services, which ought to be consecrated to sincere patriotism, with sordid riches," noting that "it is no wonder there is so little sincerity where there is so much interest." He thought that national service should be performed gratis as on the local level and countered the argument that no one would serve if not paid with the rejoinder that while a tailor could not be expected to make a coat for his sovereign without remuneration, "a gentleman, who expects a confidence to be reposed in him, by his King and country, ought to have more sentiment than a taylor. [sic]" Burgh maintained that insofar as public service warranted compensation, rewards should be honorary, rather than pecuniary. Nor should rewards be hereditary.[62] Such conditions

made men of property the inevitable candidates for public office. Burgh
expressed regret that this qualification would exclude from service able
men lacking substance, but did not dwell on the point. Essentially he
accepted the eighteenth century assumption that property promoted social
stability and a sense of responsibility. Accordingly, men of property
were the natural leaders of the nation. Burgh did not, however, equate
property with land. Although he expected the landed classes to play a
major role in the nation's councils, he was critical of the disproportionate influence exerted by such classes. In the "Remarks Historical
and Political," he conservatively suggested that the King occasionally
choose his ministers from other than the nobility or the gentry in order
to demonstrate that birth was not the sole criterion for royal favor.
Far more outspoken in the Political Disquisitions, he argued that the
preponderant influence of landed property in government unduly predisposed the government to aristocratic interests at the expense of the
mercantile and manufacturing classes. Legislation disadvantageous to
these groups resulted. The corn laws were a prime example of this. If
representation was on its proper footing, the commercial community would
play an important role in parliament. Reflecting his bias toward the
mercantile community, Burgh asserted that "the interests of merchants is
so much the interest of the nation, that there can hardly be too many
merchants in parliament."[63]

Property was not, however, the sole criterion for public service.
Ability was also necessary. Members of parliament, for example:

> ought to be men of good natural parts, education,
> and character, sound reasoners, graceful speakers,
> knowing in the three interests, viz. the landed,
> the commercial, and the monied, in general history, law, and politics, and in the history, laws,
> and politics of Britain, learned in human nature,
> and masters of the spirit and disposition of the
> inhabitants of the three kingdoms, and of the
> colonies.

Less exceptional individuals, "if honest," would be acceptable providing
parliament was independent.[64]

Franchise reform was the final requisite if the "spirit" of the
constitution was to be restored. Noting that "in antient times" all the
inhabitants of counties apparently could vote, Burgh bemoaned the restriction of the county franchise to freeholders. Representative government presupposed "the consent of the whole people, as far as it can
be obtained." Otherwise the "whole people are enslaved to the one, or
the few, who frame the laws for them." Inadequate representation made
possible the misapprehension or misrepresentation of the majority will.
Burgh charged that this had frequently occurred during Walpole's administration. "No one," he argued, "can imagine that the British or any
other constitution, ever intended confusion and absurdity; the few to
out-vote the many," the wealthy to be deprived of their just vote in
legislation.[65] Yet this was precisely the state of affairs in Britain.
Because of the over-representation of boroughs, many of which were

strongly influenced or directly controlled by a few lords or by the
court, and the attachment of the county franchise to the forty shilling
freehold, large numbers of respectable and propertied individuals were
deprived of a voice in government. Burgh himself, as a copyholder,
could not vote. There were many like him.

In a series of tables, Burgh indicated the number of votes required
in various boroughs to elect a representative to the Commons. In Wallingford, for example, there were 150 qualified voters. A majority of
their number, merely 76 people, were thus able to elect one of the 558
members of the Commons. In all, Burgh estimated that 254 members of the
Commons were elected for all practical purposes by only 5723 voters, the
majority of the qualified voters in boroughs such as Wallingford. Altogether the boroughs and Cinque Ports accounted for 382 of the representatives in the Commons. Yet it was notorious, Burgh justly observed,
that, with the exception of some of the larger cities, themselves gross-
ly underrepresented, boroughs, especially burgage boroughs, were highly
amenable to influence and manipulation. Obviously, "the easiness of
bribing a small handful of voters, who have the privilege of sending
two members [to parliament,] is ruinous to the independency of the house
of commons." Rectifying this "absurdity, would be restoring the constitution."[66]

Burgh proposed that exercise of the franchise be based on the payment of certain taxes. As the "Constitutionalist," he recommended that
all males who paid the window tax be allowed to vote. In the Political
Disquisitions he went even further. Consistently sympathetic with the
industrious poor whose contribution to the national well being was reflected in their payment of direct or indirect taxes, Burgh boldly stated that he could see "no argument" against allowing these poor a voice
in selecting their representatives. Otherwise "an immense multitude of
people are utterly deprived of all power in determining who shall be the
protectors of their lives, their personal liberty, their little property
. . . and the chastity of their wives and daughters, etc." It was especially unfair to bar the poor from "determining who shall be the law-
givers of their country" when "they have a very heavy share in raising
the taxes which support government." Burgh estimated that the sumptuary
taxes paid by the poor equaled a "heavy land-tax."[67]

Although his position was a logical outgrowth of his belief that a
financial stake in society entitled a citizen to certain rights, as well
as responsibilities, Burgh's defense of what closely approximated universal manhood suffrage was highly unusual, even in reform circles. It
was commonly argued that the franchise of the poor would be peculiarly
amenable to the influence of those upon whom they depended. Indeed
Burgh himself criticized the franchise as it was presently constituted
on the grounds that "beggarly boroughs" inhabited by poor people elected
many of the representatives to the Commons at the behest of the court or
powerful nobles. But this objection would be overcome "if the state
were on a right foot, and parliament free from court-influence." Burgh
realized, however, that the issue was highly controversial and consequently did not press it.[68] It would be sufficient, he conceded, if the
franchise were broadened to include those who paid direct taxes.

Further reflecting his conviction that a man's influence in the political sphere should be proportioned to his financial stake in the body
politic's welfare, Burgh sanctioned plural voting as the natural right
of men who had more to secure.[69] He expected widening the franchise to
"render bribery impracticable" and at last give the commercial and manufacturing interests the influence they so richly deserved.[70]

In addition to broadening the electoral base, Burgh also proposed
a system of proportional representation. The current distribution of
seats in the Commons made possible the over-representation of some communities, especially the "beggarly boroughs," at the expense of more
heavily populated and prosperous areas. One of Burgh's favorite examples of this injustice was a comparison of the "inconsiderable counties"
of Cornwall and Devon with the county of Middlesex, including London,
Westminster, and Southwark. The wealth of Cornwall and Devonshire, and
consequently their contribution to revenue was approximately one-tenth
that of Middlesex and its cities. Yet the less prosperous and produc-
tive territories elected 70 members of parliament compared to 10 for
the wealthy Middlesex area. Instead of the current distinction among
cities, boroughs, counties, Cinque Ports, and universities, Burgh recommended that seats in parliament be distributed on a county basis in pro-
portion to the county's contribution to the public expense.[71]

In his stimulating study, Party Ideology and Popular Politics at
the Accession of George III, John Brewer argues that the Stamp Act debate was "crucial" to the emergence of representation as an issue in
radical politics during the late 1760s. The fact that as early as 1762
James Burgh, one of the foremost spokesmen for reform, advocated increasing merchant representation in parliament, redistributing parliamentary
seats on the basis of contributions to the land tax, and extending the
franchise to all those who paid a specified amount of tax, suggests that
Brewer was too quick to dismiss the role of the indigenous Commonwealthman tradition in this debate.[72] English radicals hardly needed the
Stamp Act crisis in America to alert them to the inequities in their own
government. What the American crisis did do, in conjunction with the
Middlesex election controversy, was to point up the grave dangers inherent in those inequities.

As a final hedge against undue influence over elections, Burgh advocated the use of the secret ballot. He was a longstanding enthusiast
of this device. Not only did it mitigate bribery, but it helped prevent
personal feuds and animosities. If Burgh's other reforms were adopted,
however, influence would no longer be a factor in elections and the ballot would be less important. Accordingly, in the wake of criticism of
the ballot as an encouragement to irresponsible exercise of the franchise, Burgh did not insist on its adoption.[73]

Having outlined a program of reform, Burgh next addressed himself
to the problem of implementing it. Popular violence was certainly one
means. But Burgh believed it should be the last, rather than the first
resort. Grievances could most simply be redressed by parliament which
already enjoyed the constitutional authority to do so.[74] Parliament,
however, had given little indication that it would reform itself of its

own volition. Parliament's stand admittedly posed problems. Historically, Burgh mistakenly observed, parliaments were established to curb the power of kings and ministers, but the people unfortunately neglected to "reserve to themselves a regular and constitutional method of exerting their power in curbing parliaments, when necessary."[75] The situation, though complicated, did not preclude action.

Given parliament's failure to legislate reform of its own accord, Burgh suggested two alternative methods of peacefully prompting the legislature to redress grievances. The most preferable, but the least likely to occur entailed the King's placing himself at the head of the reform movement. Burgh urged George III to be a true "patriot king." Rhetorically he queried:

> What if the most illustrious and most amiable
> personage of this country should make it his
> peculiar glory to take the lead in a scheme,
> whose grand object is infinitely superior to
> every party view, and which would establish
> that state in whose happiness no one is so much
> interested as himself, on a foundation never more
> to be shaken, either by popular discontent, on
> one hand, or by the combinations of the Great
> on the other? From such a leader, and the power-
> ful following which his appearance at the head of
> such a scheme would command, what effects might
> not be expected?

Such service would justly earn the monarch the title of "Father of his country."[76]

Yet, after fourteen futile years, even Burgh with his persistent faith in the king's good intentions apparently had little confidence that George III would head the cause of reform. He thus proposed extraparliamentary action as the most feasible alternative for redressing grievances. A national political association should be immediately organized to pressure parliament into reform.

Associations were not a new concept in British history. Political associations were "as old as the alliance of barons that imposed Magna Carta on an unwilling King John, as old as the medieval commune."[77] In Burgh's own day, however, most English associations were non-political. The Society for the Encouragement of Arts, Manufactures and Commerce was the most prominent of many such organizations.[78] Not until the 1760s did political association once more assume an important role in British life. The Stamp Act Congress; the Irish Association which was erroneously thought by many, including Burgh, to have secured the 1768 act that limited Irish parliaments to eight years; and the Wilkite Society of Supporters of the Bill of Rights (1769) all reflected a new political consciousness.[79]

James Burgh was no recent enthusiast of association.[80] His dramatic appeal for the creation of a "GRAND ASSOCIATION FOR RESTORING THE

CONSTITUTION"[81] represented the culmination of a life-long belief that
associations were an important instrument of change. The consistency
with which he supported this tactic has never received attention.
Throughout his long career Burgh recommended the formation of a variety
of associations, largely for moralistic purposes. In Britain's Remembrancer he exhorted the Quality and Gentry [to] enter into an Association, to live mostly in the Country upon their Estates, and within their
Incomes; to countenance the publick Worship of God and to support a due
Decorum in their own Families." He assured them their action would ban-
ish "Extravagance and Impiety" from Britain. He also urged the citizens
of London to associate for the purpose of restoring "the frugal, the industrious, the virtuous and religious Manners of our Fathers against a
Flood of Deism, of French Poppery [sic] , and of bewitching Pleasure,
which overruns the land." In the Dignity of Human Nature he reminded
his audience that "whoever understands human nature, knows, of what consequences associations are." It was at this same time that Burgh himself unsuccessfully attempted to organize a "Grand Association consisting of persons conspicuous for their characters, and Stations, who could
easily have procured the assistance of the able pens in the three kingdoms for carrying on a periodical publication in support of virtue and
truth." Failure likewise ensued from his efforts to organize an "Association against the iniquitous practices of Engrossers, Forestallers,
Jobbers, etc. and for reducing the Price of Provisions, especially Butchers Meat."[82] Despite these rebuffs, Burgh persisted in his support of
association, though bemoaning the fact that contemporaries "have not yet
come to a resolution for associating, petitioning, or instructing."[83]
Inevitably, Burgh's politicization led him to urge the formation of political associations. Against the background of the petition movement
of 1769 spearheaded by the Bill of Rights Society, he proposed the organization of a "general national association of Free Britons," to restore the state. Men of property, untainted by "the wages of iniquity,"
were exhorted to lead the cause of reform in their respective counties.
Petitions from throughout the land in support of annual parliaments with
rotating membership, a place-bill, and adequate representation should be
submitted to parliament.[84] Again Burgh's advice bore no fruit.

Undaunted, Burgh reiterated these recommendations in the Political
Disquisitions. Fearful of popular violence, he proposed instead:

> to apply the power of the people, guided, limited,
> and directed by men of property, who are interested
> in the security of their country, and have no
> income, by place or pension, to indemnify them for
> bringing slavery and ruin upon their country--to
> apply their power--(if found absolutely necessary)
> to prevent the application of the same power unre-
> strained, unlimited, and directed by mere caprice,
> or the spirit of party.[85]

In addition to men of property, Burgh's national association should in-
vite the support of "all friends of liberty, all able commanders." Paro-
chial committees should be organized to enlist the support of "all persons whose names are in any tax-book, and are willing to join." A "grand

committee" should be instituted in the three kingdoms and in the American colonies. Ideally the impetus behind this movement should come from the king, but failing this, the independent nobles, or if need be, responsible Londoners, should lead the cause.[86]

One of the first responsibilities of the association would be to ascertain the "undoubted sense of the people, on the state of public affairs," as a preliminary to procuring petitions, signed by a majority of the people of property, in support of the reforms already delineated.[87] Burgh did not underestimate the difficulty this entailed. His political philosophy demanded majority support behind any constitutional alterations. Minority rule was tyranny. Yet his own experiences made him painfully aware that the people were not easily aroused. He had bitterly observed in _Crito_ that "the independent people of our hopeful age will not bestir themselves for their own interest; though they have it . . . in their power, in a constitutional way, to obtain of their governors, redress of grievances." Popular inertia and timidity were the boon of tyrants and the bane of reformers.[88]

If the public would but arouse itself, there was little question in Burgh's mind that their efforts would be successful. "I doubt whether any court ever was desperate enough to resist the united demand of a whole people, not yet enslaved." In any contest between government and the majority of the people, "the decision may prove difficult, but it is most likely to be in favor of liberty . . . For if the cause be unquestionably good, the people will soon have purse, and army, and every thing else in their hands." Convinced that right must triumph, Burgh did not specify how the people would do this. Moreover, obviously hopeful that petitioning would accomplish its purpose, he did not delineate any course of action should it fail. He maintained that from a practical viewpoint it was best to deal with such contingencies as they occurred.[89] And undoubtedly Burgh's fear of revolution made him shrink from considering alternative actions--a common reaction among English reformers.

That Burgh would have procrastinated about the use of force in the wake of the almost certain rejection of petitions is quite probable. In the interest of speculation, an even more pertinent point of consideration concerns his response to the certain lack of majority support for his reform proposals. Possibly he would have followed the lead of colonial revolutionaries and repudiated, at least temporarily, the restrictive demand of the Lockean contract theory that the will of the majority prevail for good or ill. Burgh's qualification that the popular will must conform to the dictates of prudence and morality offered him the means of doing so without being accused of inconsistency. There is no evidence to support this thesis, however, and much to refute it. Burgh's belief in majority rule and his fierce opposition to oligarchy make doubtful his participation in a minority attempt to force the alteration of the constitution without popular approval. Although the righteousness of Burgh's position made him hopeful that the people would respond to his call for reform, he acknowledged:

By the readiness of the people to enter into

associations, it may be effectually determined,
whether the majority are desirous of the proposed reformations . . . the true criterion
between rebellion and reformation consists not
in the atrociousness of the abuses to be re-
formed, but in the concurrence of the people in
desiring reformation.[90]

In the wake of hostilities in America Burgh's criticisms of the
government and sympathetic discussion of colonial grievances were hardly
calculated to engender a favorable response among Englishmen. Not until
1780 had disillusionment with the government's conduct of the war grown
sufficiently to occasion a serious effort at extra-parliamentary action
through association. Even widespread disaffection with wartime policy,
however, proved inadequate to arouse popular enthusiasm for the cause of
reform. Ultimately, Wyvill, Jebb, and Cartwright experienced defeat as
had Burgh in his efforts to provoke mass enthusiasm for reform. The i-
deas which Burgh had so tenaciously championed required a period of fer-
mentation during which the economic pressures of industrialization and
the heady example of the French Revolution stirred the masses to support
the changes advocated earlier by the reform minority for whom Burgh
spoke.

James Burgh's misfortune is that he stood in the vanguard of a movement in infancy. He was one of the earliest and most vigorous spokesmen for reform in George III's reign. Avoiding the extremism of Wilkes
and Junius, he nonetheless offered the public an impassioned critique of
contemporary politics coupled with specific reform proposals designed to
safeguard the constitution and popular liberties. The simplicity and
superficiality of Burgh's analysis was largely a by-product of his two-
dimensional moralistic perspective, reinforced by the naivete of the political amateur. A man who could maintain that "politics are only common sense applied to matters of public concern"[91] obviously had little
experience managing men and did not sufficiently appreciate the complex-
ity of situations or the legitimacy of intellectual diversity. There
was no middle ground between right and wrong for Burgh. But the relatively unsophisticated character of Burgh's political commentary
did not adversely affect its popular impact. Quite the contrary. The
very simplicity and repetitiveness of his arguments enhanced their prop-
aganda value. The culmination of Burgh's efforts, the Political Disquisitions, was undoubtedly the most thorough exposition of the radical
platform prior to the American Revolution. The work's heavy reliance on
other sources enhanced, rather than detracted from its value as a sum-
mary of the radical position. Readers could hardly fail to be impressed
with the copious documentation Burgh used to substantiate his arguments.

Although Burgh was essentially a propagandist for ideas long current in Commonwealthman circles, he enjoys a special place in the reform
movement. He particularly wished to be remembered as the progenitor of
an association "as useful toward the promoting of a right way of thinking and living" as the Society for Arts, Manufactures and Commerce was
for promoting its goals.[92] His aspiration has been realized. Burgh's
lifelong interest in association climaxed by his call in 1775 for a

GRAND ASSOCIATION distinguishes him as one of the most important fore-
fathers of the political association movement of the late eighteenth and
the nineteenth centuries--a movement significant in itself and as a contributor to the evolution of modern political parties.[93] In terms of the
development of English radicalism, Burgh well deserved the tribute Daniel Isaac Eaton paid him when he proposed to include Burgh's works in a
projected series of Political Classics.

CONCLUSION:

THE SUM OF THE MAN

In making a final assessment of James Burgh, it is clear that the relative neglect he has experienced at the hands of historians is not warranted on the basis of the popularity or significance of his writings in his own day. It stems instead from several considerations. The paucity of easily accessible biographical data in the form of diaries or correspondence undoubtedly discouraged research on Burgh. Moreover, his commitment to a life of retirement and his insistence on retaining the status of a private citizen--attitudes encouraged by his youthful failures at the University and in business, by his sensitivity to the pitfalls of pride, and by his inclination to defer to the leadership of the great--led Burgh to publish most of his works anonymously and to shun the public spotlight. As a consequence, although many of his publications achieved tremendous sales by eighteenth century standards, they did not secure to their author the degree of personal recognition that might reasonably have accrued to him. By his own choice, Burgh remained "behind the scenes" for the most part. Until the publication of the Political Disquisitions his reputation was greatest among a limited, albeit prestigious, circle of friends and acquaintances, foremost of whom were the Honest Whigs. The Disquisitions secured Burgh a substantial degree of public recognition, at least within the Anglo-American reform movement. And to date it is largely on the basis of this work that his historical reputation has rested. Without question, the tome was the most comprehensive expression of the reform perspective prior to the American Revolution. On both sides of the Atlantic it quickly achieved the status of a classic authority. Had Burgh lived on after its publication to enjoy the plaudits of his peers and, more importantly, to continue propagandizing on behalf of reform during the crucial war years, he would certainly have achieved an even greater prominence in the reform movement, rivaling that of Price and Cartwright.

But historians, of course, must judge Burgh on what he did achieve and not on the basis of "what might have been." Within these parameters Burgh's variegated career proves more instructive and important than has hitherto been recognized.

101

In the first place, it is essential to remember that Burgh was a moralist and educator as well as a political reformer. His interests were wide ranging, but always rooted in his religious and moral convictions. Nor is Burgh atypical of eighteenth century Anglo-American reformers in this eclecticism. His example serves as a reminder that "specialization" was largely an alien concept at that time, even among reformers. Catharine Macaulay, for example, first achieved prominence as a republican historian and political pamphleteer, but in her last years wandered into the realm of metaphysics and education. Granville Sharp was initially preoccupied with the issue of slavery and only gradually took up the cause of America and parliamentary reform. Joseph Priestley enjoyed a reputation as an educational innovator and scientist before becoming a political activist. Likewise, Richard Price was a noted moralist and statistician prior to his involvement in political causes. The list could go on and on. Fundamental to the careers of all of these individuals, however, was their moral fervor.

Moreover, although the moralistic bent of reformers like Burgh was admittedly exaggerated, it was far more typical of a century generally stereotyped as the "age of enlightenment" than that designation would suggest. The critical acclaim and substantial sales enjoyed by Burgh's diatribes against public and private immorality are indications of the continued fascination and importance that religious and moral questions held for the reading public during the eighteenth century. Voltaire's religious attitudes harbingered the future; Burgh's were a truer reflection of his generation's sentiments.

This is not to say that "reason" was not prized by Burgh and his contemporaries. Quite the contrary. Burgh's life provides a particularly good example of the force of reason as an ideal in the eighteenth century. A keen admirer of Newtonian physics, as were his comrades, the Honest Whigs, Burgh attempted to rationalize all situations. Although often impressed with the irrational side of man, he emphasized the intelligibility of the human condition. Despite his frequent allusions to the impending disaster awaiting the British nation, he optimistically believed in the solubility of problems through the use of reason. His sorry attempts to rationalize his faith poignantly underscore the tensions between faith and reason that prevailed during the century. But however far Burgh wandered from his Calvinistic roots, he maintained an abiding concern for moral and religious issues that was certainly derived from his upbringing in the Reverend Andrew Burgh's home and church. He measured his own life and all aspects of his society with a moral yardstick acquired in his youth. A believer in moral absolutes, he viewed the world simplistically in terms of right and wrong. Although this perspective sometimes occasioned superficiality in his analysis of his society, it imbued Burgh's writings with a passion and directness that were persuasive and undoubtedly contributed to his effectiveness as a propagandist and to his popularity with the general reading public.

With the exception of his manual on rhetoric which is now recognized as a major contribution to the development of the elocutionary movement in England and America, Burgh's "thoughts on education" and his

commentaries on a host of social problems that agitated reform-minded
men and women of his generation have been largely ignored by historians.
These compositions were tremendously popular with Burgh's contemporaries. Some were even reprinted well into the nineteenth century. They
are a valuable index of eighteenth century tastes and attitudes on such
diverse topics as education, attitudes towards women, poor relief, the
growth of humanitarianism, and penal reform. Too often the role of men
like Burgh in preparing the public mind for fundamental social reform is
overlooked. Such writers are frequently far more influential at a popular level than the stellar figures of an age. By popularizing the theories of the Condorcets or the Lockes they make possible the eventual
acquiescence of society in what would otherwise be revolutionary and
disruptive changes.

Previous studies slighted Burgh's role as moralist, educator, and
social commentator, but his reputation as a radical grew considerably
from the time when Herbert Butterfield described the Disquisitions as a
"curious compilation" and its author as a "fanatic on the subject of associations."[1] All of the recent works on English radicalism and the i-
deological origins of the American Revolution recognize the important
place of the Disquisitions in these movements. Nonetheless, Burgh remained a shadowy figure. The process whereby he became a radical was
unexplored; important nuances of his political philosophy were unknown;
the scope of his radical actions was insufficiently appreciated; and the extent of his influence was not fully evaluated. When fleshed out, Burgh's
political career highlights certain features of late eighteenth century
English radicalism that have not been sufficiently appreciated.

John Wilkes's altercation with the government in 1763 and the
Stamp Act Debate of 1765 marked the beginning of overt popular political agitation during George III's reign, but Burgh's example is a reminder that the foundations for that agitation had been laid, in some
cases, years before these episodes. Burgh's radicalization was initiated by his disillusioning encounter in 1754 with avaricious and ambitious grandees. This discrete experience was doubtless approximated
in the lives of other radicals. Catharine Macaulay and her brother John
Sawbridge, for example, grew up in a family whose hostility toward arbitrary government was rooted in the punishment their paternal grand-
father received as a consequence of his role in the South Sea Bubble.[2]
This familial tradition predisposed the grandchildren to place the worst
interpretation on episodes like the Wilkes affair.

What is particularly striking about Burgh's evolution as a political radical is the role played by George III in the process. Isaac
Kramnick has noted the fascination that Bolingbroke's "patriot king"
held for Commonwealthmen during Walpole's administration. But virtually no attention has been paid to this theme in studies of radicalism
during the reign of George III. Perhaps Burgh's enduring enthusiasm for
a patriot king was simply an anachronism. But the author of a 1783 pamphlet that advocated associating to "restore the ancient constitution"
by shortening the duration of parliaments and securing an equal representation echoed Burgh's hopes that "A Patriot King may annihilate

Faction and, supported by the confidence of a grateful People, smile at the impotent struggles of pseudo-patriots." Likewise, the republican historian, Catharine Macaulay, argued as late as 1790 that if a country would have a king, he should not be a constitutional cipher, but a "patriot king."[3] Nostalgia for a patriot king was a logical corollary of the Commonwealthman's commitment to the "mixed" constitution which was thought to be imperilled by undue aristocratic influence. The theme was also altogether reasonable in light of the fundamentally conservative aspiration of English radicals, like Burgh, to restore some mythic yesteryear when virtue flourished and an harmonious equilibrium governed men's social and political relationships. At the least Burgh's longing for a patriot king enhances our appreciation of just how innately conservative the radical movement was. And certainly there is a need for further research to determine the pervasiveness of the patriot king theme.

The accession of the long anticipated patriot king encouraged Burgh to dream of the millennium. The aggravated factionalism that characterized the first years of the new reign profoundly disturbed and disillusioned Burgh. More importantly, it effected his active involvement in political affairs for the first time in his lengthy literary career. Here again, Burgh's experience highlights a factor in the revitalization of late eighteenth century English radicalism that has generally been overlooked. That this variation on the "rising expectations" syndrome contributed significantly to the initial turmoil and radical agitation of the period seems altogether plausible. Indisputably, it played a major role in Burgh's metamorphosis into a political radical.

Once radicalized, Burgh produced a variety of compositions that consistently enunciated standard Commonwealthman philosophy. In particular, his support for a more equal representation based upon the principle of taxation antedated the Stamp Act debate and in no wise was dependent upon that crisis. Burgh's example calls attention to the vitality of the indigenous Commonwealthman tradition and qualifies John Brewer's thesis that the Stamp Act debate was "crucial" to the emergence of equal representation as a radical goal in the late 1760s.

With the publication of An Account of the Cessares Burgh became one of the earliest spokesmen for reform in George III's reign. As his disillusionment with factionalism and aristocratic influence over parliament intensified, Burgh increasingly emphasized popular action in the form of "associating, petitioning, or instructing,"[4] as the most viable mode for securing reform and regeneration. Although he occasionally alluded to the possibility of more violent means, Burgh was not a revolutionary. Assuredly the fact that he had benefited from the very real opportunity for prosperity and social mobility to be found in England served as a moderating influence in his life. In addition, his Calvinistic background with its patriarchal overtones and emphasis on social stability encouraged his deference to authority, respect for social order, and healthy horror of mob violence. The latter sentiment was undoubtedly reinforced by the fearful example of revolution and civil war in the seventeenth century and the Jacobite uprisings of his own age. Finally, Burgh aspired not to destroy the existing order and create anew.

Instead, he advocated radical reforms to achieve a conservative goal--
the restoration of the ancient constitution. The paradox of his posture
was typical of late eighteenth century English radicalism and contributed to its nonrevolutionary character.

A lifelong enthusiast of association as an instrument of change,
Burgh advocated the formation of associations to secure parliamentary
reform as early as 1767. He reiterated this appeal in the "Constitutionalist" letters, published in 1769-1770. Convinced by the Middlesex
election controversy that the constitution had been subverted and that
the liberties of the people and survival of the empire were endangered,
he repeatedly urged his extensive newspaper audience to support fundamental parliamentary reform. Simultaneously he vigorously agitated for
the repeal of the Townshend Revenue duties. Colin Bonwick to the contrary, Burgh was keenly aware of the interdependence of Anglo-American
grievances and as "Constitutionalist" and "The Colonist's Advocate" he
forcefully underscored the long-range peril goverment's policies in
America posed to liberty in the mother country.

That Burgh was specifically encouraged to undertake both newspaper
series as part of organized political campaigns by London radicals and
colonial patriots is an intriguing possibility. Burgh's friendship with
Catharine Macaulay was sufficiently close to encourage rumors that she
inherited his unpublished manuscripts. And Mrs. Macaulay's brother, Alderman Sawbridge, was a key figure in the effort to expand the petitions
of 1769-1770 into an appeal for fundamental parliamentary reform. Moreover, Burgh's longstanding friendship with Benjamin Franklin, the prime
lobbyist for repeal of the Townshend duties, naturally suggests that
Franklin encouraged Burgh to become "The Colonist's Advocate." Whatever
the truth of such conjectures, it is clear that within reform circles
Burgh early established a reputation as a radical spokesman and that he
was much more involved in radical agitation than has generally been appreciated. His reputation as a radical should not solely rest on the
Political Disquisitions.

The Disquisitions, of course, was the capstone of Burgh's career.
The tome quickly secured the status in England and in America of a monu-
mental reference work with the authority of a political classic. An impressive number of America's founding fathers and virtually all the key
figures in the English reform movement were indebted to the work.

Burgh's heavily documented picture of British corruption confirmed
the colonial conception of a degenerate mother country dominated by avaricious aristocrats whose quest for power and enrichment threatened the
liberties of Englishmen on both sides of the Atlantic. In the after-
math of revolution, Burgh's opinions on such subjects as political parties, standing armies, and the nature of power continued to influence
Americans from the backwoods of Kentucky to the towns of New England.
The scope of the Disquisitions enabled both Federalists and Antifederalists to cull arguments from the book in support of their conflicting
positions on the constitutional structures of the new nation. The peace
of 1783 did not sever the intellectual bonds between American patriots
and English radicals.

Burgh's fellow reformers in England drew on his statistics and documentation to substantiate the case for annual parliaments, a more equal parliamentary representation based on franchise reform, the secret ballot, and the elimination of placemen and pensioners. In particular they were influenced by Burgh's proposal for the formation of a GRAND ASSOCIATION. Although essentially a propagandist for ideas long familiar in Commonwealthman circles, Burgh enjoys special distinction as one of the most important progenitors of the political association movement of the late eighteenth and nineteenth centures.

For most of his contemporaries, however, James Burgh was the proverbial prophet crying in the wilderness. They were not yet ready to attend his message. Repeated frustration and disappointment led Burgh in his discouragement to remark exaggeratedly that "mankind are a worthless and ungrateful set of beings, for a man to wear himself out in serving." His persistent efforts in their behalf belied this severe judgment. Despite the seeming futility of his endeavors he continued to "honour virtue and truth, . . . to detest and disgrace corruption and villainy . . . to raise the standard of liberty higher, and to unfurl it wider than . . . [had] been attempted by any private person before." A man of his moral convictions could do no less. Failure was made bearable by his philosophical observation: "I am myself a worthless being, compared with my own ideas of worth, and with those in scripture; and if I do not lay myself out in the service of mankind, whom shall I serve? My insignificant self? That would be sordid indeed."[5]

Lacking the vantage point of the twentieth century historian, James Burgh died without the consolation of knowing that his largely selfless efforts to improve his age were fruitful. Together with a host of contemporaries who labored on behalf of diverse causes ranging from the reclamation of prostitutes, the alleviation of poverty, and the upgrading of female education, to the redistribution of parliamentary seats and a more equitable franchise, James Burgh laid the necessary groundwork for the nineteenth century "age of reform."

NOTES

INTRODUCTION: The Much Neglected Mr. Burgh

[1]Basil Williams, The Whig Supremacy, 1714-1760, XI (2nd rev. ed. by
C.H. Stuart; Oxford History of England Series; Oxford: Clarendon Press,
1962), p. 1.

[2]The foregoing survey of the Commonwealthmen is drawn from Caroline
Robbins, The Eighteenth-Century Commonwealthman; Studies in the Transmission, Development and Circumstance of English Liberal Thought from
the Restoration of Charles II until the War with the Thirteen Colonies
(New York: Atheneum, 1968; first published Cambridge: Harvard University Press, 1959).

[3]In addition to Robbins' book see also Colin Bonwick, English Radicals and the American Revolution (Chapel Hill: The University of North
Carolina Press, 1977).

[4][James Burgh], Crito, or Essays on Various Subjects, II (London:
Printed for Messrs. Dodsley in Pal-Mall; Becket and DeHandt in the
Strand; White in Fleet-Street; Payne, in Paternoster Row; and Cooke,
near the Royal Exchange, 1767), 1. Hereafter an author's name which
does not appear on the title page of a book will only appear in brackets
in the first citation of that book.

[5]Robbins, Eighteenth-Century Commonwealthman, p. 365; Eugene Black,
The Association: British Extraparliamentary Political Organization, 1769-
1793 (Cambridge: Harvard University Press, 1963), p. 29n. See also
Douglas Adair, "The Authorship of the Disputed Federalist Papers," Wil-
liam and Mary Quarterly, I (July, 1944), 261; Felix Gilbert, To the
Farewell Address: Ideas of Early American Foreign Policy (Princeton:
Princeton University Press, 1961), p. 36; Randolph G. Adams, Political
Ideas of the American Revolution,(3rd ed.; New York: Barnes and Noble,
1958), p. 184; Herbert Butterfield, George III, Lord North, and the People, 1779-1780 (London: G. Bell and Sons, LTD, 1949), p. 259ff; Alpheus
Thomas Mason, The States Rights Debate: Antifederalism and the Constitution (Englewood Cliffs, New Jersey: Prentice-Hall, Inc., 1964), p. 8;
Bernard Bailyn, The Ideological Origins of the American Revolution (Cambridge: The Belknap Press of Harvard University, 1967), p. 41; H. Trevor
Colbourn, "John Dickinson, Historical Revolutionary," Pennsylvania Magazine of History and Biography, LXXXIII (July, 1959), 283-286; John

Brewer, <u>Party Ideology and Popular Politics at the Accession of</u>
<u>George III</u> (Cambridge: Cambridge University Press, 1976), p. 214; and
Bonwick, <u>English Radicals</u>, pp. 8, 75.

[6]The fullest published treatments of Burgh heretofore available
are: Andrew Kippis, <u>Biographica Britannica or the Lives of the Most Em-</u>
<u>inent Persons who have flourished in Great Britain and Ireland, From the</u>
<u>Earliest Ages to the Present Times: Collected from the Best Authorities,</u>
<u>Printed and Manuscript, and Digested in the Manner of Mr. Bayle's His-</u>
<u>torical and Critical Dictionary</u>, III (London: John Rivington, 1784),13-
16; John Nichols, <u>Literary Anecdotes of the Eighteenth Century</u>, com-
<u>prising Biographical Memoirs of William Bowyer, Printer and many of his</u>
<u>learned friends; An Incidental View of the Progress and Advancement of</u>
<u>Literature in This Kingdom During the Last Century; and Biographical An-</u>
<u>ecdotes of a Considerable Number of Eminent Writers and Ingenious Art-</u>
<u>ists; with a very Copious Index</u>, II (London: printed for Nichols, Son,
and Bently, at Cicero's <u>Head</u>, Red-Lion-Passage, Fleet-Street, 1812) 263-
267; Robbins, <u>Eighteenth-Century Commonwealthman</u>, pp. 363-368; Ian
Christie, <u>Wilkes, Wyvill, and Reform: The Parliamentary Reform Movement</u>
<u>in British Politics, 1760-1785</u> (London: Macmillan & Co., 1962), pp. 53-
57; Oscar and Mary Handlin, "James Burgh and American Revolutionary Theory," <u>Proceedings of the Massachusetts Historical Society</u>, LXXIII (January-December, 1961), 38-57; and Carla H. Hay, "Benjamin Franklin, James
Burgh and 'The Colonist's Advocate' Letters," <u>William and Mary Quarter-</u>
<u>ly</u>, XXXII (January, 1975), 111-124.

[7]J[ames] B[urgh], <u>The Dignity of Human Nature or, A brief Account</u>
<u>of the certain and established Means for attaining the True End of our</u>
<u>Existence in Four Books I. Of Prudence. II. Of Knowledge. III. Of</u>
<u>Virtue. IV. Of Revealed Religion</u>, I (a new ed.; London: Printed for J.
Johnson and J. Payne, in <u>Pater-noster-row</u>; and T. Cadell, in <u>The Strand</u>,
1767; first published London: Printed for J. and P. Knaston, in Ludgate
Street; J. Whiston and B. White, in Fleet-Street; A. Millar in the
Strand; R. and J. Dodsley, in Pall-Mall; and J. Ward in Cornhill, 1754),
94. All citations are from the 1767 London edition.

[8]Lawrence Stone, <u>The Family, Sex and Marriage in England, 1500-1800</u>
(New York: Harper & Row, 1977).

CHAPTER ONE: A Moralist in Babylon

[1]Andrew Burgh spelled his name "Brugh." A.J. Tait, City Librarian,
Sandeman Public Library, Perth, Scotland to C.H. Hay (August 10, 1965).
When or why James Burgh altered his spelling of the family name is not
known. For convenience' sake his spelling will be used for all members
of the family.

[2]According to the _Fasti_ of the Church of Scotland, Andrew Burgh received his M.A. from St. Andrews University July 23, 1697 and was ordained a Minister January 8, 1701. G.R. Barbour (for the Curator of Historical Records, Scottish Record Office) to C.H. Hay (August 5,1965).

[3]Andrew Kippis, _Biographica Britannica_, III, 14. The extent of Burgh's contact with his illustrious cousin is a matter of speculation. In 1758 William Robertson came to London in conjunction with the publication of his history of Scotland. He was widely feted. That the two cousins visited together on that occasion seems probable, but is not documented. Although Robertson's friend, Alexander Carlyle, has left a rather detailed account of this episode, no mention is made of Burgh. _Autobiography of the Rev. Dr. Alexander Carlyle, Minister of Inveresk Containing Memorials Of The Men And Events Of His Time_ (Edinburgh and London: William Blackwood and Sons, 1860). Only once did Burgh himself refer to Robertson, his "much esteemed friend and relation," although he cited Robertson's books occasionally. [James Burgh], _Political Disquisitions: or, An Enquiry into Public Errors, Defects, and Abuses. Illustrated by, and established upon Facts and Remarks extracted from a Variety of Authors, ancient and modern. Calculated to draw the timely Attention of Government and People to a due Consideration of the Necessity, and the Means, of Reforming those Errors, Defects, and Abuses; of Restoring the Constitution, and Saving the State_ (3 vols.; London: Printed for E. and C. Dilly in the Poultry, 1774-1775), III, 15, 124; II, 300, 367, 369.

[4][James Burgh], _Crito, or Essays on Various Subjects_, I (London: Printed for J. Dodsley in Pall Mall, 1766), 139-140. Burgh's reference to himself as a "gentleman" is not to be brushed aside as a meaningless appelation. Dorothy Marshall has observed: "Nor was the designation 'gentleman' one of empty form accorded to any male as a common courtesy by an equalitarian age. On many an eighteenth-century tomb the word 'gentleman' was inscribed to denote the place which the deceased had filled in the world he had now left." _English People in the Eighteenth Century_ (London: Longmans, Green and Co., 1956), p. 51. In his will James Burgh again described himself as a "Gentleman." Burgh, _Will_, 1775; Alexander 334; Somerset House Records, Principal Probate Registry (London, England). The author wishes to thank Professor Carl Cone for initially referring her to this document.

[5]The Burgh union was terminated July 14, 1736 by Andrew's death at approximately fifty-nine years of age. Margaret Burgh survived her husband until July 15, 1771. G.R. Barbour to C.H. Hay (August 5, 1965).

[6]John Burgh matriculated as a second year student in Session 1720-1721; he received his B.A. degree in 1721. R.G. Cant, Keeper of the Muniments, St. Andrews University, St. Andrews, Scotland to C.H. Hay (May 9, 1966). He attempted to serve as minister at Foulis Wester in 1730. Unlike his father, however, he failed to secure the approval of the congregation before accepting the presentation. He was called before the synod of Perth and Stirling April 15, 1731 where he declared his sorrow for his "'foolish, rash and inconsiderat [sic] step'" which he blamed on "'infirmity, precipitancy and the several encouragements

. . . [he] then had to accept.'" This caused him to neglect obtaining
certain knowledge of the congregation's sentiments on his appointment.
On October 13, 1731, he was censured by the synod and his presentation
voided. Apparently he never secured another presentation as there is
no further reference to him in the Fasti. Minutes of the synod of Perth
and Stirling (CH2/449/8), pp. 80-5, 95-101 as noted in Barbara L.H.
Horn, Assistant Keeper, Scottish Record Office, to C.H. Hay (July 12,
1971). Andrew Kippis notes Burgh's residence at St. Andrews. His source
for the information was a letter from Burgh's sister to his wife. Biographia Britannica, III, 14. St. Andrews University, however, has no
record of Burgh's enrollment. The Keeper of the Muniments at St. Andrews acknowledges, on the other hand, that Burgh could have been a student at the University without having formally registered. R.G. Cant to
C.H. Hay (May 6, 1966).

[7]Kippis, Biographia Britannica, III, 14.

[8]James Burgh has been erroneously designated by several historians
as the recipient of an honorary degree from Oxford University in
recognition of his supposed answer to the Rev. Mr. Lindsey's Apology for
resigning the vicarage of Catterick. See Thomas Cromwell, Walks Through
Islington (London: Printed for Sherwood, Gilbert, and Piper, Paternoster Row, 1835), p. 55; John Nelson, The History and Antiquities of the
parish of ISLINGTON, in the county of Middlesex; including Biographical
Sketches of the Most Eminent and Remarkable Inhabitants with Some Account of Several Objects of Interest in the Adjoining Parishes (2nd ed.;
London: Printed for and sold by the Author, Middle Row Place, Holborn;
K.J. Ford, Bookseller, 117 Upper Street, Islington; Rodwell and Martin,
New Bond-Street; and John Major, Fleet Street, 1823), p. 49; William Robinson, The History and Antiquities of the Parish of Stoke Newington in
the County of Middlesex (London: John Bowyer Nichols and Son, 25 Parliament Street, 1842), p. 90n. Oxford University, however, has no record
of such a degree having been conferred on Burgh. R.E. Clifford (of Oxford University Registry) to C.H. Hay (August 9, 1965). The actual recipient of the degree was William Burgh (1741-1808), an Irish politician involved in the Yorkshire movement, who received a DCL from Oxford
on April 9, 1788 for his 1774 publication "A Scriptural Confutation of
the Arguments against the one Godhead of the Father, Son, and Holy
Ghost produced by the Rev. Mr. Lindsey." Sir Leslie Stephen, ed., Dictionary of National Biography, III (London: Oxford University Press,
1885-1890; reprinted 1921-1922), 331-332.

[9]Kippis, Biographia Britannica, III, 14.

[10][James Burgh], Youth's Friendly Monitor: Being a Set of DIREC-
TIONS, PRUDENTIAL, MORAL, RELIGIOUS, and SCIENTIFIC. First drawn up for
a Farewel [sic] Present, by the Master of an Academy near London, to his
Pupils on their removing from under his Care. To which is prefixed, An
Account of the extraordinary Proceedings of some Persons, which occa-
sioned the Publication of this Tract, contrary to the Author's original
Intention. Together with THEOPHILUS, A CHARACTER worthy of Imitation
(London: Printed for M. Cooper at the Globe in Paternoster-row, 1754);
Youth's Friendly Monitor, p. 5. These two pieces were published together

but each has its own pagination. Accordingly, they will henceforth be cited separately.

[11]The exact date of Burgh's arrival in London is unknown. As his brother John was still alive in 1731, it had to be later than this. Burgh had been in England at least a year, and probably longer than that, before writing Britain's Remembrancer in 1745. Most likely he came to London in the early 1740s when he was around twenty-five years old.

[12]Frederick A. Pottle, ed., Boswell's London Journal 1762-1763 (New York: McGraw-Hill Book Co., 1950), p. 294.

[13]Liberals as well as "King's Friends" were vulnerable to anti-Scot sentiment. The editor of a London newspaper felt constrained to assure his readers that the republican historian Catharine Macaulay who had lately been "censured as a North Briton" was in fact an Englishwoman. Gazetteer and New Daily Advertiser, February 22, 1769. Henceforth this publication will be cited as the Gazetteer.

[14]Burgh, Political Disquisitions, I, 215.

[15]Ibid., III, 336-377; [James Burgh], "Constitutionalist," Gazetteer, V, September 1, 1769; [XV], December 27, 1769.

[16]Anthony Lincoln has analysed this subject in his Some Political and Social Ideas of English Dissent, 1763-1800 (Cambridge: University Press, 1938).

[17]Pottle, Boswell's London Journal, pp. 43-45.

[18][James Burgh], PROPOSALS (Humbly offered to the PUBLIC) For an ASSOCIATION Against The Iniquitous Practices Of ENGROSSERS, FORESTAL-LERS, JOBBERS, etc. And For Reducing The PRICE OF PROVISIONS, Especially BUTCHERS MEAT (London: Printed for J. Payne, at the Feathers, Pater-noster-Row; and Richardson and Urquhart, under the Royal Exchange, 1766) pp. 12-14.

[19][James Burgh], Britain's Remembrancer: Being Some thoughts on the proper improvement of the present juncture. The character of this age and nation. A brief view, from history, of the effects of the vices which now prevail in Britain; upon the greatest empires and states of former times, etc. (7th ed.; Boston: Printed by Benjamin Mecom at the New Printing Office in Boston, 1759; first published London: Printed for M. Cooper, at the Globe in Pater-noster Row; and Sold at the Pamphlet-Shops in London and Westminster, 1746), pp. 43-44. All citations are from the Mecom edition. American editions of Britain's Remembrancer o-mitted the phrase "the Danger not over" from the title.

[20]Nichols, Literary Anecdotes, II, 263. Other than Onslow, Nichols does not identify these friends; nor does he specify the nature of On-slow's assistance to Burgh.

[21]Kippis, Biographia Britannica, III, 14.

[22]Ibid. Kippis's information was based on the recollections of Burgh's widow. See also, Burgh, Youth's Friendly Monitor, p. iii.

[23]The fifty page pamphlet sold for 6d and was first advertised in The Daily Advertiser (London) January 31, 1746.

[24]Burgh, Britain's Remembrancer, pp. 6-7, 32-38, 41.

[25]Burgh, Youth's Friendly Monitor, p. iv; British Museum General Catalogue of Printed Books, XXX (London: Published by the Trustees of the British Museum, 1965), column 76; Roger Pattrell Bristol, The American Bibliography of Charles Evans, XIV (Worcester, Mass.: American Antiquarian Society, 1959), p. 59; Nichols, Literary Anecdotes, II, 263; Kippis, Biographia Britannica, III, 14. John Brewer notes that sales of 5000 copies constituted "spectacular success" for eighteenth century pamphlets. Party Ideology and Popular Politics, p. 146.

[26]Burgh,"Constitutionalist," IX, Gazetteer, October 21, 1769; Youth's Friendly Monitor, p. xii.

[27]Burgh, Crito, II, 211; Political Disquisitions, III, 417; Dignity of Human Nature, II, 198.

[28]The Monthly Review; or Literary Journal, XXXIV (April, 1766), 303; XXXVII (July, 1767), 15-16; LI (November, 1774), 348; Kippis, Biographia Britannica, III, 16.

[29]Burgh, "Constitutionalist," IX, Gazetteer, October 21, 1769; Crito, II, 12.

[30]Burgh, Political Disquisitions, II, vi-vii; Dignity of Human Nature, I, 246; II, 269.

[31]Bailyn, Ideological Origins, p. 23. In his "A Reply to the Essay on Population By the Rev. T. R. Malthus In a Series of Letters. To which are Added, Extracts from the Essay, with Notes," William Hazlitt noted the value of a heavily documented work such as Burgh's Political Disquisitions: "But without much learning in one's self, it is easy to take advantage of the learning of others. By the help of a common-place book which is all that is wanted in these cases (and I am fortunate enough to have such a one by me in the collections of 'that honest chronicler,' James Burgh) I might soon swell the size of these letters to a bulk, which the bookseller would not like." P.P. Howe, ed., The Complete Works of William Hazlitt, I (London: J.M. Dent & Sons, LTD, [1930]), 265.

[32]Kippis, Biographia Britannica, III, 14.

[33]Frank Brady, Frederick Pottle, eds., Boswell in Search of a Wife, 1766-1769 (New York: McGraw-Hill Co., 1956), p. 161; Burgh, Dignity of Human Nature, I, 4, 200; Verner Crane, "The Club of Honest Whigs: Friends of Science and Liberty," William and Mary Quarterly, XXIII (April, 1966), 219-220; Burgh, Theophilus, p. 13; George W. Corner, ed.,

The Autobiography of Benjamin Rush; His "Travels Through Life" together with his Commonplace Book for 1789-1813 (Princeton: Published for The American Philosophical Society by Princeton University Press, 1948), pp. 60-61; Geoffrey Scott, Frederick Pottle, eds., Private Papers of James Boswell from Malahide Castle; In the Collection of Lt.-Colonel Ralph Heyward Isham, VII (New York: privately printed, 1930), 193-194; Kippis, Biographia Britannica, III, 15; Nichols, Literary Anecdotes, II, 266-267.

[34] Published in 1747 shortly after Burgh moved to Stoke Newington, the English edition sold for 1s. The Daily Advertiser, July 9, 1747. All citations are from the American edition by Rogers and Fowle (Boston: 1749).

[35] Kippis, Biographia Britannica, III, 14, 15.

[36] Samuel Lewis, The History and Topography of the Parish of Saint Mary, Islington in the County of Middlesex (London: Printed for the Author by Gilbert and Rivington; Published by J.H. Jackson, 1842), p. 311n; Robinson, History of . . . Stoke Newington, p. 12; map of Carew Mildmay estate, British Museum 3465 (27), referred to the author by Professor Carl Cone.

[37] Lewis, History . . . of the Parish of Saint Mary, p. 314; Peter William Clayden, Samuel Sharpe, Egyptologist and Translator of the Bible (London: Kegan Paul, Trench and Co.; Paternoster Square, 1883), p. 15.

[38] Carl B. Cone, Torchbearer of Freedom: The Influence of Richard Price on Eighteenth Century Thought (Lexington: University of Kentucky Press, 1952), p. 28.

[39] Peter William Clayden, The Early Life of Samuel Rogers (Boston: Roberts Brothers, 1888), p. 4.

[40] Stone, The Family, Sex and Marriage, pp. 325ff.

[41] Burgh, Britain's Remembrancer, pp. 48-50.

[42] Page Smith, Daughters of the Promised Land: Women in American History (Boston: Little, Brown, 1970), pp. 35ff.

[43] Burgh, Dignity of Human Nature, I, 99; Crito, I, 43. Hannah Burgh was a niece of Mrs. Sarah Seabrooke who, in turn, was the sister-in-law of George Streatfield, a wealthy Dissenter. Upon his death in 1756, Mr. Streatfield willed Hannah Burgh £400, a rather sizable sum. Mrs. Seabrooke died in 1770, naming Hannah Burgh her executrix and heir to the residue of her not inconsiderable estate. George Streatfield, Will, 1757; Herring 32, Somerset House Records, Principal Probate Registry (London, England). Sarah Seabrooke, Will, 1770; Jenner 278, Somerset House Records, Principal Probate Registry (London, England). Professor Carl Cone generously supplied the author with these statistics.

[44] Burgh, Youth's Friendly Monitor, p. 11; Kippis, Biographia

Britannica, III, 14; obituary notice in the <u>Gentleman's Magazine</u>, LVIII (December, 1788), 1131. Mary Wollstonecraft met Hannah Burgh in 1783. The older woman encouraged Mary to open a school at Newington Green and secured some twenty pupils for it in three weeks time. On several occasions she came to Mary's financial assistance. According to William Godwin, Mary never forgot Hannah Burgh's services and always paid tribute to her virtues. Eleanor Flexner, <u>Mary Wollstonecraft</u> (New York: Penguin Books, 1972), pp. 46-48; William Godwin, <u>Memoirs of Mary Wollstonecraft</u> (New York: Haskell House Publishers LTD, 1969) pp. 28-29.

[45] Burgh, <u>Dignity of Human Nature,</u> I, 102-103, 105-106, 97.

[46] Burgh averaged eight to ten hours per day meeting his academic responsibilities. <u>Ibid</u>., II, 484.

[47] Burgh's school is consistently described as an academy. Technically, an academy was designed to serve as the nonconformist counterpart of Oxford and Cambridge. The average student would thus be about twelve to eighteen. Apparently, however, Burgh's academy admitted younger children. The Rogers boys, who were under the usual age for admission to academies, attended Burgh's school and were privately tutored by him after his retirement to Islington. Clayden, <u>Samuel Rogers</u>, pp. 9-10, 16. Moreover, Burgh has much to say about the education of young children. Officially, nonconformists were prohibited from conducting schools for young children. H.C. Barnard, <u>A History of English Education from 1760</u> (2nd ed.; London: University of London Press, 1961), p. 28.

[48] Herbert McLachlan, <u>English Education under the Test Acts; Being the History of the Nonconformist Academies</u> (Manchester: Manchester University Press, 1931), p. 76.

[49] Burgh, <u>Dignity of Human Nature</u>, I, 217.

[50] Burgh, <u>Youth's Friendly Monitor</u>, pp. 52-53.

[51] Burgh, <u>Dignity of Human Nature</u>, II, 160.

[52] As a copyhold tenant of Carew Mildmay, Esquire, Burgh paid the third highest rent in Newington Green--twenty-six pounds per year. The annual land tax assessment on Burgh's home based on its rental value was 31.6d. Land Tax Assessment Books, Middlesex Record Office, Box 2015-2025, p. 15. Moreover, on behalf of himself and his "young gentlemen" (his pupils), Burgh contributed a substantial sum to the Newington Green chapel each year. On June 30, 1755, he contributed two guineas for himself and four pounds, one shilling on behalf of the young gentlemen. The amount of the contribution remained relatively constant until about 1760 when it began to increase, apparently reflecting an increased enrollment in his school. By 1763 Burgh was contributing ten guineas annually to the Chapel for himself and his charges. Newington Green Meeting Account Books; property of the Newington Green Chapel; Books I-II. The author wishes to thank Professor Carl Cone for providing her with this information. At the time of his retirement, Burgh had a

"competent, though not a large fortune." Andrew Kippis attributed its moderate nature to the fact that Burgh's "mind was always far raised above pecuniary views." Biographia Britannica, III, 15. Burgh's financial success as a schoolmaster was unusual. As he himself noted, educators were generally underpaid. Dignity of Human Nature, I, 221-222; Crito, I, 150.

[53] This routine was pursued by Theophilus, Burgh's fictional model of moral conduct and was certainly autobiographical.

[54] Newington Green Meeting Account Books, Book II.

[55] Clayden, Samuel Rogers, p. 15.

[56] Burgh, Dignity of Human Nature, I, 173.

[57] Burgh, Political Disquisitions, I, 103, 117; II, 90; III, 85.

[58] Ibid., II, 341.

[59] One of the youthful recipients of the original essay was a native of Amsterdam who may have had the work printed in Dutch. Burgh, Youth's Friendly Monitor, pp. iv, v, 2. Harvard Library has a copy of the private printing which was entitled Directions, prudential, moral, religious and scientific, for the use of the youth at a Boarding-school near London. Being the Master's Farewel [sic] Present to his Pupils, on their removing from under his care. National Union Catalogue, Library of Congress.

[60] Leonard Labaree, ed., The Papers of Benjamin Franklin, IV (New Haven, Conn.: Yale University Press, 1961), 404n. The Hymn had two London editions and raised "a very pretty sum" for its orphaned beneficiary. Burgh, Youth's Friendly Monitor, p. xii.

[61] Kippis, Biographia Britannica, III, 14. There are no extant copies of this pamphlet which sold for 1d or 6d a dozen "to such publick spirited People as will give them away." The Daily Advertiser, April 22, 1751.

[62] Burgh, Youth's Friendly Monitor, p. v; Dignity of Human Nature, I, iii.

[63] Burgh, Youth's Friendly Monitor, p. v.

[64] Burgh, Dignity of Human Nature, I, iii-iv.

[65] Burgh, Crito, II, 19.

[66] The noble lord was probably Lord Waldegrave, who succeeded Thomas Hayter as preceptor to the princes in 1752, or possibly Lord Bute.

[67] Burgh, Crito, II, 208-209.

[68]"The Free Enquirer" appeared in *The General Evening Post* from about late May, 1753 until possibly June of 1755. Precision on this point is impossible since most issues of this newspaper for these years are no longer extant. At least 76 essays out of a projected 104 were published. See the papers for October 29-31 and November 19-21, 1754. Andrew Kippis noted Burgh's association with the series. *Biographia Britannica*, III, 15.

[69]Burgh, *Crito*, II, 212.

[70]"The Free Enquirer," LXXIV, *General Evening Post*, October 29-31, 1754.

[71]Burgh, *Crito*, II, 212-213; see also *Dignity of Human Nature*, I, 168-169; *Theophilus*, pp. 11-12.

[72]*The Monthly Review*, VII, (October, 1752), 317-318.

[73]Burgh retitled the work *Youth's Friendly Monitor: Being a Set of DIRECTIONS, PRUDENTIAL, MORAL, RELIGIOUS, and SCIENTIFIC . . .* See pp. ix-x and *The Whitehall Evening-Post; or, London Intelligencer*, August 29-31, 1754. Apparently the two booksellers in question were J. Hodges and R. Baldwin who published an edition of *Youth's Friendly Monitor* in 1754. *National Union Catalogue*, Library of Congress. An American edition, based on one of the pirated versions, was published by Nathaniel Patten at Hartford, Conn. in 1787.

[74]Burgh, *Youth's Friendly Monitor*, p. v; *Dignity of Human Nature*, I, iv, 1; II, 485.

[75]*The Daily Advertiser*, January 4, 1754, March 25, 1754, April 18, 1754; *The Whitehall Evening-Post*, March 30-April 2, 1754. Published in one volume, the first edition was printed for J. and P. Knaston, J. Whiston and B. White, A. Millar, R. and J. Dodsley, and J. Ward.

[76]Two new editions were subsequently published in London: J. Johnson and J. Payne brought out a two-volume edition in 1767 and Charles Dilly brought out an edition in 1794. *British Museum Catalogue*, XXX, column 76. The work was early made accessible to colonials. Harvard Library had acquired a copy by 1773 and the Library Company of Philadelphia owned it by 1770. H. Trevor Colbourn, *The Lamp of Experience: Whig History and the Intellectual Origins of the American Revolution* (Chapel Hill: University of North Carolina Press, 1965), pp. 200, 207. There were eventually at least five complete American editions. *National Union Catalogue*, Library of Congress. Moreover, parts of the treatise were incorporated into an 1846 volume published at Philadelphia under the title of *Rules for the Conduct of Life. By James Burgh. To which is added, the proper method of preserving health. By Lewis Cornaro. With an introduction by J.P. Durbin, D.D.* A second edition of this tome appeared in 1851. *National Union Catalogue*, Library of Congress. There was even a German translation of the *Dignity of Human Nature* in 1778: *Der Werth des Menschen, aus dem Englischen ubersetzt-Braunschweig, in der furste.* (Waisenhaus-Buchhandlung, 1778), 2 vols.

<u>Catalogue General Des Livres Imprimes De La Bibliotheque Nationale</u>, XXI
(Paris: Imprimerie Nationale, 1905), column 643.

[77]<u>The Monthly Review</u>, XI (August, 1754), 81, 86. Kippis, <u>Biograph-
ia Britannica</u>, III, 16. In his biography of Samuel Rogers, Peter Clayden remarked that Burgh "wrote a work entitled 'Political Disquisitions,'
but was best known as the author of a book 'On the Dignity of Human Nature,'" p. 7. Burgh's obituary notice in the <u>Gazetteer</u> also cited the
<u>Dignity of Human Nature</u>, together with the <u>Political Disquisitions</u>, as
Burgh's most notable publications. August 28, 1775.

[78]As late as 1832 a London bookseller could thus advertise the
work. <u>Richard Baynes's select general Catalogue of Books, Old and New
. . .</u> (London: Richard Baynes, 1832).

[79]Burgh, <u>Dignity of Human Nature</u>, I, 174; II, 485; see also, Burgh,
<u>Youth's Friendly Monitor</u>, p. v.

[80]John Nichols, not always a completely reliable source, asserted
Burgh wrote two pamphlets in 1758: <u>Political Speculations</u>, supposedly
published in that year, and <u>The Rationale of Christianity</u>, published in
1760. <u>Literary Anecdotes</u>, II, 265. No copies of pamphlets with these
titles and publication dates are known to exist. Neither <u>The Daily Ad-
vertiser</u>, <u>The London Chronicle</u>, nor <u>The Monthly Review</u> carried notices
of their publication.

CHAPTER TWO: The Moralist Politicized

[1]Brewer, <u>Party Ideology and Popular Politics</u>, p. 23; <u>The Public
Advertiser</u> (London), October 29, November 1, 1760.

[2]Colin Bonwick's recent study, <u>English Radicals and the American
Revolution</u>, makes no mention of this dimension of politics in the 1760s.
John Brewer makes only a passing reference to it. <u>Party Ideology and
Popular Politics</u>, p. 23.

[3]Burgh, <u>Dignity of Human Nature</u>, I, vii-viii; Burgh, "Remarks Historical and Political Collected from Books and Observation. Humbly presented to the King's most excellent Majesty." (1762). British Museum
King's MS433, pp. 6-7.

[4]Burgh, <u>Political Disquisitions</u>, III, 386, 416.

[5]Reconstructing the club's membership and activities is difficult
as club records are incomplete and unexact. Verner Crane concludes that
there were twenty to twenty-five members. "The Club of Honest Whigs,"
214, 218-219. See also Cone, <u>Torchbearer of Freedom</u>, p. 54 and Carl Van

Doren, _Benjamin Franklin_ (New York: The Viking Press, 1964; first published, 1938), p. 421.

[6]Scott and Pottle, _Private Papers of James Boswell_, VIII, 121.

[7]Oscar and Mary Handlin, "James Burgh and American Revolutionary Theory," 43.

[8]Quoted in Burgh, _Political Disquisitions_, I, xvi-xvii. Thomas Gordon was an English political writer of the early eighteenth century who is most famous for his collaboration with John Trenchard on the _Independent Whig_ and _Cato's Letters_.

[9]Burgh, _Youth's Friendly Monitor_, p. 15; _Dignity of Human Nature_, I, 18.

[10][James Burgh], _The Art of Speaking. Containing I. An Essay; in which are given rules for expressing properly the principal Passions and Humours, which occur in Reading, or public Speaking; and II. Lessons taken from the ancients and Moderns (with Additions and Alterations where thought useful) exhibiting a Variety of Matter for practice;--the emphatical words printed in Italics; with Notes of Direction referring to the Essay. To which are added; A Table of the Lessons; and an Index of the Various Passions and Humours in the Essay and Lessons_ (5th ed.; Newbury-Port, Mass.: Printed by John Mycall, for William Green, of Boston, 1782; first published London: Printed for T. Longman, J. Buckland, and W. Fenner, in Pater-noster Row; J. Waugh, in Lombard-street; E. Dilly in the Poultry; and T. Field in Cheapside, 1761), pp. 4, 42, 57-58. All citations are from the 1782 William Green edition.

[11]From the _Spectator_, no. 907; quoted in Warren Guthrie, "The Development of Rhetorical Theory in America 1635-1850-V. The Elocution Movement--England," _Speech Monographs_, XVIII (March, 1951), 19.

[12]Mary Margaret Robb, _Oral Interpretation of Literature in American Colleges and Universities; A Historical Study of Teaching Methods_ (New York: The H.W. Wilson Company, 1941), pp. 31, 70; Guthrie, "Development of Rhetorical Theory," 23, 25.

[13]Burgh, _The Art of Speaking_, p.6.

[14]_The Monthly Review_, XXVI (March, 1762), 199; _British Museum Catalogue_, XXX, column 76.

[15]Guthrie, "Development of Rhetorical Theory," 25; Bristol, _American Bibliography of Charles Evans_, XIV, 59; _National Union Catalogue_, Library of Congress. Harvard Library had acquired an autographed copy of the first London edition by 1767. And it was among the books read by the Harvard speaking club between 1770-1781. Guthrie, "Development of Rhetorical Theory," 25. From 1788 through 1800 it was one of the "most popular" books in the college and society libraries at Brown. _Ibid._, 21. Even on the fringes of American civilization, the work enjoyed a reputation. In a letter to the editor of _The Georgia State_

Gazette or Independent Register (Augusta), a correspondent signing himself "Juvenis" referred to Burgh as "a great master of eloquence" and quoted from *The Art of Speaking* to indicate the importance of oratory. April 25, 1787.

[16] *The Pennsylvania Packet or The General Advertiser* (Philadelphia), April 3, 1775.

[17] Frederick Haberman, "English Sources of American Elocution," chapter V, *History of Speech Education in America; Background Studies*, ed., Karl R. Wallace (New York: Appleton-Century-Crofts, Inc., 1954), p. 115. See Noah Webster, *An American Selection of Lessons in Reading and Speaking, calculated to improve the Minds and refine the Taste of Youth . . . To which is Prefixed, Rules in Elocution, and Directions for expressing the principal Passions of the Mind* (3rd ed.; Philadelphia: Young and Mc-Culloch, 1787), pp. 16-19. Webster's general directions for expressing certain Passions or Sentiments were taken from *The Art of Speaking*. Haberman's reference to the pirating of Burgh has been investigated by William Parrish. In 1783 a Philadelphia printer published a volume entitled *Rhetorical Grammar* which was attributed to Thomas Sheridan. Actually the book, published without Sheridan's authorization, was a combination of the preface to Sheridan's *General Dictionary* (London: 1780) and Burgh's introductory essay to *The Art of Speaking*. In an excellent piece of detective work, Parrish divulged "The Burglarizing of Burgh, or The Case of the Purloined Passions," *The Quarterly Journal of Speech*, XXXVIII (December, 1952), 431-434. Parrish speculated that the fact that Burgh's work was published anonymously made it vulnerable to such piracy. Though most editions of *The Art of Speaking* did fail to identify the author, the first edition attributed the work to the author of the *Dignity of Human Nature*. *The London Chronicle*, December 24-26, 1761, p. 621.

[18] Frederick Haberman, "The Elocutionary Movement in England, 1750-1850," unpublished Ph.D. thesis (Cornell, 1947), p. 111; quoted in Donald E. Hargis, "James Burgh and The Art of Speaking," *Speech Monographs*, XXIV (November, 1957), 275. Hargis's article provides a thorough analysis of *The Art of Speaking*.

[19] The handwriting deteriorates markedly after the first eighty pages; abbreviations, erasures, and crossed-out words become frequent.

[20] Burgh told only his wife about the manuscript which is dated August 13, 1762. "Remarks Historical and Political," pp. i-ii.

[21] *Ibid.*, pp. 2-5, 17-18, 52-53, 80, 132, 222.

[22] *Ibid.*, pp. 191, 96, 103-106.

[23] There is no marginalia to indicate that the manuscript was ever read nor is there any reference to it in the King's correspondence. Elizabeth Cuthbert, Assistant Registrar, Royal Archives, Windsor Castle to C.H. Hay (January 4, 1974).

[24][James Burgh], An Account of the First Settlement, Laws, Form of Government, and Police of the Cessares, A People of South America: in Nine Letters, from Mr. Vander Neck, one of the Senators of that Nation, to his Friend in Holland with notes by the editor (London: Printed for J. Payne, at the Feathers, Pater-noster-row, 1764), p.v.

[25]Ibid., p. 121.

[26]Jacob Viner, "Man's Economic Status," Chapter 2 in James L. Clifford, ed., Man Versus Society in 18th-Century Britain; Six Points of View (New York: W.W. Norton & Co., 1972), p. 48.

[27]The Monthly Review, XXXIV (April, 1766), 303-308; The London Chronicle, September 2-4, 1766, p. 231; "XYZ," ibid., October 21-23, 1766, p. 393.

[28]J.D. Chambers, G.E. Mingay, The Agricultural Revolution 1750-1880 (New York: Schocken Books, 1966), pp. 35, 39, 111; T.S. Ashton, Economic Fluctuations in England 1700-1800 (Oxford: Clarendon Press, 1959), p. 22.

[29]The London Chronicle received numerous letters of protest. See "Roni," September 9-11, 1766, p. 253; "P.S.," September 13-16, 1766, p. 269; "A Well-Wisher to the Aggrieved," September 16-18, 1766, p. 280; "A Little Farmer," September 16-18, 1766, p. 274; "Leicestershire," September 20-23, 1766, p. 289; "A Cornish Tinner," September 20-23, 1766, p. 293; "Britophilus," October 2-4, 1766, p. 329; "O. Jacques," ibid.; "Thoughts relative to exorbitant Price of Provisions," October 21-23, 1766, p. 396; and "T.J.," October 30-November 1, 1766, p. 425.

[30]Burgh, PROPOSALS . . . For An ASSOCIATION, pp. 2-7.

[31]Ibid., pp. 17-23.

[32]The Monthly Review, XXXV (August, 1766), 148.

[33]Burgh, Crito, II, 20, 8, 188.

[34]Gentleman's Magazine, XXXVII (May, 1767), 262; The Monthly Review, XXXVII (July, 1767), 9-16; The London Chronicle, May 14-16, 1767, p. 465; June 23-25, 1767, pp. 601-602; August 6-8, 1767, p. 129; "Forewarned is Forearmed," ibid., July 28-30, 1767, p. 103; [anonymous], ibid., August 22-25, 1767, p. 189; Political Register, I (1767), 484.

[35]See below, pp. 35-36.

[36]"Philopaulus," The London Chronicle, March 12-15, 1768, p. 244. Boswell identified Burgh as "Philopaulus." Frederick Pottle, James Boswell, The Earlier Years, 1740-1769 (New York: McGraw-Hill Book Co., 1966), p. 547.

[37]The meeting occurred about March 30, 1768. The two again dined together on May 14th in the company of William Rose, Benjamin Franklin, and Sir John Pringle. Brady and Pottle, Boswell in Search of a Wife,

p. 161; Scott and Pottle, Private Papers of James Boswell, VII, 193-194.

[38]Corner, Autobiography of Benjamin Rush, pp. 60-61. Mrs. Macaulay and Burgh were highly complimentary of each other's work. After Burgh's death it was alledged by one of the historian's critics that she had inherited Burgh's unpublished writings and was palming them off as her own. She indignantly denied the charge. See [Anonymous] in The St. James's Chronicle; or, British Evening-Post (London), August 25-27, 1778 and Catharine Macaulay to The Bath Chronicle, September 3, 1778.

[39]Bonwick, English Radicals and the American Revolution, p. 117.

[40]Burgh, Crito, I, 24-25.

[41]Quoted in Christie, Wilkes, Wyvill and Reform, p. 32.

[42]Burgh, Political Disquisitions, I, 206-207.

[43]See the Gazetteer for July 15, August 7, August 18, August 28, September 1, September 15, September 27, October 6, October 21, October 27, November 4, November 16, November 28, December 7, December 27, February 28, March 14, May 12, May 21, May 25, 1769-1770. Colin Bonwick claims that "alone among the Commonwealthmen [Joseph] Priestley expressed his views in a public pamphlet" on the Wilkes controversy. English Radicals and the American Revolution, p. 117. This statement requires clarification or qualification in light of Burgh's "Constitutionalist" letters.

[44]Burgh, "Constitutionalist," I, Gazetteer, July 15, 1769.

[45]"Constitutionalist" letters were reprinted in The London Chronicle, August 29-31, 1769, p. 212; March 13-15, 1770, p. 255; May 24-26, 1770, p. 500; The Middlesex Journal (London), August 8-10, 1769, September 16-19, 1769; and The Kentish Gazette (Canterbury), July 19-22, 1769. In "Constitutionalist," IX, October 21, 1769 and XII, November 16, 1769, Burgh expressed his appreciation to various correspondents with The Public Advertiser and The London Chronicle as well as the Gazetteer. In addition to Burgh's specific acknowledgements, the series prompted a number of sympathetic letters from correspondents to the Gazetteer, including "An Exclusioner," July 29, 1769; "Another Constitutionalist," September 7, 1769; "A Freeholder of Kent," and "W.B.," October 19, 1769; "Cambro-Britannus," October 26, 1769; "Amor Patriae Meae," October 28, 1769; "J.O.," November 2, 1769; "A Briton," and "L.R.B.," November 8, 1769; "A Freeholder," December 28, 1769, January 15, 1770; "Card," January 6, 1770; "Mat Meanwell," January 23, 1770; "DOUBLE-FEE," June 18, 1770; and a series of rebuttals from "Brecknock," September 18, September 28, October 5, October 10, October 26, November 2, November 22, December 26, January 2, January 5, January 17, 1769-1770.

[46]Burgh, "Constitutionalist," XI, Gazetteer, November 4, 1769.

[47]Burgh, Political Disquisitions, II, 90, 277.

[48]Andrew Kippis first identified James Burgh as "The Colonist's Advocate." Biographia Britannica, III, 15. In his 1950 edition of Benjamin Franklin's Letters to the Press, 1758-1775 (Chapel Hill: University of North Carolina Press), p. 167, Verner Crane attributed the letters to Benjamin Franklin. For a resolution of this controversy see Hay, "Franklin, Burgh, and 'The Colonist's Advocate' Letters," 111-124.

[49]Crane, Franklin's Letters to the Press, p. 285. The London Chronicle, Middlesex Journal, and Public Advertiser carried very little commentary on colonial matters in general during the months of January through March when the question of repealing the Townshend duties was being debated in parliament. Other than "The Colonist's Advocate" letters, the most extended comment on the issue of repeal was the letters of "Old Mentor," written in rebuttal to "The Colonist's Advocate." See the Public Advertiser, January 9, 11, 18, February 17, and 23, 1770. The London Chronicle published excerpts from "The Colonist's Advocate" January 30-February 1, 1770, p. 112 and February 20-22, 1770, p. 180.

[50]Burgh, "Constitutionalist," XVIII, Gazetteer, May 12, 1770.

[51]This announcement was contained in an advertisement which appeared in January of 1773 probably in the newspapers or as an appendix to some recent publication. John Nichols has preserved excerpts of the notice in Literary Anecdotes, II, 265-266.

[52]Burgh, Political Disquisitions, I, vii-ix.

[53]Charles Francis Adams, ed., The Works of John Adams with a Life of the Author, IX (Boston: Little Brown and Co., 1854), 351. Ian Christie, Wilkes, Wyvill and Reform, p. 53. The first two volumes were both published prior to the 1774 general election. See advertisements in The Daily Advertiser, February 1, 1774 and The London Chronicle, June 9-11, 1774, p. 559. Colin Bonwick mistakenly states that volume II appeared too late for this purpose. English Radicals and the American Revolution, p. 75.

[54]Burgh's academy was taken over by his assistant, Mr. Cockburn. After moving to Islington Burgh continued to contribute three guineas to the Green Chapel until his death. See Newington Green Meeting Account Books, III; Kippis, Biographia Britannica, III, 15; Clayden, Samuel Rogers, pp. 9-10, 16; "Journal of Josiah Quincy, Jun., During His Voyage and Residence in England from September 28th, 1774, to March 3d, 1775," Proceedings of the Massachusetts Historical Society, L (1916-1917), 467; The Works of Augustus Toplady, A.B. New Edition, With an Enlarged Memoir of the Author, VI (London: Printed for William Baynes and Son, Paternoster Row; and H.S. Baynes, Edinburgh, 1825), 220-221.

[55]The third volume of the Political Disquisitions, published in early February, 1775, contained the following notice: "When the Author wrote the General Preface to these Disquisitions, he proposed to lay before the Public more than three volumes of the materials he had collected. What these three volumes contain, is the most interesting to the

Public; and his health daily breaking, disqualifies him for proceeding farther at present."

[56] An advertisement in The London Chronicle, February 9-11, 1775, p. 140, quotes the price of Dilly's edition in England as 6s. per volume, 18s. for the set. An advertisement in the Pennsylvania Packet, June 12, 1775, lists this English edition at 42s. per set and the American edition at 30s. a set for subscribers and 36s. for non-subscribers.

[57] John Nichols, Illustrations of the Literary History of the Eighteenth Century Consisting of Authentic Memoirs and Original Letters of Eminent Persons; and intended as a sequel to The Literary Anecdotes, VI (London: Printed by and for J.B. Nichols and Son, 25 Parliament-Street, Westminster, 1831), 61. Josiah Quincy lent his copy to a Mr. Hollis. "Letters to Josiah Quincy, Jr.," Proceedings of the Massachusetts Historical Society, L (October, 1916-1917), 491.

[58] Lewis Patton and Peter Mann, eds., The Collected Works of Samuel Taylor Coleridge, I ("Bollinger Series"; London and Princeton: Routledge and Kegan Paul Ltd and Princeton University Press, 1971), xlvii. Harvard Library had two sets of the Disquisitions by 1790 and the Library Company of Philadelphia had a set by 1807. Colbourn, The Lamp of Experience, p. 201; Catalogue of Books belonging to the Library Company of Philadelphia (Philadelphia: n.p., 1807).

[59] "An Independent Whig," St. James's Chronicle, January 17-19, 1775; "Indignatus," London Evening-Post, July 21-23, 1778; Pennsylvania Packet, November 13, 1775; The Monthly Review, L (February, 1774), 109-122; LI (November, 1774), 344-355; LII (August, 1775), 109-115; The Critical Review, XXXVII (February, 1774), 89-93; XXXIX (January, 1775), 28-32; XXXIX (March, 1775), 178-181; The London Magazine, XLIII (April, 1774), 195; XLIII (July, 1774), 340-342; XLIV (March, 1775), 146-147; Gentleman's Magazine, XLIV (December, 1774), 585-586; and "C.," The Scots Magazine (Edinburgh), XXXVI (February, 1774), 90. John Brewer stresses the importance of review magazines like The Monthly Review (circulation 3,000) and Gentleman's Magazine (circulation 10,000) in extending a publication's audience far beyond those who purchased the work. Party Ideology and Popular Politics, p. 147.

[60] "H.S.B.M.," The Kentucky Gazette (Lexington), November 26, 1791.

[61] Baron Johan van der Capellen included an extract from the Disquisitions in his introduction to a Dutch translation of Richard Price's Additional Observations on the Nature of Civil Liberty and the War with America. Richard Price, Nader Aanmerkingen Over Den Aart en De Waorde Der Burgerlyke Vryheid en eener Vrye Regeering benevens, trans. by Johan Derk Baron van der Capellen (Lyden: L. Herdingh, 1777), pp. 30-48.

[62] "C.," The Scots Magazine, XXXVI (February, 1774), 90.

[63] Letter of James Boswell to the Rev. W.J. Temple, April 28, 1776, in response to a query of Temple's about the Disquisitions. Letters of James Boswell to the Rev. W.J. Temple with an introduction by Thomas

Seccombe, (London: Sidgwick and Jackson, LTD, 1908), p. 188.

^{64}Timothy L.S. Sprigge and Ian Christie, eds., The Correspondence of Jeremy Bentham, I (University of London: The Athlone Press, 1968), 246. Parr's remark is quoted in Nichols, Illustrations of the Literary History of the Eighteenth Century, VI, 61.

^{65}Catharine Macaulay, An ADDRESS to the PEOPLE of England, Scotland, and Ireland, on the present Important Crisis of AFFAIRS (2nd ed.; London: Printed for Edward and Charles Dilly, 1775), pp. 22-25. John Wilkes' speech to Parliament, March 21, 1776, as quoted in S. MacCoby, ed., The English Radical Tradition, 1763-1914 (New York: New York University Press, 1952), p. 30. Richard Price, Observations on the Nature of Civil Liberty, The Principles of Government, and the Justice and Policy of the War with America (8th ed.; London: Printed for T. Cadell, in the Strand, 1778), p. 10n.; Observations on the Importance of the American Revolution and The Means of Making it a Benefit to the World (London: n.p., 1784), p. 54n. The Life and Works of Thomas Paine, ed. by William M. Van der Weyde, II (New Rochelle, New York: Thomas Paine National Association, 1925), 166. Ian Christie, Wilkes, Wyvill and Reform, pp. 146, 186. Alison G. Olson, The Radical Duke (London: Oxford University Press, 1961), p. 52. John Disney, The Works Theological, Medical, Political, and Miscellaneous, of John Jebb, M.D., F.R.S. with Memoirs of the Life of the Author (London: n.p., 1787), II, 436, 468n., 502; III, 286-287. Capel Lofft, Letter to the Society for Constitutional Information ([London]: Printed and Distributed Gratis By the Society for Constitutional Information, 1782), p. 55. Robbins, Eighteenth-Century Commonwealthman, p. 398. Minutes of SCI, September 20, 1782, TS11/1133, f. 110. See also Joseph Towers, TRACTS on POLITICAL and OTHER SUBJECTS, I (3 vols., London: W. Davies and T. Cadell et al, 1796), 172, 176.

^{66}John Cartwright, The Legislative Rights of the Commonalty Vindicated; or, Take your Choice! (2nd ed.; London: J. Almon, 1777), pp. xi-xiv, xxix-xxx, 17, 39-40, 51-53, 110-111, 198-199. John Osborne contends that Burgh "received scant mention from Cartwright in his writings." John Cartwright (Cambridge: At the University Press, 1972), p. 22. This simply is not true of Take your Choice! in which Cartwright first issued his call for an association.

^{67}Bonwick, English Radicals and the American Revolution, pp. 134, 285n.

^{68}Patton and Mann, The Collected Works of Coleridge, I, xlvii-xlviii, 270ff. Hazlitt, Works, I, 265-281. John T. Rutt, ed., The Theological and Miscellaneous Works of Joseph Priestley, LL.D. F.R.S. etc. in 25 vols. (printed by G. Smallfield, Hackney, [1832]), XXII, 144n., 227n., 385-386n., 392n.; XXV, 89n., 101n. William Morgan, Memoirs of the Life of The Rev. Richard Price (London: Printed for R. Hunter and R. Rees, 1815), p. 96n. THOMAS G. STEVENSON'S CATALOGUE of Historical Books for sale (Edinburgh, 1842), p. 31. See also John Longley, An ESSAY Toward Forming a More Complete Representation of the COMMONS of GREAT BRITAIN (London: J. Johnson, 1795), p. 13.

[69]Advertisement prefixed to [Arthur O'Connor's], THE MEASURES OF MINISTRY TO PREVENT A REVOLUTION ARE THE CERTAIN MEANS OF BRINGING IT ON (3rd. ed.; London: Printed for D.I. Eaton, at the Cock and Swine, No. 74, Newgate Street, 1794).

[70]Bonwick, English Radicals and the American Revolution, pp. 40-42, 65-66. Richard Henry Lee, Life of Arthur Lee, I (2 vols.; Boston, 1829), 196, 199, 200. Catharine Macaulay to James Otis, April 27, 1769, Warren-Adams Letters, I (2 vols.; Boston, 1917, 1925), 7-8. Colbourn, "John Dickinson, Historical Revolutionary," 284.

[71]C.F. Adams, Works of John Adams, IX, 351.

[72]Dickinson was responsible for the importation of Catharine Macaulay's History of England into America in contravention of the colonial embargo on British goods. Lee, Life of Arthur Lee, II, 30.

[73]Colbourn, The Lamp of Experience, p. 19. Volumes one and two of the American edition were first advertised for sale June 5, 1775; volume three was available October 9, 1775. See the Pennsylvania Packet for those dates.

[74]H. Trevor Colbourn, "Thomas Jefferson's Use of the Past," William and Mary Quarterly, XV (January, 1958), 65n.

[75]Pennsylvania Packet, November 13, 27, 1775. See also The New-York Journal; or The General Advertiser (New York), June 22, November 23, 1775 and The New York Gazette; and the Weekly Mercury (New York), June 26, 1775.

[76]Merrill Jensen, ed., Tracts of the American Revolution, 1763-1776 (Indianapolis: Bobbs-Merrill Co., 1967), p. 307. In a letter of January 5, 1816 to Dr. J. Morse, Adams remarked that in the days prior to the Revolution "Cato's Letters and the Independent Whig, and all the writings of Trenchard and Gordon, Mrs. Macaulay's History, Burgh's Political Disquisitions, Clarendon's History of the Civil War, and all the writings relative to the revolutions in England became fashionable reading." Adams, Works of John Adams, X, 202. See also J.E.A. Smith's The History of Pittsfield, (Berkshire County) Massachusetts, From the Year 1734 to the Year 1800 (Boston: Published by Lee and Shepard, 1869), pp. 225-226.

[77]Oscar and Mary Handlin, "James Burgh and American Revolutionary Theory," 38. The evidence, however, will not sustain the Handlins' sweeping assertion that the Disquisitions had even more influence upon the "common folk" than upon the leadership of the revolutionary generation.

[78]Bailyn, Ideological Origins, p. ix.

[79]Cited in Colbourn, The Lamp of Experience, p. 187.

[80]One of Jefferson's sets of the Disquisitions is now in the Rare

Book Room of the Library of Congress. There are random pencil markings throughout the volumes. H. Trevor Colbourn, "Jefferson's Use of the Past," 65n.; Colbourn, The Lamp of Experience, p. 221; The Writings of Thomas Jefferson, ed. by Andrew Lipscomb, VIII (Washington, D.C.: Thomas Jefferson Memorial Association of United States, 1905), 32. Henry Stephens Randall, The Life of Thomas Jefferson, I (New York: Derby and Jackson, 1858), 53,55.

[81] The Federalist, ed. with an introduction and notes by Jacob E. Cooke, (Cleveland: World Publishing Co., Meridian paperbacks, 1961), p. 382. Adair, "The Authorship of the Disputed Federalist Papers," 260. Robert Green McClosky, ed., The Works of James Wilson, I (Cambridge: The Belknap Press of Harvard University, 1967), 107-108. Jackson Turner Main, The Antifederalists; Critics of the Constitution, 1781-1788 (Chapel Hill: for the Institute of Early American History and Culture at Williamsburg, Va. by the University of North Carolina Press, 1961), pp. 8-11. "Argus," The Independent Chronicle and Universal Advertiser (Boston), April 18, 1782. "A Democratic Federalist," Maryland Gazette or Baltimore Advertiser, October 26, 1787. [Anonymous], ibid., September 4, 1787. "Rough Hewer," [Abraham Yates], New York Gazetteer, March 22,1785, reprinted in The Newport Mercury (Rhode Island), April 9, 1785. "The Examiner," Massachusetts Gazette (Springfield), September 18, 1782, cited in Main, Antifederalists, p. 78n. "H.S.B.M.," The Kentucky Gazette, November 26, 1791, December 24, 1791; "XYZ," ibid., February 18, 1792. Abijah Bigelow, The Voter's Guide: or the Power, Duty, & Privileges of the Constitutional Voters in the Commonwealth of Massachusetts (Leominster, Mass.: J. Wilder, 1807), pp. 113, 139-141.

[82] Letter of John Adams to James Burgh, December 28, 1774. Adams, Works of John Adams, IX, 351, 558-559.

[83] Kippis, Biographia Britannica, III, 15. Bunhill Fields Burial Registry, 23; Public Record Office (London, England); R.b. 4/3984, #223. Professor Cone supplied the author with this information.

[84] James Burgh, Will.

[85] Bunhill Fields, Burial Registry, 29; R.b. 4/3987, #9. Professor Cone supplied the author with this information.

[86] Gentleman's Magazine, XLV (August, 1775), 407; The Daily Advertiser, August 29, 1775; Gazetteer, August 28, 1775; The London Chronicle, August 26-29, 1775, p. 203; Public Advertiser, August 28, 1775.

[87] Burgh, Political Disquisitions, III, 417.

CHAPTER THREE: The Man of Faith

[1] Bonwick, English Radicals and the American Revolution, pp. 14-15.

126

[2] Burgh, _Crito_, II, 114.

[3] Burgh, _Dignity of Human Nature_, I, 200, 261-263; II, 24-25, 35, 50, 61-64, 216, 247; _An Account of the Cessares_, p. 61.

[4] Burgh, _Britain's Remembrancer_, p. 39; _Thoughts on Education_, p. 29; _Dignity of Human Nature_, II, 306, 461; _Youth's Friendly Monitor_, pp. 41-43; _Political Disquisitions_, I, 112, 402.

[5] Burgh, _Thoughts on Education_, p. 31.

[6] Burgh, _Crito_, I, xvi-xvii. In his utopian essay, however, Burgh did endorse the exclusion of papists from political life on the grounds that their religion advocated the destruction of Protestantism and thus, it was assumed, of Protestant states. _Account of the Cessares_, p. 51.

[7] Burgh, _Political Disquisitions_, I, 470; III, 225, 330, **398**; _Britain's Remembrancer_, p. 25.

[8] Burgh even argued that subjects had no more right to dictate a king's religion than the king had to do the converse. Burgh, _Dignity of Human Nature_, I, 292-293; _Crito_, I, xi; _Political Disquisitions_, III, 202; "Remarks Historical and Political," pp. 32ff., 226.

[9] Burgh, _Political Disquisitions_, II, 36-37. The Feathers Tavern petition requested that Anglican clerics no longer be required to subscribe to the 39 articles. Likewise, lawyers and physicians should be dispensed from subscription as a prerequisite for receiving a degree at Oxford or Cambridge. The petition, organized by a quasi-political association, the Feathers Tavern Association, was presented to Parliament in 1772.

[10] Burgh, _Britain's Remembrancer_, p. 24; _Thoughts on Education_, pp. 29, 37; _Dignity of Human Nature_, II, 308, 314; "The Free Enquirer," LXXV, _General Evening Post_, November 5-7, 1754; _Crito_, II, 106-108.

[11] Burgh, _Dignity of Human Nature_, II, 388-390.

[12] Burgh, _Crito_, II, 172-173, 241-242; _Political Disquisitions_, I, 379; II, 258.

[13] Caroline Robbins has suggested that Burgh might have been a deist in "'When It is that Colonies May Turn Independent:' An Analysis of the Environment and Politics of Francis Hutcheson (1694-1746)," _William and Mary Quarterly_, XI (April, 1954), 250n.

[14] Burgh, _Dignity of Human Nature_, II, 3, 240-247, 307-317, 346, 372, 377, 412; _Crito_, I, 189, 269; II, 224; _Thoughts on Education_, pp. 29-30, 58n.; _Political Disquisitions_, I, xx; III, 176.

[15] "A CHRISTIAN," _London Evening-Post_, March 3-5, 1774.

[16] Burgh, _Crito_, I, 270-271; II, 168-169, 224; _Dignity of Human_

<u>Nature</u>, II, 376. In <u>Thoughts on Education</u> Burgh had severely censured the Deists for denying the expiatory nature of the Redemption. p. 29.

[17]Burgh, <u>Crito</u>, I, 151, 275, 278; II, 124ff., 145, 160, 177.

[18]<u>The Critical Review</u>, XXIII (June, 1767), 447-448; see also <u>ibid.</u>, XXII (July, 1766), 59. Kippis, <u>Biographia Britannica</u>, III, 15. See also <u>The Monthly Review</u>, XXXVII (July, 1767), 15; Alexander Chalmers, <u>The General Biographical Dictionary</u>, VII (new edition; London: J. Nichols and Son, 1813), 322 for additional critical remarks. In a letter of July 8, 1774 to Catharine Macaulay, Augustus Toplady described a recent conversation with the ailing Burgh on the subject of God's response to moral evil. Toplady concluded that Burgh was "much better qualified for political disquisitions, than either for theological or for metaphysical ones." <u>Works</u>, VI, 221.

[19]Burgh's most thorough discussion of the nature of truth in general and of moral truth in particular is in <u>Dignity of Human Nature</u>. See I, 88, 142, 200; II, 4-6, 18, 20-21, 131.

[20]Burgh, <u>Crito</u>, II, 208, 211.

CHAPTER FOUR: The Educator

[1]Cone, <u>Torchbearer of Freedom</u>, p. 10.

[2]Unless otherwise specifically noted, the general discussion of dissenting education that follows is drawn from McLachlan, <u>English Education under the Test Acts</u>.

[3]Lincoln, <u>Some Political and Social Ideas of English Dissent</u>, p.68.

[4]Not until 1779 did Dissenters receive a general authorization to teach and even then endowed schools were not included in this act.

[5]Burgh, <u>Britain's Remembrancer</u>, pp. 24-25. Burgh felt that the very size of the universities fostered a breakdown of discipline, neglect of studies, and dissipation. <u>Political Disquisitions</u>, III, 154. John Locke and Thomas Sheridan shared Burgh's concern about the corruption of English youth. John Locke, <u>Some THOUGHTS Concerning EDUCATION</u>, printed in <u>The Works of John Locke in Nine Volumes</u>, VIII (12th ed.; London: Printed for C. and J. Rivington; T. Egerton, J. Cut; J. and A. Arch; Longman and Co.; W.T. Clarke; J. Mawman; Baynes and Son; Harding and Co.; Baldwin and Co.; Harvey and Darton; R. Scholey; J. Bohn; J. Collingwood; T. Tegg; G. and W.B. Whittaker; G. Mackie; W. Mason; Hurst, Robinson, and Co.; J. Hearne; J. Brumby; Simpkin and Marshall; S. Prowett; W. Pickering; R. Saunders; J. Parker, Oxford; and Stirling and

Slade, Edinburgh, 1824), iv.; Thomas Sheridan, A.M., A PLAN of EDUCATION for the Young Nobility and Gentry of GREAT BRITAIN. Most humbly addressed to The Father of His People. (London: Printed for E. and C. Dilly, in the Poultry, 1769), pp. iv, xii-xvii.

[6] Burgh, Dignity of Human Nature, I, 184, 271.

[7] Ibid., 184.

[8] Burgh, Thoughts on Education, p. 11.

[9] Burgh, Dignity of Human Nature, I, 189; Sheridan, PLAN of EDUCATION, p. 53; Joseph Priestley, LLD. FRS., MISCELLANEOUS OBSERVATIONS RELATING TO EDUCATION. more especially, as it respects the CONDUCT of the MIND. To which is added, An Essay on a course of Liberal Education for Civil and Active Life. (Cork: Printed by T. White, No. 55, opposite the West Gate of the Exchange, 1780), pp. 9-12. See also, Locke, THOUGHTS concerning EDUCATION, p. 58.

[10] Burgh, Thoughts on Education, p. 11.

[11] In his THOUGHTS concerning EDUCATION, Locke remarked:"The little, or almost insensible impressions on our tender infancies have very important and lasting consequences . . .," p. 7. Similarly, Jean Pierre de Crousaz stressed the importance of pre-school years in a youngster's development and severely criticized the contemporary custom of treating children as frivolous playthings during this crucial formative period. New MAXIMS concerning the EDUCATION of YOUTH and a DISCOURSE concerning PEDANTRY. Both translated from French into English by the Reverend Mr. GEORGE STEPHEN TACHERON (London: Printed for the TRANSLATOR, and sold by T. COOPER, at the Globe in Pater-Noster-Row; M. CHASTEL, at the Golden Bull, Compton-street, Soho; and by the Booksellers of London and Westminster, 1740), pp. 3-5.

[12] Burgh, Dignity of Human Nature, I, 198; Thoughts on Education, p. 10.

[13] Burgh, Political Disquisitions, I, 1-2.

[14] Burgh, Dignity of Human Nature, I, 116. Sheridan, Locke, and John Clarke shared Burgh's sentiments. Sheridan, PLAN of EDUCATION, pp. 79-81; Locke, THOUGHTS concerning EDUCATION, pp. 37, 41, 44; John Clarke, An ESSAY upon the EDUCATION of YOUTH in GRAMMAR-SCHOOLS. In which the Vulgar Method of Teaching is examined, and a New one proposed, for the more Easy and Speedy Training up of Youth to the Knowledge of the Learned Languages; together with History, Chronology, Geography etc. (2nd ed. With very LARGE ADDITIONS; London: Printed for ARTHUR BETTESWORTH, at the Red Lion in Pater-Noster-Row, 1730), pp. 132, 134.

[15] Whereas Locke preferred that a child be educated at home by a tutor, rather than being exposed to the bad example of other children at school, Priestley, John Clarke, and Sheridan all shared Burgh's enthusiasm for some form of group education. Locke, THOUGHTS concerning

129

EDUCATION, p. 54; Priestley, MISCELLANEOUS OBSERVATIONS, pp. 48-52;
Clarke, ESSAY upon . . . EDUCATION, p. 204; Sheridan, PLAN of EDUCATION,
p. 52.

[16]Burgh, Crito, I, 76; see also Dignity of Human Nature, I, 213.
Burgh severely criticized Rousseau's educational theories in Crito. He
found the philosopher's ideas almost wholly "impracticable." Crito, I,
72 ff; see also Account of the Cessares, p. 68.

[17]Burgh, Dignity of Human Nature, I, 214-215.

[18]Burgh, Dignity of Human Nature, I, 204, 208; Burgh, Thoughts on
Education, pp. 33-42.

[19]Burgh, Thoughts on Education, p. 36.

[20]Burgh, Dignity of Human Nature, I, 297-298. Locke had stressed
this point in his THOUGHTS concerning EDUCATION, p. 86.

[21]Burgh, Crito, I, 155.

[22]Ibid., 158, 161.

[23]Burgh, Dignity of Human Nature, I, 225.

[24]Ibid., 218-219. See also Priestley, MISCELLANEOUS OBSERVATIONS,
pp. 41-43.

[25]Burgh, Thoughts on Education, p. 12.

[26]Herbert McLachlan maintains that only at the Warrington Academy
was French a regular part of the curriculum. English Education under
the Test Acts, p. 36. It seems probable, however, that Burgh would have
followed his own advice and included French as a regular part of the
curriculum in his own academy.

[27]Burgh, Dignity of Human Nature, I, 226. Both Locke and Sheridan
recommended instruction in French. Locke, THOUGHTS concerning EDUCA-
TION, p. 152; Sheridan, PLAN of EDUCATION, p. 88.

[28]Burgh, The Art of Speaking, pp. 4, 42, 57-58; Dignity of Human
Nature, I, 231.

[29]Burgh, Dignity of Human Nature, I, 228-229.

[30]McLachlan, English Education under the Test Acts, p. 35.

[31]Burgh, Dignity of Human Nature, I, 233.

[32]Ibid., 234, 247, 248.

[33]McLachlan, English Education under the Test Acts, p. 40; Robbins,
Eighteenth-Century Commonwealthman, p. 238.

[34]Burgh, Thoughts on Education, p. 15.

[35]Burgh, Youth's Friendly Monitor, p. 9.

[36]Burgh, Dignity of Human Nature, I, 234-235. Hebrew Hutchisson is most probably John Hutchinson (1674-1737), an anti-Newtonian, whose followers were criticized for their sermons decrying reason and natural religion. Hutchinson believed the Hebrew language was formed by God.

[37]Burgh, Dignity of Human Nature, I, 235-236.

[38]Ibid., 236-237.

[39]Burgh, Thoughts on Education, p. 14. Thomas Sheridan believed that music was a waste of time and often led to mingling with bad company. PLAN of EDUCATION, p. 172.

[40]Burgh, Thoughts on Education, p. 14; Dignity of Human Nature, I, 238.

[41]Burgh, Thoughts on Education, p. 36. Burgh incorporated such a list into the postscript of Youth's Friendly Monitor. Included were over one hundred titles on everything from chemistry to logic.

[42]Burgh, Thoughts on Education, pp. 53-57; Dignity of Human Nature, I, 124, 128, 146.

[43]See for example, excerpts from A LETTER from a FATHER to his DAUGHTER at a BOARDING-SCHOOL in the General Evening Post, January 18-20, 1774; S. Whyte, "Thoughts on Education," in ibid., October 13-15, 1772; "No Macaroni," ibid., October 8-10, 1772; [Anonymous], The Morning Chronicle, and London Advertiser, September 14, 1774; "R.," Monthly Review, XXIX (November, 1763), 372; "H.," ibid., XLV (August, 1771),81; Critical Review, XVI (November, 1763), 329-330; Catharine Macaulay, Letters on Education (London: C. Dilly, 1790), pp. 142, 201-208. Lawrence Stone has briefly discussed changes in eighteenth century attitudes towards female education as part of the evolution of the "companionate marriage" in The Family, Sex and Marriage, pp. 343-360.

[44]Eleanor Flexner suggests that Mary Wollstonecraft who was befriended by Burgh's widow, Hannah, was in fact influenced by Burgh's arguments on female education. Mary Wollstonecraft, pp. 48, 161-162.

[45]Writing to the American educator, Ezra Stiles, January 20, 1762, Chauncy Whittelsey commented: "Should you make any Progress in the Affair of a Colledge [sic] I should be glad to hear of it; I heartily wish you Success therein; I was not long since reading a Treatise wrote by one Burgh; . . . [who] maintains, that 40 or 50 is as many Students, or Pupils, as should belong to one College or Academy at a time." Franklin Bowditch Dexter, Extracts from the Itineraries and Other Miscellanies of Ezra Stiles, D.D., LL.D. 1755-1794 With a Selection from his Correspondence (New Haven: Yale University Press, 1916), p. 584.

CHAPTER FIVE: The Social Critic

[1]Burgh, Political Disquisitions, III, 150.

[2]Burgh, Dignity of Human Nature, I, 185.

[3]Gordon S. Wood has succinctly summarized the attitude of Whig theorists in particular on the subject of public immorality and its impact on the body politic. The Creation of the American Republic, 1776-1787 (Chapel Hill: University of North Carolina Press, 1969), pp. 28-36; 65-70.

[4]Burgh, Political Disquisitions, III, 30; see also ibid., 380; An Account of the Cessares, p. 43.

[5]Burgh, Dignity of Human Nature, I, 185; II, 123.

[6]M. Dorothy George, London Life in the Eighteenth Century (New York: Harper Torchbooks; Harper & Row, 1965 [originally published London: Kegan Paul, Trench, Trubner & Co., Ltd., 1925]), p. 1.

[7]Price believed that England's population was declining as a result of the debilitating effects of luxury on the populace. George, London Life, p. 23.

[8]Burgh, Political Disquisitions, III, 64.

[9]Burgh, Thoughts on Education, p. 19; Political Disquisitions, III, 17, 31, 60-61. Burgh's suspicions about luxury were by no means peculiar to himself. A correspondent with the London Chronicle, "J___H___," wrote "When I reflect on the universal depravity of manners that prevails among my countrymen, and view the progress of luxury and corruption among the people, together with that visible decline of honour and real patriotism among the modern great, I cannot but fear for the event." September 9-11, 1766. See also "BX," The London Chronicle, November 4-6, 1766, p. 444; "J.W.," Gazetteer December 12, 1769; "West Indian," ibid., September 26, 1769.

[10]Burgh, Britain's Remembrancer, p. 15; Account of the Cessares, p. 98n.

[11]Burgh, Dignity of Human Nature, II, 155-159, 164-168; "Remarks Historical and Political," pp. 90, 198; Political Disquisitions, III, 99, 223.

[12]Henry Fielding, Amelia (2 vols; London: Frank Cass & Co. LTD, 1967), II, 180-181. Burgh, Dignity of Human Nature, II, 167. Burgh recommended to the King that masquerades be prohibited. "Remarks Historical and Political," p. 28.

[13]Burgh, Dignity of Human Nature, I, 76.

[14]Ibid., 64-65, II, 164; Youth's Friendly Monitor, p. 6; "Remarks Historical and Political," p. 49; Crito, II, 71-72.

[15]Burgh, "Remarks Historical and Political," p. 14.

[16]John Osborne, John Cartwright, pp. 14, 61.

[17]Burgh, Dignity of Human Nature, II, 178; "Remarks Historical and Political," pp. 16, 122-124, 136-137, 198, 201; Crito, I, 50.

[18]Burgh, Dignity of Human Nature, I, 79-80. He favored more rigorous penalties for those who went bankrupt because of negligence or extravagance. "Remarks Historical and Political" pp. 139-140.

[19]Robbins, Eighteenth-Century Commonwealthman, pp. 14-16; Bonwick, English Radicals and the American Revolution, p. 13.

[20]Burgh, Dignity of Human Nature, I, 32.

[21]Burgh, Dignity of Human Nature, II, 177; "Remarks Historical and Political," p. 47; Account of the Cessares, p. 7n.

[22]Robbins, Eighteenth-Century Commonwealthman, p. 15.

[23]Burgh, "Remarks Historical and Political," pp. 121-122.

[24]Burgh, Account of the Cessares, pp. 7-8n.

[25]Ibid., p. 82; "Remarks Historical and Political," p. 154; Crito, II, 92-95; PROPOSALS . . . For An ASSOCIATION; Political Disquisitions, III, 387.

[26]Burgh, Crito, I, 54; II, 71, 89-90; "Remarks Historical and Political," pp. 165-168; Political Disquisitions, III, 226-227. In his discussion of the paradoxical development of slavery and freedom in colonial America, Edmund S. Morgan cites James Burgh as an example of this same paradox operating in England. Morgan contends that Burgh endorsed the virtual enslavement of the poor. This interpretation represents a fundamental misunderstanding of Burgh's attitude toward the poor. It ignores both the moralistic foundation of Burgh's reaction to idlers and Burgh's advocacy of agrarian reform to improve the lot of the poor. Burgh certainly believed there would always be poor people and that their labor was vital to the economy, but he most certainly did not want to keep them impoverished, let alone virtually "enslave" them, in order to ensure national prosperity. American Slavery, American Freedom: The Ordeal of Colonial Virginia (New York: W.W. Norton & Company, 1975), pp. 324, 370, 382.

[27]Burgh, Dignity of Human Nature, I, 288; "Remarks Historical and Political," pp. 25, 27, 48, 52-53, 55, 58, 200, 228; Account of the Cessares, pp. 54, 82; Crito, I, 58, II, 75, 93, 99, 101-103; Political Disquisitions, III, 160-167, 170-171.

[28]Burgh, <u>Dignity of Human Nature</u>, II, 160; <u>Account of the Cessares</u>, pp. 50, 110n.; <u>Crito</u>, I, 56.

[29]Burgh, <u>Dignity of Human Nature</u>, II, 160; "Remarks Historical and Political," pp. 51-52, 147-150; <u>Crito</u>, I, 46, 47.

[30]Burgh, <u>Political Disquisitions</u>, III, 30, 139-140.

[31]<u>Ibid.</u>, 228-229.

[32]<u>Ibid.</u>, 179-180, 191.

CHAPTER SIX: The Political Disquisitor

[1]See Gordon Wood, <u>Creation of the American Republic</u>, pp. 28-36 for specific examples of this line of reasoning.

[2]Burgh, <u>Thoughts on Education</u>, pp. 15-16; <u>Dignity of Human Nature</u>, I, 164, 254-255; II, 195-206; "The Free Enquirer," XXIII, <u>General Evening Post</u>, October 30-November 1, 1753 ; XXVII November 27-29, 1753 .

[3]Robbins, <u>Eighteenth-Century Commonwealthman</u>, p. 177.

[4]Isaac Kramnick, <u>Bolingbroke and His Circle; The Politics of Nostalgia in the Age of Walpole</u> (Cambridge: Harvard University Press, 1968), pp. 95-96, 163ff., 236ff.

[5]Burgh, <u>Crito</u>, 208-213; <u>Dignity of Human Nature</u>, II, 198.

[6]Burgh, "Remarks Historical and Political," pp. 3-6, 21.

[7]Burgh, "The Free Enquirer," XXVII, <u>General Evening Post</u>, November 27-29, 1753 ; XXIII, October 30-November 1, 1753 .

[8]Burgh, <u>Crito</u>, II, 49-50.

[9]<u>Ibid.</u>, I, 4-6; <u>Dignity of Human Nature</u>, I, 164, II, 205-206; <u>Thoughts on Education</u>, p. 16; "The Free Enquirer," XXIII, <u>General Evening Post</u>, October 30-November 1, 1753 ; "Remarks Historical and Political," p. 21; <u>Political Disquisitions</u>, III, 332.

[10]Burgh, <u>Political Disquisitions</u>, I, 49-50, 374; II, 48; III, 183, 433.

[11]Burgh, <u>Political Disquisitions</u>, II, 459.

[12] Burgh, _Account of the Cessares_, pp. 26-27; _Thoughts on Education_, p. 15; _Political Disquisitions_, I, 2.

[13] Burgh, _Political Disquisitions_, I, 1-2.

[14] Burgh, _Account of the Cessares_, pp. 26, 39.

[15] Burgh, _Political Disquisitions_, I, 106, III, 10, 234; "Constitutionalist," II, _Gazetteer_, August 7, 1769 , X, October 27, 1769 , XVIII, May 12, 1770; _Dignity of Human Nature_, I, 2.

[16] Burgh, _Account of the Cessares_, p. 25.

[17] Burgh, _Crito_, II, 233-234; "Remarks Historical and Political," p. 184; _Account of the Cessares_, p. 25; _Political Disquisitions_, I, 253.

[18] Burgh, _Political Disquisitions_, I, 116-117; "Remarks Historical and Political," p. 59.

[19] Burgh, _Political Disquisitions_, I, 3-4; III, 277.

[20] _Ibid._, I, 221.

[21] _Ibid._, III, 267. Burgh told the King that "the government of Engl. has long been more an _Oligarchy_ than anything else. A set of great _Officers_ of _State_ have governed King, Lords and Com.ˢ" As an example of such undue influence, Burgh cited the Pelham-Newcastle ultimatum to George II that forced the King to repudiate Lords Granville and Bath. "Remarks Historical and Political," pp. 2-3.

[22] In the "Remarks Historical and Political," p. 5, Burgh argued that the English constitution "acknowledged neither cabinet-council, prime Minister, Favourite, nor Junto."

[23] Burgh, _Political Disquisitions_, III, 183; II, 48.

[24] R.R. Palmer, _The Age of the Democratic Revolution, A Political History of Europe and America, 1760-1800: The Challenge_, vol. I (Princeton: Princeton University Press, 1959), 71-72.

[25] Wood, _Creation of the American Republic_, p. 31. Burgh, _Political Disquisitions_, I, 376.

[26] Burgh, _Political Disquisitions_, I, 399, 403.

[27] Burgh, _Crito_ , II, 29.

[28] Sydenham's remarks were made in the course of a 1744 parliamentary debate on annual parliaments. Quoted in Burgh, _Political Disquisitions_, III, 48. Burgh was horrified by the prevalence of perjury in England as it damned its perpetrator to eternal perdition and tended "to ruin all virtue." "The Free Enquirer," _General Evening Post_, XXIII, October 30 - November 1, 1753 ; XXVII, November 27-29, 1753 ; XXVIII,

December 11-13, 1753; XXXI, January 1-3, 1754; XXXIV, January 22-24, 1754.

[29] Burgh, Political Disquisitions, I, 268, 280; II, 79.

[30] Ibid., I, 226-227, 270-271, 277; II, 110; "Constitutionalist,"VI, Gazetteer, September 15, 1769.

[31] Burgh, Political Disquisitions, I, xiii; Dignity of Human Nature, II, 199.

[32] Burgh, Political Disquisitions, III, 320.

[33] Burgh, Crito, I, 33-35.

[34] Burgh, Political Disquisitions, I, 270.

[35] Ibid., II, 348-353, 369, 396, 449.

[36] Ibid., 406.

[37] Ibid., 401-402; Crito, II, 104. Burgh was contradictory in de-lineating the composition of the militia. At one point he indicated that householders whose homes contained ten or more windows should form its ranks and described a militia consisting of other than men of prop-erty as a mongrel army. Political Disquisitions, II, 401-402. Else-where he recommended that all males be trained for service in the mili-tia. Ibid., 347.

[38] Burgh, Political Disquisitions, II, 36-37; see also "Constitu-tionalist," I, Gazetteer, July 15, 1769.

[39] Bonwick, English Radicals and the American Revolution, p. 119. Burgh, "The Colonist's Advocate," VI, January 29, 1770 in Crane, Benja-min Franklin's Letters to the Press, p. 185; "Constitutionalist," V, Gazetteer, September 1, 1769.

[40] Burgh, "Remarks Historical and Political," p. 230.

[41] Burgh, Political Disquisitions, I, 221.

[42] Handlin, "James Burgh and American Revolutionary Theory," 50-51.

[43] Burgh, Political Disquisitions, II, 284, 286-287, 297, 310, 319, 320.

[44] Ibid., II, 319, 328; "Constitutionalist," V, Gazetteer, Septem-ber 1, 1769.

[45] Burgh, Political Disquisitions, II, 310.

[46] Ibid., 274, 295-297, 314-316, 319; Crito, II, 41-42; "Constitu-tionalist," IV, Gazetteer, August 28, 1769.

[47] Burgh, *Political Disquisitions*, II, 322-323.

[48] Bonwick, *English Radicals and the American Revolution*, p. 82.

[49] Burgh, *Political Disquisitions*, I, 200, 447-448; II, 439; III, 277-278, 430, 435.

[50] *Ibid.*, III, 425, 434-435.

[51] Burgh, *Dignity of Human Nature*, II, 204; "Constitutionalist,"XVII *Gazetteer*, March 14, 1770 . Burgh warned the King that the people would have no recourse but rebellion if the three estates tried to enslave them. "Remarks Historical and Political," p. 180.

[52] Burgh, *Political Disquisitions*, II, 3.

[53] Republicanism was espoused by the historian Catharine Macaulay, her brother, Alderman John Sawbridge, John Stevenson, another London politician and East India Company merchant, Thomas Hollis and his cousin Timothy Hollis, Thomas Brand, Richard Baron, and Sylas Neville. Robbins, *Eighteenth-Century Commonwealthman*, p. 358.

[54] Burgh, *Political Disquisitions*, I, 9, 50. Burgh further commented in the *Disquisitions* that republican government "is undoubtedly preferable to . . . [monarchical, as in Britain], supposing a state to be *setting* its form of government . . .." II, 18; see also I, 116-117. But as late as *Crito*, II, 36-37 he had observed that "the wit of man will never devise any form of government preferable to *limited* monarchy, with a house of lords, and another of commons, rightly *regulated*, and duly *balanced* against one another."

[55] Burgh, "Constitutionalist," I, *Gazetteer*, July 15, 1769), IV, August 28, 1769.

[56] *Ibid.*, I, July 15, 1769 ; *Political Disquisitions*, I, 185.

[57] Burgh, *Crito*, II, 19.

[58] Burgh, *Political Disquisitions*, I, 87-88, 94, 130. Burgh recommended annual parliaments to the King. "Remarks Historical and Political," p. 66.

[59] Burgh, "Constitutionalist," I, *Gazetteer*, July 15, 1769 ; "Remarks Historical and Political," pp. 66-67; *Crito*, II, 39-40, 76; *Political Disquisitions*, I, 129, 152.

[60] Burgh, "Constitutionalist," I, *Gazetteer*, July 15, 1769.

[61] Burgh, *Political Disquisitions*, II, 42.

[62] *Ibid.*, 92; "Remarks Historical and Political," pp. 9, 12; *Crito*, II 65.

[63]Burgh, "Remarks Historical and Political," p. 186; Political Disquisitions, II, 81; I, 51-54.

[64]Burgh, Political Disquisitions, I, 62-63.

[65]Ibid., 3, 27, III, 346; Crito, II, 25; "Constitutionalist," III, Gazetteer, August 18, 1769 . See also "Remarks Historical and Political," p. 59.

[66]Burgh, Political Disquisitions, I, 40-45, 68-69; "Constitutionalist," III, Gazetteer, August 18, 1769 . See also Crito, II, 23-25.

[67]Burgh, "Constitutionalist," I, Gazetteer, July 15, 1769; Political Disquisitions, I, 37-38. In the Account of the Cessares all citizens (protestant males, 21 years or older, married or widowers) enjoyed the franchise, p. 50. But Burgh apparently envisioned such citizens as householders, p. 52. See also "Remarks Historical and Political," p. 66.

[68]Burgh, Political Disquisitions, I, 36-38. Major John Cartwright criticized Burgh for compromising on the issue of granting the franchise to the poor. Take Your Choice!, pp. 39-40.

[69]Burgh, "Remarks Historical and Political," p. 67; Crito, II, 38; Political Disquisitions, I, 49. Interestingly, in his utopian essay Burgh specifically repudiated plural voting. Undoubtedly he deemed it inappropriate in an ideal society where everyone shared equally in the community's property. Account of the Cessares, p. 48.

[70]Burgh, Crito, II, 24-25, 38.

[71]Ibid., 23-24, 37-38; "Constitutionalist," I, Gazetteer, July 15, 1769 ; Political Disquisitions, I, 39; "Remarks Historical and Political," p. 68.

[72]Brewer, Party Ideology and Popular Politics, pp. 20, 207; Burgh, "Remarks Historical and Political," pp. 60-68, 107.

[73]Burgh recommended the ballot in "The Free Enquirer," XXVII, General Evening Post, November 27-29, 1753 ; Dignity of Human Nature, II, 199, 200; Account of the Cessares, p. 89; Crito, II, 37; "Constitutionalist," III, Gazetteer, August 18, 1769 ; Political Disquisitions, I, 176.

[74]Burgh, "Constitutionalist," VI, Gazetteer, September 15, 1769 . Oscar Handlin has maintained that Burgh believed "reform could only come from [parliament];" that the people "could do no more than urge it to adhere to the true spirit of the constitution." "James Burgh and American Revolutionary Theory," 54. On the contrary, though Burgh hoped petitions would suffice to move parliament to embrace reform, he warned that "when p_____s desert their duty, the people must look to themselves." The time had not yet come for such a response, but wisdom suggested that parliament "quench a rising flame before it becomes a conflagration." "Constitutionalist," XVII, Gazetteer, March 14, 1770.

[75]Burgh, Political Disquisitions, I, 6.

[76]Burgh, "Constitutionalist," [XV], Gazetteer, December 27, 1769, III, August 18, 1769; see also Political Disquisitions, I, 486; III,190, 433.

[77]Black, The Association, p. 1.

[78]Other associations were the Game Association (Daily Advertiser; January 9, 1758); Brethren of the laudable Association of Antigallicans (Daily Advertiser; May 17, 1760); Swaffham Association; Gentlemen associated for the Protection of their Tenants (The London Chronicle; September 14-16, 1766, p. 239).

[79]Black, The Association, p. 29.

[80]Caroline Robbins seems to imply that Burgh was indebted to An Historical Essay on the English Constitution (probably written by Obadiah Hulme) for his interest in association. Eighteenth-Century Commonwealthman, pp. 363-364. Although Burgh quoted from the Essay to bolster his call for an association (Political Disquisitions, III, 429), his interest in associations long antedated the Essay, published in 1771.

[81]Burgh, Political Disquisitions, III, 428-429.

[82]Burgh, Britain's Remembrancer, pp. 41, 43; Dignity of Human Nature, II, 255; Crito, II, 208; PROPOSALS . . . For An ASSOCIATION, p. 8ff.

[83]Burgh, Crito, II, 83, 18.

[84]Burgh, "Constitutionalist," III, Gazetteer, August 18, 1769; IV, August 28, 1769; VI, September 15, 1769.

[85]Burgh, Political Disquisitions, III, 426.

[86]Ibid., 428-429; 432-433.

[87]Ibid., 434-435. Interestingly, Burgh indicated that the first task of the association would be securing public credit. He did not, however, elaborate on how this was to be accomplished.

[88]Burgh, Crito, II, 18-19; "Constitutionalist," X, Gazetteer, October 27, 1769; Political Disquisitions, III, 378-379.

[89]Burgh, "Constitutionalist," II, Gazetteer, August 7, 1769; Political Disquisitions, III, 435, 449.

[90]Burgh, Political Disquisitions, III, 429-430.

[91]Burgh, "Remarks Historical and Political," p. 4.

[92]Burgh, Crito, II, 211.

[93]Black, The Association, p. 4.

CONCLUSION: The Sum of the Man

[1] Butterfield, _George III, Lord North, and the People_, pp. 259-260.

[2] Alexander Stephens, _Memoirs of John Horne Tooke_, II (2 vols.; New York: 1968; originally published London: 1813), 282-283.

[3] _A SOLEMN APPEAL to the GOOD SENSE OF THE NATION: Pointing OUT The Immediate Necessity Of A CORDIAL COALITION Between The KING AND THE PEO- PLE_ (London: W. Flexner, 1783), p. 13.   Macaulay, _Letters on Education_, pp. 224-225, 229, 272-273.

[4] Burgh, _Crito_, II, 83, 18.

[5] Burgh, _Political Disquisitions_, III, 174, 417.

BIBLIOGRAPHY

PRIMARY SOURCES

Manuscripts:

British Museum:
    James Burgh. "Remarks Historical and Political Collected from
Books and Observations. Humbly Presented to the King's most excellent
Majesty," (1762). King's MS 433.
    Map of Carew Mildmay estate, 3465 (27).

Library of Congress:
    National Union Catalogue.

Middlesex Record Office:
    Land Tax Assessment Books, Box 2015-2025, 1767-1780.

Public Record Office (London, England):
    Bunhill Fields Burial Registry, 23; R.b. 4/3984, January 11, 1771-
April 9, 1778, #223. 29; R.b. 4/3987, May 3, 1778-December 25, 1794.#9.
    Minutes of the Society for Constitutional Information, Ts 11/1133.

Somerset House Records, Principal Probate Registry (London, England):
    James Burgh, Will, 1775; Alexander 334. George Streatfield, Will,
1757; Herring 32. Sarah Seabrooke, Will, 1770; Jenner 278.

Printed Primary Sources: Diaries, Memoirs, Correspondence, Documents,
                          Pamphlets and Books.

Adams, Charles Francis. The Works of John Adams with a Life of the Au-
    thor. 10 vols.; Boston: Little Brown & Co., 1850-1856.
Adams, John. Diary and Autobiography of John Adams. Editor in chief L.
    H. Butterfield. 4 vols.; "The Adams Papers"; Cambridge: Belknap
    Press of Harvard University Press, 1961.
Bailyn, Bernard (ed.). Pamphlets of the American Revolution, 1750-1776.
    Vol. I; Cambridge: The Belknap Press of Harvard University, 1965.
[Baynes, Richard]. Richard Baynes's select Catalogue of Books, Old and
    New . . . (on sale). London: Richard Baynes , 1832.
Beloff, Max (ed.). The Debate on the American Revolution, 1761-1783.
    2nd ed.; London: Adam & Charles Black, 1960.
Bibliotheca Parriana; A Catalogue of the Library of the Late Reverend
    and Learned Samuel Parr, LL.D., Curate of Hatton, Prebendary of St.
    Paul's, etc. London: n.p., 1828.

[Bigelow, Abijah]. "Letters of Abijah Bigelow, Member of Congress, to
His Wife, 1810-1815," Proceedings of the American Antiquarian Society, XL, new series (1930), 305-406.
_____. The Voter's Guide: or, the Power, Duty & Privileges of the
Constitutional Voters in the Commonwealth of Massachusetts. to
which are added, original remarks with various extracts from His-
torians, and the writings and public speeches of eminent political
characters in this and other countries, tending to explain the
causes of the Rise and Fall of Republican Governments. Leominster,
Mass.: J. Wilder, 1807.
Boswell, James. Boswell in Search of a Wife, 1766-1769. Edited by
Frank Brady and Frederick A. Pottle. New York: McGraw-Hill, 1956.
_____. Boswell's London Journal, 1762-1763. Introduction and
Notes by Frederick A. Pottle. New York: McGraw-Hill Book Co., 1950.
_____. Letters of James Boswell to the Rev. W.J. Temple. With an
introduction by Thomas Seccombe. London: Sidgwick & Jackson, LTD,
1908.
_____. Private Papers of James Boswell from Malahide Castle; In
the Collection of Lt.-Colonel Ralph Heyward Isham. Prepared for
the press by Geoffrey Scott, and Frederick A. Pottle. 18 vols.;
Mount Vernon, N.Y.: privately printed by W.E. Rudee, 1928-1934.
Burgh, James. An Account of the First Settlement, Laws, Form of Government, and Police of the Cessares, A People of South America: in
Nine Letters, from Mr. Vander Neck, one of the Senators of that Nation, to his Friend in Holland, With Notes by the Editor. London:
Printed for J. Payne, at the Feathers, Pater-noster row, 1764.
_____. The Art of Speaking. Containing I. An Essay; in which are
given rules for expressing properly the principal Passions and Humours, which occur in Reading, or public Speaking; and II. Lessons
taken from the Ancients and Moderns (with Additions and Alterations
where thought useful) exhibiting a Variety of Matter for practice;
--the emphatical words printed in Italics; with Notes of Direction
referring to the Essay. To which are added; A Table of the Lessons;
and an Index of the Various Passions and Humours in the Essay and
Lessons. 5th ed.; Newbury-Port, Mass.: Printed by John Mycall, for
William Green, of Boston, 1782 [originally published London: Printed for T. Longman, J. Buckland, and W. Fenner, in Pater-noster Row;
J. Waugh, in Lombard-street; E. Dilly in the Poultry; and T. Field
in Cheapside, 1761].
_____. Britain's Remembrancer, Being Some Thoughts on the proper
Improvement of the present Juncture. The Character of this Age and
Nation. A Brief View, from History of the Effects of the Vices
which now prevail in Britain, upon the greatest Empires and States
of former Times. Remarkable Deliverances this nation has had in
the most imminent Dangers; with suitable Reflections. Some Hints,
shewing what is in the Power of the several Ranks of People, and of
every Individual in Britain, to do toward securing the State from
all its Enemies. Boston: Reprinted by Benjamin Mecom, at the New
Printing Office, 1759 [originally published London: Printed for M.
Cooper, at the Globe in Pater-noster-Row, 1746].
_____. "Constitutionalist," The Gazetteer and New Daily Advertis-
er (London), I-XX, 1769-1770.

_____. Crito, or Essays on Various Subjects. Vol. I; London: Printed for J. Dodsley in Pall Mall, 1766; Vol. II; London: Printed for Messrs. Dodsley in Pall-Mall; Becket and De Handt, in the Strand; White, in Fleet-Street; Payne, in Paternoster Row; and Cooke, near the Royal Exchange, 1767.

_____. The Dignity of Human Nature. or, A brief Account of the certain and established Means for attaining the True End of our Existence. In Four Books. I. Of Prudence. II. Of Knowledge. III. Of Virtue. IV. Of Revealed Religion. 2 vols.; A new edition; London: Printed for J. Johnson and J. Payne, in Pater-noster-row; and T. Cadell, in The Strand, 1767 [originally published London: Printed for J. and P. Knaston, in Ludgate Street; J. Whiston and B. White, in Fleet-Street; A. Millar in the Strand; R. and J. Dodsley, in Pall-Mall; and J. Ward in Cornhill, 1754].

_____. "The Free Enquirer," General Evening Post (London), 1753-1754.

_____. An Hymn to the Creator of the World. The Thoughts taken Chiefly from Psal. civ. To which is added in Prose, an Idea of the Creator from His Works. 2nd ed.; London: Printed and Sold by M. Cooper, in Pater-noster-row; and the Pamphlet Shops in London and Westminster, 1750.

_____. "Philopaulus." The London Chronicle, March 12-March 15, 1768, p. 244.

_____. Political Disquisitions: or, An Enquiry into Public Errors, Defects, and Abuses. Illustrated by, and established upon Facts and Remarks extracted from a Variety of Authors, ancient and modern. Calculated To draw the timely Attention of Government and People to a due consideration of the Necessity, and the Means, of Reforming those Errors, Defects, and Abuses; of Restoring the Constitution, and Saving the State. 3 vols.; London: Printed for E. and C. Dilly in the Poultry, 1774-1775.

_____. Political Disquisitions . . .. Vol. III; Philadelphia: Printed and Sold by Robert Bell, in Third Street and William Woodhouse in Front Street, 1775.

_____. PROPOSALS (Humbly offered to the PUBLIC) for an ASSOCIATION Against The Iniquitous Practices of ENGROSSERS, FORESTALLERS, JOBBERS, etc. And For Reducing The PRICE OF PROVISIONS, Especially BUTCHERS MEAT. London: Printed for J. Payne, at the Feathers, Paternoster-Row; and Richardson and Urquhart, under the Royal Exchange 1766.

_____. Thoughts on Education, Tending chiefly To recommend to the Attention of the Public, some Particulars relating to that Subject; which are not generally considered with the Regard their Importance deserves. Boston: Reprinted and Sold by Rogers and Fowle in Queen-Street, 1749 [originally published London: Printed for G. Freer, at the Bible in Bell-Yard, Temple-Bar; and sold by M. Cooper, at the Globe in Pater-noster-Row; and Mrs. Amey, at the Gazette, Charing Cross, 1747].

_____. Youth's Friendly Monitor: Being a Set of DIRECTIONS, PRUDENTIAL, MORAL, RELIGIOUS, AND SCIENTIFIC. First drawn up for a Farewel [sic] Present, by the Master of an Academy near London, to his Pupils on their removing from under his Care. To which is prefixed, An Account of the extraordinary Proceeding of some Persons,

which occasioned the Publication of this Tract, contrary to the
Author's original Intention. Together with THEOPHILUS, A CHARACTER
worthy of Imitation. London: Printed for M. Cooper at the Globe
in Paternoster-row, 1754.

Burton, John Hill. Life and Correspondence of David Hume. Reprinted;
New York: Burt Franklin, 1967 [originally published Edinburgh:
n.p., 1846].

[Carlyle, Alexander]. Autobiography of the Rev. Dr. Alexander Carlyle,
Minister of Inveresk Containing Memorials Of The Men And Events of
His Time. Edinburgh and London: William Blackwood and Sons, 1860.

Cartwright, John. American Independence the Interest and Glory of Great
Britain . . .. Philadelphia: Printed and Sold by Robert Bell in
Third-Street, 1776.

_____. The Legislative Rights of the Commonalty Vindicated; or,
Take Your Choice! 2nd ed.; London: J. Almon, 1777.

A Catalogue of a valuable and useful collection of books, in English and
Foreign Divinity, Classics . . . on sale by W. Ridge. Worcester,
Mass.: n.p., 1832.

Catalogue of Books, amounting at the Retail Price to Over 100,000 Dol-
lars, which are now offered for Sale in General at Fifty Per Cent
Discount, at the Literary Rooms 48, Cornhill, Boston. n.p.: S. Eth-
eridge, Printer, 1822.

Catalogue of Books, belonging to the Apprentices' Library Company of
Philadelphia. n.p.: Jesper Harding, 1823.

Catalogue of Books belonging to the Library Company of Philadelphia . . ..
Philadelphia: n.p., 1807.

Catalogue of Books in the Massachusetts Historical Library, Boston: S.
Hall, 1796.

Catalogue of Books in the Washington Library. Washington: n.p., 1835.

Catalogue of Historical Works, Belonging to the Old South Church and Society, in the Rooms of the Massachusetts Historical Society, n.p.,
n.d.

Catalogue of the Books belonging to the Charleston Apprentice's Library
Society. Charleston: n.p., 1841.

A Catalogue of the Entire Library of the Late Granville Sharp, Esq. Author of various Tracts on the Slave Trade, etc. etc. . . .. London:
n.p., 1813.

Catalogue of the Library of Rev. Thomas Prince, Former Pastor of Old
South Church, Boston. Boston: Crocker & Brewster, 1846.

Catalogue of the library of the late Dr. Joseph Priestley . . ., for
sale by Thomas Dobson. Philadelphia: n.p., 1834.

Catalogue of the . . . Valuable Library of the late William Priestman,
Esq. Philadelphia: n.p., 1831.

A Catalogue of the Washington Collection in the Boston Athenaeum. Boston: n.p., 1897.

The Charter and Bye-Laws, of the New-York Society Library; with a catalogue of the Books belonging to the Library. New York; n.p., 1773.

[Churchill, Awnsham (comp.).] A Collection of Voyages and Travels,
some Now first Printed from Original Manuscripts, others Now First
Published in English. In Six Volumes. With a General Preface,
giving an Account of the Progress of Navigation, from its first Beginning. Vol. III; London: Printed, by Assignment from Mess^r
Churchill, For John Watthol, over-against the Royal-Exchange in

Cornhill; Thomas Wotton, at the Queen's-Head and Three Daggers o-
ver-against St. Dunstan's-Church, in Fleet-Street; Samuel Birt, in
Ave-Mary-Lane, Ludgate-Street; Daniel Browne, at the Black-Swan,
without Temple Bar; Thomas Osborn, in Gray's Inn; John Shuckburgh,
at the Sun, next the Inner-Temple Gate, in Fleet-Street; and Henry Lintol, at the Cross-Keys, against St. Dunstan's-Church, in
Fleet-Street, 1732.

Clarke, John. An Essay upon the EDUCATION of YOUTH in GRAMMAR-SCHOOLS.
In which the Vulgar Method of Teaching is examined, and a New one
proposed, for the more Easy and Speedy Training up of Youth to the
Knowledge of the Learned Languages; together with History, Chrono-
logy, etc. 2nd ed. with very LARGE ADDITIONS; London: Printed for
ARTHUR BETTESWORTH, at the Red Lion, in Pater-Noster-Row, 1730.

The Constitution of the Hartford Library Company; Extracts from the By-
Laws, and a Catalogue of the Books. Hartford, Conn.: Hudson &
Goodwin, 1797.

Cooke, Jacob E. (ed.). The Federalist. Cleveland: Meridian paperbacks,
1961.

Corner, George W., (ed.). The Autobiography of Benjamin Rush; His
"Travels Through Life" together with his Commonplace Book for 1789-
1813. Princeton: Published for the American Philosophical Society
by Princeton University Press, 1948.

Cushing, H.A., (ed.). The Writings of Samuel Adams. 4 vols.; New York:
n.p., 1904-1908.

de Crousaz, Jean Pierre. New MAXIMS concerning the EDUCATION of YOUTH
and a DISCOURSE concerning PEDANTRY. Both translated from French
into English By the Reverend Mr. GEORGE STEPHEN TACHERON. London:
Printed for the TRANSLATOR, and sold by T. COOPER, at the Globe in
Pater-Noster-Row; M. CHASTEL, at the Golden Bull, Compton-street,
Soho; and by the Booksellers of London and Westminster, 1740.

Dexter, Franklin Bowditch (ed.), Extracts from the Itineraries and Other
Miscellanies of Ezra Stiles, D.D., LL.D. 1755-1794 With a Selection from his Correspondence, New Haven: Yale University Press,
1916.

[Dickinson, John]. A New Essay [By the Pennsylvania Farmer] On the Constitutional Power of Great Britain over the Colonies in America;
with the Resolves of the Committee from the Provinces of Pennsylvania and Their Instructions in Assembly. Philadelphia: n.p.,1774.

Disney, John. The Works Theological, Medical, Political, and Miscellaneous of John Jebb, M.D. F.R.S. with Memoirs of the Life of the Author. 3 vols.; London: n.p., 1787.

Farrand, Max. The Records of the Federal Convention. 3 vols.; New Haven: n.p., 1911.

Fielding, Henry. Amelia. Vol. II.; n.p.: Frank Cass & Co. LTD, 1967.

Franklin, Benjamin. The Papers of Benjamin Franklin. Edited by Leonard
W. Labaree. 19 vols. to date. New Haven: Yale University Press, 1959-.
_____. The Works of Benjamin Franklin in Twelve Volumes. Edited by
John Bigelow. New York: G.P. Putnam's Sons, 1904.
_____. The Writings of Benjamin Franklin. Edited by Albert Henry
Smyth. 10 vols.; New York: Macmillan Co., 1905-1907.

Grattan, Henry. Speeches of the Right Honourable Henry Grattan in the
Irish and In the Imperial Parliament. Edited by his son. Vol. I;
London: n.p., 1822.

145

Hales, Stephen. A NEW-YEARS-GIFT TO DRAM-DRINKERS, BEING An EARNEST AD-
     DRESS to THEM; Reprinted out of his 2d Volume on VENTILLATORS. To
     which is Prefixed an EPISTLE to THEM, By WILLIAM HENRY, D.D. F.R.S.
     Dean of Killaloe and Chaplain to his EXCELLENCY GEORGE, EARL OF
     HALIFAX LORD Lieutenant of Ireland. Dublin: Printed for SAMUEL
     PRICE Bookseller in Dame-Street, 1762.
Howe, P.P. (ed.). The Complete Works of William Hazlitt. I. London: J.
     M. Dent and Sons, LTD, [1930].
Jefferson, Thomas. The Writings of Thomas Jefferson. Edited by Andrew
     Lipscomb. 20 vols. in 10; Washington, D.C.: Thomas Jefferson Me-
     morial Association of U.S., 1905.
[Junius]. The Letters of the Celebrated Junius. 2 vols.; London: n.p.,
     1783.
Kippis, Andrew, et al. Biographia Britannica or The Lives of the Most
     Eminent Persons who have flourished in Great Britain and Ireland
     From the Earliest Ages to the Present Times: Collected from the
     Best Authorities, Printed and Manuscript, and Digested in the Man-
     ner of Mr. Bayle's Historical and Critical Dictionary. Vol. III;
     London: John Rivington, 1784.
Leland, John. A View of the Principal Deistical Writers That Have Ap-
     peared in England In The Last And Present Century: With Observa-
     tions Upon Them, And some Account of The Answers That Have Been
     Published Against Them. In Several Letters To A Friend. 2 vols.;
     London: Longman, Hurst, Rees and Orme, Thomas Turnball, Printer,
     Edinburgh, 1807.
"Letters to Josiah Quincy, Jr.," Proceedings of the Massachusetts His-
     torical Society, L, 3rd series (1916-1917), 472-496.
Lofft, Capel. Letters addressed to the Society for Constitutional In-
     formation. [London:] Printed and Distributed Gratis By The Society
     For Constitutional Information, 1782.
Longley, John. An ESSAY Toward Forming a More Complete Representation
     of the COMMONS of GREAT BRITAIN. (London: J. Johnson, 1795).
Macaulay, Catharine. An ADDRESS to the PEOPLE of England, Scotland, and
     Ireland, on the present Important Crisis of AFFAIRS. 2nd ed; Lon-
     don: Printed for Edward and Charles Dilly, 1775.
_____. Letters on Education (London: C. Dilly, 1790).
MacCoby, S. (ed.). The English Radical Tradition, 1763-1914. New York:
     New York University Press, 1957.
McCloskey, Robert Green (ed.). The Works of James Wilson. 2 vols.;
     Cambridge, Mass.: The Belknap Press of Harvard University, 1967.
Nichols, John. Illustrations of the Literary History of the Eighteenth
     Century Consisting of Authentic Memoirs and Original Letters of Em-
     inent Persons; and intended as a sequel to The Literary Anecdotes.
     Vol. VI; London: Printed by and for J.B. Nichols and Son, 25, Par-
     liament-Street, Westminster, 1831.
_____. Literary Anecdotes of the Eighteenth Century comprising Bi-
     ographical Memoirs of William Bowyer, Printer and many of his
     learned friends; An Incidental View of the Progress and Advance-
     ment of Literature in This Kingdom During the Last Century; and Bio-
     graphical Anecdotes of a Considerable Number of Eminent Writers and
     Ingenious Artists; with a very Copious Index. Vol. II; Red-Lion-
     Passage, Fleet-Street, 1812.
[O'Connor, Arthur]. The Measures of Ministry to Prevent a Revolution,

Are the Certain Means of Bringing It On. 3rd ed.; London: Printed
    for D.I. Eaton, at the Cock and Swine, No.74, Newgate Street,1794.
Price, Richard. ["Correspondence"]. Proceedings of the Massachusetts
    Historical Society, L, 3rd Series (1916-1917), 472-496.
_____. Nadere Aanmerkingen Over Den Aart en De Waarde Der Burger-
    lyke Vryheid en eener Vrye Regeering benevens. Trans. by Johan
    Derk van der Capellen. Leyden: L. Herdingh, 1777.
_____. Observations on the Importance of the American Revolution
    and The Means of making it a Benefit to the World. London: n.p.,
    1784.
_____. Observations on the Nature of Civil Liberty, The Princi-
    ples of Government, and the Justice and Policy of the War with A-
    merica. 8th ed.; London: Printed for T. Cadell, in the Strand,1778.
Priestley, Joseph. MISCELLANEOUS OBSERVATIONS RELATING TO EDUCATION.
    more especially, as it respects the CONDUCT of the MIND. To which
    is added, An Essay on a course of Liberal Education for Civil and
    Active Life. Cork: Printed by T. White, No.55, opposite the West
    Gate of the Exchange, 1780.
[Quincy, Josiah, Jun.] "Journal of Josiah Quincy, Jun., During His Voy-
    age and Residence in England from September 28th, 1774, to March
    3rd, 1775," Proceedings of the Massachusetts Historical Society,
    L, 3rd series (1916-1917), 433-471.
Rutt, John T. (ed.). The Theological and Miscellaneous Works of Joseph
    Priestley, LL.D. F.R.S. etc. in 25 vols. Printed by G. Smallfield,
    Hackney, [1832].
Sheridan, Thomas. A PLAN of EDUCATION for the Young Nobility and Gentry
    of GREAT BRITAIN. Most humbly addressed to The Father of His People.
    London: Printed for E. and C. Dilly, in the Poultry, 1769.
A SOLEMN APPEAL to the GOOD SENSE OF THE NATION: Pointing OUT The Immedi-
    ate Necessity OF A CORDIAL COALITION Between The KING AND THE PEO-
    PLE (London: W. Flexner, 1783).
Sprigge, Timothy L.S. & Christie, Ian, (eds.). The Correspondence of
    Jeremy Bentham. Vol. I. London: The Athlone Press, 1968.
Stephens, Alexander. Memoirs of John Horne Tooke. 2 vols.; New York:
    1968; originally published London: 1813.
Towers, Joseph. TRACTS on POLITICAL and OTHER SUBJECTS. 3 vols.; Lon-
    don: W. Davies and T. Cadell, et al, 1796.
[Tucker, Josiah]. A Series of Answers to certain Popular Objections, A-
    gainst Separating from the Rebellious Colonies and Discarding Them
    Entirely: being the Concluding Tract of the Dean of Gloucester on
    the Subject of American Affairs. Gloucester: R. Raikes, 1776.
Van der Weyde, William M. (ed.). The Life and Works of Thomas Paine, 10
    vols.; New Rochelle, New York: Thomas Paine National Historical As-
    sociation, 1925.
Warren-Adams Letters, 2 vols.; Boston: 1917, 1925.
Webster, Noah, jun. Esq. An American Selection of Lessons in Reading
    and Speaking, Calculated to improve the Minds and refine the Taste
    of Youth . . . .. To which is prefixed, Rules in Elocution, and Di-
    rections for expressing the principal Passions of the Mind. 3rd ed.;
    Philadelphia: Young and M'Culloch, 1787.
[Wilkes, John]. The Speeches of Mr. Wilkes in the House of Commons n.p.:
    1786.
The Works of Augustus Toplady, A.B. New Edition, With an Enlarged Mem-

oir of the Author. Vol. VI. London: Printed for William Baynes
and Son, Paternoster Row; and H.S. Baynes, Edinburgh, 1825.
Wyvill, Christopher. (ed.). POLITICAL PAPERS, chiefly respecting the
attempt of the County of York, and other Considerable Districts,
Commenced in 1779, and Continued During Several Subsequent Years,
to Effect a Reformation of the Parliament of Great-Britain. 4 vols;
York: Printed by W. Blanchard: Sold by J. Johnson, St. Paul's
Church-Yard, London, and J. Todd, York, 1794-1802.

Printed Primary Sources: Newspapers and Periodicals

(British)

The Bath Chronicle
The Critical Review
The Daily Advertiser
The Gazetteer and New Daily Advertiser
General Evening Post
Gentleman's Magazine
The London Chronicle
London Evening-Post
The London Magazine
The Monthly Review
The Morning Chronicle, and London Advertiser
The Public Advertiser
The St. James's Chronicle; or British Evening-Post
The Scots Magazine
The Whitehall Evening-Post; or, London Intelligencer

(American)

The Boston-Gazette and Country Journal
The Brunswick Gazette and Weekly Monitor (New-Brunswick, New Jersey)
The Connecticut Courant, and Hartford Weekly Intelligencer
The Connecticut Courant, and Weekly Intelligencer (Hartford)
The Connecticut Journal (New Haven)
The Georgia State Gazette or Independent Register (Augusta)
The Independent Chronicle and the Universal Advertiser (Boston, Mass.)
The Kentucky Gazette (Lexington)
The Maryland Gazette; or, the Baltimore Advertiser
The Maryland Journal and the Baltimore Advertiser
The Massachusetts Gazette or the Springfield and Northampton Weekly Ad-
vertiser.
The New-Hampshire Spy (Portsmouth)
The Newport Herald (Rhode Island)
The Newport Mercury (Rhode Island)
The New-York Gazette; and the Weekly Mercury
The New York Gazetteer (New York)
The New-York Journal, and Daily Patriotic Register
The New-York Journal, and Weekly Register
New-York Journal; or, The General Advertiser
The Norfolk and Portsmouth Journal (Virginia)
The North-Carolina Gazette (Newbern)
The Pennsylvania Gazette (Philadelphia)

The Pennsylvania Packet, and Daily Advertiser (Philadelphia)
The Pennsylvania Packet or The General Advertiser (Philadelphia)
The Providence Gazette and Country Journal (Rhode Island)
The South Carolina Gazette (Charlestown)
The Virginia Gazette
The Virginia Independent Chronicle (Richmond)
Virginia Journal, and Alexandria Advertiser

SECONDARY SOURCES

Books:

Adams, Randolph G. Political Ideas of the American Revolution; Britan-
    nic-American Contributions to the Problem of Imperial Organization,
    1765-1775. 3rd ed.; New York: Barnes & Noble, 1958.
Aiken, John, et al. General Biography of Lives. Vol. II; London: J.
    Johnson . . ., 1801.
Ashton, T.S. Economic Fluctuations in England, 1700-1800. Oxford:
    Clarendon Press, 1959.
_____. An Economic History of England: The 18th Century.   1st
    rev. ed.; London: Methuen & Co. LTD, 1966.
Bailyn, Bernard. The Ideological Origins of the American Revolution.
    Cambridge: The Belknap Press of Harvard University Press, 1965.
Barnard, H.C. A History of English Education from 1760. 2nd ed.; Lon-
    don: University of London, 1961.
Black, Eugene Charlton. The Association: British Extra-parliamentary
    Political Organization, 1769-1793. Cambridge: Harvard University
    Press, 1963.
Bonwick, Colin. English Radicals and the American Revolution. Chapel
    Hill: The University of North Carolina Press, 1977.
Brauer, George C., Jr. The Education of a Gentleman: Theories of Gen-
    tlemanly Education in England, 1660-1775. New York: Bookman Asso-
    ciates, 1959.
Brewer, John. Party Ideology and Popular Politics at the Accession of
    George III. Cambridge: Cambridge University Press, 1976.
Bristol, Roger Pattrell (comp.). The American Bibliography of Charles
    Evans. Vol. XIV; reprinted Glouster, Mass.: Peter Smith, 1967 [or-
    iginally published Glouster, Mass.: American Antiquarian Society,
    1959].
British Museum Catalogue of Printed Books. Vol. XXX; London: Published
    by the Trustees of the British Museum, 1965.
Butterfield, Herbert. George III, Lord North and the People, 1779-1780.
    London: G. Bell and Sons, LTD, 1949.
Catalogue General Des Livres Imprimes De La Bibliotheque Nationale. Vol.
    XXI; Paris: Imprimerie Nationale, 1905.
Chalmers, Alexander. The General Biographical Dictionary. Vol. VII;
    new ed.; London: J. Nichols and Son, 1813.
Christie, Ian R. Wilkes, Wyvill and Reform: The Parliamentary Reform
    Movement in British Politics, 1760-1785. London: Macmillan & Co.,
    1962.
Clarke, D.M. British Opinion and the American Revolution. Cambridge:
    n.p., 1930.

149

Clayden, Peter William. The Early Life of Samuel Rogers. Boston: Robert Brothers, 1888.

_____. Samuel Sharpe, Egyptologist and Translator of the Bible. London: Kegan Paul, Trench & Co.; Paternoster Square, 1883.

Colbourn, H. Trevor. The Lamp of Experience: Whig History and the Intellectual Origins of the American Revolution. Chapel Hill: University of North Carolina Press, 1965.

Cone, Carl. The English Jacobins; Reformers in Late 18th Century England. New York: Charles Scribner's Sons, 1968.

_____. Torchbearer of Freedom: The Influence of Richard Price on Eighteenth Century Thought. Lexington: University of Kentucky Press, 1952.

Crane, Verner W. (ed.). Benjamin Franklin's Letters to the Press, 1758-1775. Chapel Hill: University of North Carolina Press, 1950.

Cromwell, Thomas Kitson. Walks Through Islington. London: Printed for Sherwood, Gilbert, Piper, Paternoster Row, 1835.

Fischer, David Hackett. The Revolution of American Conservatism; The Federalist Party in the Era of Jeffersonian Democracy. New York: Harper & Row, 1965.

Flexner, Eleanor. Mary Wollstonecraft. New York: Penguin Books, 1972.

Gay, Peter (ed.). Deism, An Anthology. Princeton: D. Van Nostrand Co., Inc., 1968.

George, M. Dorothy. London Life in the Eighteenth Century. New York: Harper Torchbooks, 1965 [originally published London: Kegan Paul, Trench & Co. LTD, 1925].

Gilbert, Felix. To the Farewell Address: Ideas of Early American Foreign Policy. Princeton: Princeton University Press, 1961.

Godwin, William. Memoirs of Mary Wollstonecraft. New York: Haskell House Publishers LTD, 1969.

Guttridge, G.H. English Whiggism and the American Revolution. Berkeley: n.p., 1942.

Harrison, Wilfred. Conflicts and Compromise; History of British Political Thought, 1593-1900. London: Collier-Macmillan Limited, 1965.

Jacobson, David L. (ed.). The English Libertarian Heritage, from the Writings of John Trenchard and Thomas Gordon in The Independent Whig and Cato's Letters. New York: The Bobbs-Merrill Co., Inc., 1965.

Keep, Austin Baxter. History of the New York Society Library. n.p.: Printed for the Trustees by the De Vinne Press, 1908.

Kramnick, Isaac. Bolingbroke and His Circle; The Politics of Nostalgia in the Age of Walpole. Cambridge: Harvard University Press, 1968.

Lee, Richard Henry. Life of Arthur Lee 2 vols.; Boston: 1829.

Lewis, Samuel. The History and Topography of the Parish of Saint Mary, Islington in the County of Middlesex. London: Printed for the Author by Gilbert & Rivington; Published by J.H. Jackson, 1842.

Lincoln, Anthony. Some Political and Social Ideas of English Dissent, 1763-1800. Cambridge: University Press, 1938.

Lynd, Staughton. Intellectual Origins of American Radicalism. New York: Vintage Books, 1969 [originally published Random House, 1968].

MacCoby, S. English Radicalism, 1762-1785. London: George Allen & Unwin, 1955.

McLachlan, Herbert. English Education under the Test Acts: Being the History of the Nonconformist Academies, 1662-1820. Manchester:

Manchester University Press, 1931.

Maier, Pauline. From Resistance to Revolution: Colonial Radicals and the Development of American Opposition to Britain, 1765-1776. New York: Alfred A. Knopf, 1972.

Main, Jackson Turner. The Antifederalists; Critics of the Constitution, 1781-1788. Chapel Hill: Printed for the Institute of Early American History and Culture at Williamsburg, Virginia by the University of North Carolina Press, 1961.

Marshall, Dorothy. English People in the Eighteenth Century. London: Longmans, Green, and Co., 1956.

Mason, Alpheus Thomas. The States Rights Debate: Anti-federalism and the Constitution. Englewood Cliffs, New Jersey: Prentice-Hall, Inc., 1964.

Mitton, Geraldine. Hackney and Stoke Newington. "The Fascination of London Series"; London: Adam and Charles Black, 1908.

Morgan, Edmund S. American Freedom, American Slavery New York: W.W. Norton & Co., 1975.

Morgan, William. Memoirs of the Life of the Reverend Richard Price. London: Printed for R. Hunter, Successor to J. Johnson, No. 72, St. Paul's Churchyard; and R. Rees, No. 62, Pall Mall, 1815.

Namier, Lewis. The Structure of Politics at the Accession of George III 2nd ed.; New York: St. Martins, 1957.

Nangle, Benjamin Christie. The Monthly Review First Series 1749-1789; Indexes of Contributors and Articles. Oxford: Clarendon Press, 1934.

Nelson, John. The History and Antiquities of the parish of ISLINGTON, in the county of Middlesex; including Biographical Sketches of the most Eminent and Remarkable Inhabitants with Some Account of Several Objects of Interest in the Adjoining Parishes. 2nd ed.; London: Printed for and Sold by the Author, Middle Row Place, Holborn; K.J. Ford, Bookseller, 117 Upper Street, Islington; Rodwell and Martin, New Bond Street; and John Major, Fleet Street, 1823.

Norris, John. Shelburne and Reform. London: Macmillan & Co., 1963.

Olson, Alison Gilbert. The Radical Duke. London: Oxford University Press, 1961.

Osborne, John. John Cartwright. Cambridge, Eng.: At the University Press, 1972.

Palmer, Robert R. The Age of the Democratic Revolution. A Political History of Europe and America, 1760-1800. Vol. I. The Challenge. Princeton: Princeton University Press, 1959.

Patton, Lewis and Mann, Peter (eds.). The Collected Works of Samuel Taylor Coleridge. Vol. I. Lectures 1795 on Politics and Religion. "Bollinger Series"; London and Princeton: Routledge & Kegan Paul, Princeton University Press, 1971.

Pole, J.R. Political Representation in England and the Origins of the American Republic. New York: St. Martins, 1966.

Pottle, Frederick A. James Boswell: The Earlier Years, 1740-1769. New York: McGraw-Hill Book Company, 1966.

Randall, Henry Stephen. The Life of Thomas Jefferson. 3 vols.; New York: Derby & Johnson, 1858.

Robb, Mary Margaret. Oral Interpretation of Literature in American Colleges and Universities; A Historical Study of Teaching Methods. New York: The H.W. Wilson Company, 1941

Robbins, Caroline. The Eighteenth-Century Commonwealthman: Studies in the Transmission, Development and Circumstances of English Liberal Thought from the Restoration of Charles II until the War with the Thirteen Colonies. New York: Atheneum, 1968 [originally published Cambridge: Harvard University Press, 1959].

Robinson, William. The History and Antiquities of the Parish of Stoke Newington in the County of Middlesex . . . . London: John Bowyer Nichols and Son, 25 Parliament Street, 1842.

Rutt, John T. The Life and Correspondence of Joseph Priestley, LL.D., F.R.S., etc. 2 vols.; London: R. Hunter, 72 St. Paul's Churchyard; M. Eaton, 187, High-Holborn; C. Fox, 67, Paternoster Row, 1831-1832.

Shaw, Ralph R. and Shoemaker, Richard H. American Bibliography, a Preliminary Checklist, 1801-1819. 22 vols.; New York: The Scarecrow Press, Inc., 1958-1966.

Smith, J.E.A. The History of Pittsfield, (Berkshire County,) Massachusetts, From the Year 1734 to the Year 1800. Boston: Published by Lee & Shepard, 149 Washington Street, 1869.

Smith, J.W. Ashley, The Birth of Modern Education; The Contribution of the Dissenting Academies, 1660-1800. London: Independent Press, LTD, 1954.

Stephen, Sir Leslie (ed.). The Dictionary of National Biography. Vol. III. London: Oxford University Press, 1921-1922 [originally published 1885-1890].

Stone, Lawrence. The Family, Sex and Marriage In England 1500-1800. New York: Harper & Row, 1977.

Thomas. Roland. Richard Price: Philosopher and Apostle of Liberty. London: Oxford University Press by Humphrey Milford, 1924.

Timbs, John. Clubs and Club Life in London, with Anecdotes of Its Famous Coffee Houses, Hostelries, and Taverns, from the Seventeenth Century to the Present. London: John Camden Holten, 1872.

Turberville, A.S. (ed.). Johnson's England: An Account of the Life and Manners of his Age. 2 vols.; Oxford: Clarendon Press, 1933.

Tyler, M.C. The Literary History of the American Revolution. 2 vols.; New York: n.p., 1897.

Van Doren, Carl. Benjamin Franklin. New York: Viking Press Compass Books edition, 1964 [originally published 1938].

Wallace, Karl R. (ed.). History of Speech Education in America; Background Studies. New York: Appleton-Century-Crofts, Inc., 1954.

Waring, E. Graham (ed.). Deism and Natural Religion, A Source Book. New York: Frederick Ungar Publishing Co., 1967.

Watson, J. Stephen. The Reign of George III, 1760-1815. "Oxford History of England Series"; Oxford: Clarendon Press, 1960.

Williams, Basil. The Whig Supremacy, 1714-1760. 2nd rev. ed. by C.H. Stuart; "Oxford History of England Series"; Oxford: Clarendon Press, 1962.

Wood, Gordon S. The Creation of the American Republic, 1776-1787. Chapel Hill: University of North Carolina Press, 1969.

Articles:

Adair, Douglas. "The Authorship of the Disputed Federalist Papers," William and Mary Quarterly, I; Part I (April, 1944), 97-122; Part II

(July, 1944), 235-264.

_____. "The New Thomas Jefferson," <u>William and Mary Quarterly</u>, III (January, 1946), 123-133.

Colbourn, H. Trevor. "John Dickinson, Historical Revolutionary," <u>Pennsylvania Magazine of History and Biography</u>, LXXXIII (July, 1959), 271-292.

_____. "Thomas Jefferson's Use of the Past," <u>William and Mary Quarterly</u>, XV (January, 1958), 56-70.

Crane, Verner. "The Club of Honest Whigs: Friends of Science and Liberty," <u>William and Mary Quarterly</u>, XXIII (April, 1966), 210-233.

Fritz, Charles Andrew. "From Sheridan to Rush: The Beginnings of English Elocution," <u>The Quarterly Journal of Speech</u>, XVI (February, 1930), 75-88.

Gilbert, Felix. "The English Background of American Isolationism in the Eighteenth Century," <u>William and Mary Quarterly</u>, I (April, 1944), 138-160.

Guthrie, Warren. "The Development of Rhetorical Theory in America, 1635-1850--V: The Elocution Movement--England," <u>Speech Monographs</u>, XVIII, no. 1 (March, 1951), 17-30.

Handlin, Oscar and Mary. "James Burgh and American Revolutionary Theory," <u>Proceedings of the Massachusetts Historical Society</u>, LXXIII (January-December, 1961), 38-57.

Hargis, Donald. "James Burgh and the Art of Speaking," <u>Speech Monographs</u>, XXIV, no. 4 (November, 1957), 275-284.

Hay, Carla H. "Benjamin Franklin, James Burgh, and the Authorship of 'The Colonist's Advocate' Letters," <u>William and Mary Quarterly</u>, XXXII, (January, 1975), 111-124.

_____. "The Making of a Radical: The Case of James Burgh," <u>Journal of British Studies</u>, XVIII, (Spring, 1979).

Lakken, Roy N. "The Concept of Democracy in Colonial Political Thought," <u>William and Mary Quarterly</u>, XVI (October, 1959), 568-580.

Lamberton, E.V. "Colonial Libraries of Pennsylvania," <u>Pennsylvania Magazine of History and Biography</u>, XLII (July, 1918), 193-234.

Laprade, W.T. Review of <u>George III, Lord North and the People</u> by Herbert Butterfield, <u>American Historical Review</u>, LVI (January, 1951), 341.

Parrish, W.M. "The Burglarizing of Burgh, or The Case of the Purloined Passions," <u>The Quarterly Journal of Speech</u>, XXXVIII (December, 1952), 431-434.

Robbins, Caroline. "'When It is that Colonies May Turn Independent:' An Analysis of the Environment and Politics of Francis Hutcheson (1694-1746)," <u>William and Mary Quarterly</u>, XI (April, 1954), 214-251.

Wolf, Edwin. "Franklin and His Friends Chose Their Books," <u>Pennsylvania Magazine of History and Biography</u>, LXXX, no. 1 (January, 1956), 11-36.

INDEX

academies, 20, 57, 114 n.47;
  curriculum, 58-64
Act of Uniformity (1662), 57
Act of Union (1707), 11
Acton, John Dalberg Acton, 1st
  baron, 81
Adams, John, 42, 43, 44, 125
  n.76; Defense of the Constitution, 44; "Novanglus," 42
Addison, Joseph, 30
"affective individualism," 4
agrarian reform, 71, 133 n.26
agriculture, 28, 33
America, 3, 31, 37, 40-44, 85,
  86-89, 95, 98, 99, 102, 105;
  American Congress, 43; American Revolution, 3, 4, 28, 30,
  41, 43, 80, 99, 101, 103;
  Constitutional Convention of
  1787, 43
Amory, Dr. Thomas, 29
amusements, 21, 64, 65, 69;
  dancing, 62, 69; gambling,
  69; masquerades, 67, 69, 75,
  132 n.12; theatre, 18, 69
ancient constitution, 90-93,
  96, 103, 105
annual parliaments, 3, 37, 83,
  91-92, 97, 106, 137 n.58
antifederalists, 43, 105
arbitration, 70
Arianism, 17, 52-53
aristocracy, 23, 24, 37, 38,
  74-75, 79, 80, 82-83, 84, 93,
  98, 103, 104, 105
aristocratic resurgence, 83
Aristotle, 16
army, 43, 85, 98
association, 38, 40, 55, 72,
  74, 86, 96-100, 104, 105, 106,
  139 n.80,87; Grand Association of 1753-54, 23-24, 74,
  78

Athanasian creed, see trinitar-
  ianism
Augusta, Princess Dowager of
  Wales, 21, 22, 23, 25
Austin, Gilbert, 31

Bailyn, Bernard, 43
Baldwin, R., 116 n.73
Baron, Richard, 137 n. 53
Bath, William Pulteney, 1st
  earl of, 135 n. 21
Beccaria, Cesare, 73
Bentham, Jeremy, 39
Bigelow, Abijah, 44
Bolingbroke, Henry St. John,
  1st viscount, 16, 23, 32, 78,
  103
Bonwick, Colin, 87, 105, 117
  n.2, 121 n.43
Boston Gazette, 42
Boston Massacre, 85
Boston Tea Party, 38, 89
Boswell, James, 11, 12, 13, 21,
  29, 35, 39, 120 n.37; Account
  of Corsica, 35
Bowyer, William, 13
Brand, Thomas, 137 n.53
Brethren of the laudable asso-
  ciation of Antigallicans,
  139 n. 78
Brewer, John, 95, 104, 112
  n.25, 117 n.2, 123 n.59
bribery, 77, 84, 92, 95
Bristol Library, 39
Buchanan, George, 41
Bunhill Fields, 44
Burgh, Andrew, 9, 10, 18, 50-
  51, 58, 102, 108 n.1, 109
  n.2, n.5
Burgh, Hannah Harding, 18-19,
  32, 44, 112 n.22, 113 n.43,
  114 n.44, 131 n.44

INDEX

Christ, Jesus, 50, 52-54
Christianity, 20, 34, 49-52, 54, 62
Church of England, 12, 29, 51
Church of Scotland, 9, 10, 49, 51
Cicero, 16
Cinque Ports, 94, 95
civil list, 84
Clarendon, George Villiers, 4th earl of, 125 n.76
Clarke, John, 129 n.15
Clarke, Samuel, 52, 62
clergy, 31, 34, 51
Coleridge, Samuel Taylor, 41; The Plot Discovered, 41
Collings, J., 29
Collinson, Peter, 29
commerce, 10-11, 27, 28, 58, 70, 86, 88, 93
Commons, House of, 3, 14, 36, 40, 42, 82, 83, 92
Commonwealthmen, 3, 4, 33, 41, 43, 49, 63-64, 71, 77-78, 80, 85, 91, 95, 99, 103,104, 106, 121 n.43
Condorcet, Marie De Caritat,103
Congregational Fund Board, 57
conspiracy, 42
constitution, British, 36, 41, 42, 43, 81-82, 86, 90-91, 93, 105, 135 n.22, 137 n.54
contract theory, 78, 82, 98
conversation, 4, 29-30
corn laws, 93
Cornwall, 95
corporal punishment, 61
correspondence, 4
corruption, 27, 28, 67, 77; political corruption, 83-85, 92
court, 36-37, 43, 64, 84, 85, 86
Coward Trust, 57
criticism of government, 23, 29, 35, 36, 37, 79
Cromwell, Oliver, 85, 92
de Crousaz, Jean Pierre, 129 n.11

crown, 43
Cunningham, Rev. Peter, 39

Davenant, Charles, 16, 85
Deane, Silas, 42
deism, 53, 65, 97, 127 n.13
Demosthenes, 62
Densham, James, 29
Devonshire, 95
Dickinson, John, 42, 125 n.72
Dilly, Charles, 35, 41
Dilly, Edward, 41, 42, 123 n.56
Dissent and Dissenters, 12, 15, 17, 33, 44, 50, 51, 57-58, 113 n.43, 114 n.47, 128 n.4
Divine Providence, 14
drunkennes, 68
Dunn, John, 21
Dutch, 84

East India Company, 38, 70, 86
Eaton, Daniel Isaac, 41, 100; Political Classics, 41
economical reform, 92
education, 3, 4, 29, 55, 57-66, 67, 102; in England, 59
egalitarianism, 70
eighteenth century, 4, 49, 57, 58, 68, 83, 93, 101-103
election bonds, 91
elocution, 4, 30-31, 63
empire, British, 13, 27, 28, 33, 35, 38, 44, 80, 89, 105
enclosure, 33, 71
Enfield, 16
England, 3, 11, 12, 14-15, 28, 104, 105, 133 n.26
English Civil War, 104
English radicals and English radicalism, 3, 36, 38, 40,41, 78, 90, 95, 103, 104, 105
Enlightenment, 102
established churches, 51
evil, 34, 53-54, 55, 128 n.18

faction and factionalism, 27, 28, 78, 79, 80, 104; see also opposition, party
"favourite," 135 n.22

INDEX

Jefferson, Thomas, 42, 43, 49,
125-126 n.80; Additional Mem-
orandun for the Convention of
Virignia, 43
Jeffries, Dr. Joseph, 29
Jews, 51, 70
John I, 96
Johnson, Samuel, 11
"Junius," 37, 99
"Junius Americanus,"37
junto, 79, 80, 82, 135 n.22

Kenross, Mr._____, 16, 17
Kentucky, 39, 105
The Kentucky Gazette, 43
king, see monarchy
King's Friends, 111 n.13
Kippis, Andrew, 4, 14, 19, 25,
29, 54, 110 n.6, 112 n.22,
115 n.52, 122 n.48
Kramnick, Isaac, 103

laissez-faire, 72
Lee, Arthur, 41
legal reform, 4, 72-73, 103
Leicester House, 78
Leland, John, 24
liberty, 28, 35, 63, 77, 80-81,
83, 86, 88, 90
liberties, 28, 36, 43, 51, 86,
91, 105
Library Company of Philadel-
phia, 116 n.76, 123 n.58
Licensing Act, 69
licentiousness, 81
Lindsey, Theophilus, 53, 110
n.8
literary piracy, 24-25
Locke, John, 4, 16, 41, 43, 52,
54, 62, 64, 78, 80, 90, 103,
128 n.5, 129 n.11, n.15
Lofft, Capel, 40
London and Londoners, 9, 11-13,
17, 29, 68, 95, 98
London Chronicle, 35
London Evening-Post, 53
Lords, House of, 82
Ludlow, Edmund, 3
Luttrell, Colonel Henry Lawes,
36

luxury, 13, 27, 67, 68, 69, 70,
132 n.7, n.9
Lyttelton, George, 22

Macaulay, Catharine, 16, 35,36,
38, 40, 41, 44, 65, 102, 103,
104, 105, 111 n.13, 121 n.38,
125 n. 72, n.76, 128 n.18,
137 n.53
Madderty, Scotland, 9, 13, 18
Madison, James, 43; The Federalist, 43
Magna Carta, 96
majority rule, 82, 90, 98
manufactures, see commerce
Mar, John Erskine, 6th or 11th
earl of, 9
marriage, 10, 18-19, 73, 131 n.
43
Marriage Act (1753), 73
Marvell, Andrew, 3
Massacre of St. George's Field,
85
Maty, Matthew, 29
mechanization, 70
merchants, 68, 70, 93
Middlesex, 16, 95
Middlesex election, 36, 80, 105
Mildmay, Carew, 114 n.52
militia, 86, 136 n.37
Milton, John, 3, 41, 60
ministers and ministry, 28, 32,
37, 38, 42, 79, 80, 82, 83,
84, 85-86, 88
miracles, 53
"mixed" government, 32, 33, 78,
81-82, 83, 104, 137 n.54
monarachy, 32, 38, 79, 82
monopolies and monopolists, 34,
70-71
Monroe, James, 43
Montesquieu, 41, 43
The Monthly Review, 24, 25, 31,
34, 35
Moore, Bernard, 43
More, Thomas, 41
Morgan, William, 41
Morris, Robert, 42
Morton, Charles, 20

national debt, 85
Navigation Acts, 89
navy, 85-86
Nedham, Marchmont, 3
Neville, Henry, 3
Neville, Sylas, 137 n.53
Newcastle, Thomas Pelham-Holles,
1st duke of, 32, 135 n.21
Newington Green, 17, 21, 27, 32,
52, 58, 78, 114 n.52
Newton, Isaac, 52, 131 n.36
Newtonian physics, 22, 59, 102
Nichols, 4, 111 n.20, 117 n.80,
122 n.51
noblesse oblige, 73, 92
non-conformist, see Dissenter
North Briton, 35
North, Frederick Lord, 38

occasional conformity, 12
oligarchy, 9, 98, 135 n.21
Onslow, Arthur, 14, 111 n.20
opposition, 23, 80
Osborne, John, 70, 124 n.66

Paine, Thomas, 40, 41, 43; Common Sense, 39, 40, 44
Palmer, William, 21
parliament, 29, 36-38, 82, 87-
88, 90-91, 95-96, 104; parliamentary elections, 35, 39, 43,
83-84; parliamentary reform,
35, 37, 38, 40, 90-95, 102,
103, 105; parliamentary representation, 37, 40-42, 83,
89, 91, 93, 97, 103,104, 106;
parliamentary representatives,
93, and their relationship to
their constituents, 91; parliamentary tyranny, 87; reapportionment of parliamentary seats, 3, 95; see also
annual parliaments, franchise
Parr, Rev. Samuel, 39
Parsons, James, 29
party, 3, 28, 29, 79, 80, 97,
100; see also faction
passions, 55
"patriot king," 27, 32, 78, 79,
80, 96, 103-104
patriots and patriotism, 27, 38,

63, 67, 77, 79, 90, 104, 132
n.9
Peace of Paris (1763), 32, 35
Peace of Paris (1783), 105
peers and peerage, see aristocracy
Pelham, Henry, 135 n.21
Pennsylvania Packet, 42
pensions and pensioners, 3, 37,
80, 84, 91-92,106
perjury, 27, 77, 84, 135 n.28
persecution, 63
petitions and petitioners, 41,
97-98, 104, 138 n.74; petitions of 1769-70, 36, 86, 87,
91
Pitt, William, Earl of Chatham,
32
Pitt, William, the younger, 40
Pittites, 79
places and placemen, 3, 37, 79,
80, 84, 85-86, 89, 91-92, 97,
106

Plato, 16, 62
plural voting, 95, 138 n.69
police, 72
politics, 27, 28, 29, 32, 99
poor, 70-72, 94, 133 n.26, 138
n.68; poor relief, 4, 67, 72,
103, 106
Pope, Alexander, 55, 63
popery, see Catholicism
popular sovereignty, 82, 87-88
population, 21, 71, 73, 132 n.7
Postlethwayt, Malachy, 91
power, 29, 43, 78, 81
prayer, 53
prerogative, 28, 32, 83, 90
The Presbyterian Fund, 57
Presbyterianism and Presbyterians, 9, 12, 17; see Calvin-
ism
Price, Rev. Richard, 17, 29,
36, 40, 41, 44, 52-53, 68,
85, 101, 102, 132 n.7
prices, 33, 71
Priestley, Joseph, 29, 41, 43,
60, 102, 121 n.43, 129 n.15
prime minister, 135 n.22
Pringle, Sir John, 29, 120 n.37

INDEX

Spectator, 59
Stamp Act, 35, 36, 95, 103, 104; Stamp Act Congress, 96
standard of living, 68
Stanley, John, 29
Stevenson, John, 137 n.53
Stiles, Ezra, 131 n. 45
Stone, Lawrence, 4, 131 n.43
Streatfield, George, 113 n.43
Swaffham Association, 139 n.78
Swift, Jonathan, 80
Sydenham, Humphrey, 84, 135 n.28

Tatler, 59
taxation, 37, 72, 86, 88-89, 94
teachers, 61
Templeman, Peter, 29
Test and Corporation Acts, iv, 51
thirty-nine articles, 12, 51
Toleration Act (1689), 59
Toplady, Rev. August, 128 n.18
Tories, 9
Townshend duties, 37, 87, 105, 122 n.49
Trenchard, John, 16, 85, 118 n.8, 125 n.76
trinitarianism, 52-53
truth, 54-55, 128 n.19
Turgot, Anne Robert Jacques, Baron De Laune, 44
Turks, 91
turnpikes, 28, 72
tyranny, 3, 28, 34, 63, 81, 98

unitarianism, 17, 53

universities, 59, 128 n.5; Cambridge, 12, 57, 114 n.47, 127 n.4; Oxford, 12, 57, 114 n.47, 127 n.9; St. Andrews, 10, 58, 101, 110 n.6; Scottish, 58

veto, 82
Voltaire, 102

Waldegrave, James Waldegrave, 2nd earl, 115 n.66
Walker, John, 31
Wallingford, 94
Walpole, Robert, 93, 103
war, 86
Warrington academy, 130 n.26
Washington, George, 42
Watson, William, 29
Webster, Noah, 31, 119 n.17
weights and measures, 70
Wesley, John, 49
Whigs, 3, 9, 29, 83, 132 n.3
Whittelsey, 131 n.45
Wilkes, John, 35, 36, 37, 40, 82, 86-88, 99, 103, 121 n.43
Wilkites, 85
William III, 83
Wilson, James, 42, 43
window-tax, 37, 94
Wollstonecraft, Mary, 65, 114 n.44, 131 n.44
women, 4, 10, 18, 65, 103, 106, 131 n.43
Wyvill, Christopher, 99

About the Author

A native of Louisville, Kentucky, Carla H. Hay received her Ph.D. degree from the University of Kentucky in 1972. She has been the recipient of an American Philosophical Society Research Grant and a National Endowment for the Humanities Summer Fellowship and has published in the William and Mary Quarterly and the Journal of British Studies. An assistant professor of history at Marquette University in Milwaukee, Wisconsin, she is currently completing a biography of the eighteenth century radical historian, Catharine Macaulay.